INDIANS, BUREAUCRATS, AND LAND

Recent Titles in
Contributions in Economics and Economic History
Series Editor: Robert Sobel

New Directions in Political Economy: An Approach from Anthropology
Madeline Barbara Leons and Frances Rothstein, editors

Moral Revolution and Economic Science: The Demise of Laissez-Faire in
Nineteenth-Century British Political Economy
Ellen Frankel Paul

Economy and Self: Philosophy and Economics from the Mercantilists to Marx
Norman Fischer

The Quality of Working Life in Western and Eastern Europe
Cary L. Cooper and Enid Mumford

The Politics of Organizational Change
Iain Mangham

Change Agents at Work
Richard N. Ottaway

Electricity for Rural America: The Fight for the REA
D. Clayton Brown

Commodities, Finance and Trade: Issues in the North-South Negotiations
Arjun Sengupta, editor

The Modern Stentors: Radio Broadcasters and the Federal Government, 1920–1934
Philip T. Rosen

J. Edgar Thomson: Master of the Pennsylvania
James A. Ward

Beyond the Adirondacks: The Story of St. Regis Paper Company
Eleanor Amigo and Mark Neuffer

Taxation of American Railroads: A Policy Analysis
Dennis L. Thompson

LEONARD A. CARLSON

INDIANS, BUREAUCRATS, AND LAND

The Dawes Act and the Decline of Indian Farming

Contributions in Economics and Economic History, Number 36

GREENWOOD PRESS
WESTPORT, CONNECTICUT•LONDON, ENGLAND

Library of Congress Cataloging in Publication Data

Carlson, Leonard A.   1947–
    Indians, bureaucrats, and land.

    (Contributions in economics and economic history;
no. 36 ISSN 0084–9235)
    Bibliography: p.
    Includes index.
      1.   Indians of North America—Land tenure.
2.   Indians of North America—Agriculture.   I.   Title.
II.   Title: The Dawes act and the decline of Indian
farming.
E98.L3C37   333.3'23'08997   80–1709
ISBN 0–313–22533–8 (lib. bdg.)

Library of Congress Catalog Card Number: 80–1709
ISBN: 0–313–22533–8
ISSN: 0084–9235

First published in 1981

Greenwood Press
A division of Congressional Information Service, Inc.
88 Post Road West, Westport, Connecticut 06881

Printed in the United States of America

10 9 8 7 6 5 4 3 2 1

Copyright Acknowledgments

Grateful acknowledgment is made to the following publishers:

The Johns Hopkins University Press for permission to reprint extracts from *The Problem of
Indian Administration* by Lewis Meriam and Associates, copyright 1928.

University of Oklahoma Press for permission to reprint extracts from *The Blackfeet: Raiders
on the Northwestern Plains* by John C. Ewers, 1958 and from *The Dawes Act and the Allotment of Indian Lands* by Delos Sacket Otis, copyright 1973.

University of Nebraska Press for permission to reprint extracts from *A History of the Santee
Sioux* by Roy W. Meyer, copyright 1967.

To My Parents

CONTENTS

ILLUSTRATIONS

TABLES

ACKNOWLEDGMENTS

Writing a book is a solitary undertaking; it is also one that requires the support and help of many people. I want to thank those who gave me help while I worked on this study.

Professor Paul David provided guidance and valuable insights throughout the work's development. Professors Warren Sanderson and John Pencavel of Stanford University assisted and encouraged me at various stages. Professors Louis Cain of Loyola University of Chicago and Mary Young of the University of Rochester offered helpful criticism of an earlier draft. My teachers, colleagues, and friends at Stanford, Emory, and elsewhere made innumerable comments and suggestions that clarified my thinking in many ways. Of course, any errors that remain are my responsibility.

The quality of my writing was improved by voluntary editorial help from Celia Huston and Bruce Richardson. Any remaining lack of clarity is my responsibility. Typing was originally launched by Barbara Funkhouser, and the final draft was cheerfully completed by Sandra Yu and Micki Powell. My parents, friends, and colleagues, throughout the writing of this study, were a never-ending source of support and patience. Special thanks go to Donald Broughton. I am grateful to all of them.

PART ONE
Federal Indian Policy and the Dawes Act

1

THE "INDIAN PROBLEM" AND THE POLICY OF ALLOTMENT

After the Civil War, the American people, Congress, and federal policymakers were forced to decide what to do with the nearly quarter of a million Indians who lived on reservations in the western United States. In 1881 Indian land under federal protection totaled more than 156 million acres, over two and one-half times the area of Georgia, the largest state east of the Mississippi. Most of this land was west of the Mississippi River and ranged in quality from arid desert to prime agricultural land. This land had been given to Indian tribes as partial compensation for lands ceded during earlier stages of the westward movement of population. The push of white settlers into previously unoccupied territory led to demands that the relatively unoccupied Indian reservations be opened to white settlement. At the same time, an increasingly influential Indian reform movement in the East advocated the adoption of programs to assimilate Indians into white culture. A variety of solutions to the "Indian problem" might have been adopted.[1] The solution actually chosen was embodied in the General Allotment Act, or Dawes Act, of 1887, which mandated a fundamental change in Indian-white relationships.

The General Allotment Act empowered the president of the United States to divide Indian reservations into 160-acre allotments, assign one allotment to each family, and open remaining lands to white settlers. Originally the lands were placed in a twenty-five-year trust, but after its passage, the law was amended to allow Indians to lease or sell their allotments to non-Indians after receiving the permission of the Office of Indian Affairs. Reformers in the 1880s were convinced that allotting land to Indians would encourage each family to farm its own land and acquire the habits of thrift, industry, and individualism needed for assimilation into white culture.

The Dawes Act, and related policies, remained in effect until the law was repealed in 1934. Although historians have concluded that the Dawes Act was a failure, the origins of that failure are not clearly understood. The Dawes Act did play a key role in opening vast amounts of Indian land to white settlers; yet, it was also a sincere if unsuccessful attempt to reform Indian property rights. This study examines the Dawes Act from both of these perspectives.

First, I consider the way in which the Dawes was carried into practice. The allotment of reservation lands began on an experimental basis in the 1860s and lasted until 1934. The federal government took three or four decades after the passage of the Dawes Act to choose some reservations for allotment, but it allotted other reservations in seeming haste as soon as the act was passed. However, some systematic reasons explain why certain reservations were allotted so much later than others. Second, I consider the impact of allotment on Indian farming. The reformers saw allotment as a way of promoting the economic advancement and cultural assimilation of Indians into white society. Allotment, however, changed Indian farming and Indian life in ways that were not foreseen by the reformers.

The allotment era saw a massive decline in Indian land holdings, and allotment was often followed by hard times for Indian farmers and ranchers. In some cases, contemporary tribal development plans have been hampered by the small amount of land left in Indian hands.[2] The slow development of Indian farming after allotment has had grave implications for modern efforts to develop reservation resources. The failure of Indian farming in the early twentieth century was in large measure a consequence of allotment.

A study of the allotment policy can further an understanding of the role of economic interests in the formation of federal policy and offer a case study of how changes in land tenure led to changes in land-use patterns and Indian welfare. In recent years, the economic theory of regulation has blossomed as a promising branch of economics and a fruitful approach to an important aspect of economic life. With few exceptions, however, these ideas have not been applied to federal Indian policy. Yet Indian policy, with its mixture of conflicts, ideals, and economic interests, offers a fertile ground for testing these propositions. Another topic of current interest is the economic theory of property rights. The reformers expected the change in land tenure brought about by allotment to promote Indian farming; the failure of allotment to provide incentives to Indian farmers has important implications for the economic theory of property rights.

Indian Policy Until 1880

Before 1850 the federal government had solved the "Indian problem" by moving Indian tribes west of the Mississippi out of the way of white settlers.

The successful war with Mexico and the discovery of gold in California in the 1840s were followed by the movement of settlers into previously undeveloped western territories. Reservations were established to guarantee diminished homes for Indians in the face of this onslaught of settlers. As new reservations were established, many tribes suffered greatly as they were uprooted and moved to areas less desired by white settlers. For all of its faults, the reservation system recognized Indian claims to tribal lands and offered protection to Indians on their diminished territory. Tribes denied the protection of reservations in Texas and California faced very real dangers of extinction.

Under the reservation system, treaties were made with each tribe called on to cede territory to the federal government. The amount of land left in tribal control depended upon the location of the land and the relative strength of the tribe in question. In some cases, the government placed tribes on reservations that were too small to allow traditional economic activities, for example, hunting. The government often provided "rations" to support the people on the reservation. The treaties sometimes included promises of schools and the payment of goods as compensation for ceded lands. Congress in the 1860s and 1870s was stingy in providing money for Indian welfare with the most generous appropriations going to potentially troublesome tribes.[3]

A number of treaties negotiated in the 1850s contained provisions calling for the future allotment of Indian lands.[4] Many of these treaties were negotiated by Commissioner George Manypenny, who was later active in the movement for Indian reform. These provisions reflected a long pro-assimilation bias in federal Indian policy. Wilcomb Washburn noted that, "Initially established as a secure, if diminished, home for the tribe, the reservation soon became [to reformers] a school where the individual Indian might be made over in the image of the white man and freed from his ties to the tribe and reservation."[5]

The Five Tribes of Oklahoma constitute a unique and important group of tribes. These tribes had originally lived in the southeastern United States and had a long tradition of settled agriculture. In the 1830s and 1840s, members of the Five Tribes were forcibly moved from their homes and resettled in what is today eastern Oklahoma. Following their removal from the Southeast, the Five Civilized Tribes established self-governing Indian nations in what was known as the Indian Territory, where they were under less direct supervision from the federal agents than other Indians. Even in this relative isolation, however, the Five Tribes were still caught up by the same problems as the rest of the United States. Some members of the Five Tribes were slaveholders and were drawn into the Civil War on the side of the South. As punishment for support of the losing side, the western half of what is today Oklahoma was ceded to the federal government as a site for reservations for other tribes.

The establishment of reservations in Oklahoma for Plains Indians and others was part of what Loring Priest called the "concentration policy."[6] This was a program of relocating many Indian tribes on reservations either in Oklahoma and the Indian Territory or in the Dakotas. A large number of tribes were resettled before the policy lost support in Congress. In the 1870s, popular opinion was aroused against removing Indian tribes by the well-publicized hardships of relocated tribes such as the Ponca and the Northern Cheyenne. In addition, congressmen in the vicinity of proposed new reservations also opposed having new Indian neighbors.

In 1867–68 a peace commission was established to bring an end to wars with the Plains tribes and to create reservations for these tribes. This commission negotiated the last formal treaties with Indian tribes. President Grant went beyond the signing of these treaties to establish what was referred to as either the "Peace Policy" or "Quaker Policy"—a curious attempt to solve persistent problems in the administration of Indian affairs by formally including religious denominations in the administration of Indian policy. On the other hand, each reservation was assigned to a particular religious group that in turn nominated one of its members to be the agent.

Grant believed religious and educational work by missionaries was the key to the assimilation of Indians. He also hoped that church appointees would help eliminate corruption in the Office of Indian Affairs. Appointments in the Indian service were assigned as political favors (the spoils system), and the jobs themselves were low paid and difficult. Often unscrupulous agents would join with outside contractors to form an "Indian ring" and cheat Indians out of promised goods and supplies. In the 1870s, two commissioners of Indian affairs resigned while under suspicion of being involved in fraudulent schemes.[7] The Board of Indian Commissioners was established in 1869 to prevent theft and oversee the formation and administration of Indian policy. The board, made up of civilian philanthropists, was another attempt to end corruption and inefficiency in the Indian service.

Hastened by clashes between rival sects, especially between the Catholics and Protestants, this curious division of authority between the civilian and the religious was gradually abandoned in the mid-1870s, and the Board of Indian Commissioners was relegated to an advisory role.

By the 1870s, the military power of Indian tribes had greatly diminished. With the destruction of the buffalo herds, the power of the Plains tribes declined, and by the second half of the decade, Indian wars were little more than desperate fights against intolerable conditions. Some Indian struggles, like the flight of the Northern Cheyenne and the attempt of Chief Joseph's band of Nez Perce to reach Canada, were sympathetically treated in the popular press. As a result, anti-Indian sentiment, fired by the Custer massacre and the Modoc War, gradually subsided in the late 1870s.

As Indians came to be more favorably viewed in the popular press, schemes to assimilate Indians also received a favorable hearing in Congress and the newspapers. On many reservations in the 1870s, the federal government established Indian police forces and also Indian-operated courts under the agent's supervision. Indian teamsters were given contracts to haul supplies and were often more successful and honest in performing these tasks than white contractors. The most widely heralded assimilationist scheme was the policy of establishing schools for the education of Indian children. The most famous Indian school of the period was in Carlisle, Pennsylvania. The school, founded by Captain James Pratt, was deliberately located far from Indian communities to force a separation of Indian children from their former way of life.

The Movement to Allot Indian Lands

Among those with an interest in Indian affairs, assimilation was the recognized goal of national Indian policy, and allotment came to be seen as the proper means of achieving that goal. In 1877 Secretary of the Interior Carl Schurz endorsed a general allotment bill. D. S. Otis noted that, "From that date onward the Indian Service as a whole worked for the speeding up of allotment under previous acts and treaties and the passage of a general law."[8] Reports from agents in the field discussed the readiness of the people on their reservations for allotment and the agents' efforts to have the idea of allotment accepted by the peoples in their charge.

Debates about Indian policy were naturally focused at the federal level. Under the Constitution, powers to regulate Indian affairs were vested in the federal government. By the 1870s, the original powers of the federal government had been expanded through precedent, law, and court decisions into an even broader authority to regulate the lives and property of Indians. In 1871 Congress assumed the right to make laws directly for Indian tribes, abolishing the system of having the Senate ratify treaties negotiated with each tribe.[9] By the time Congress formally considered a general allotment bill, the legal right of Congress to pass such legislation was clearly established.

In 1880 Senator Coke of Texas introduced a bill calling for the allotment of all Indian reservations. This law would have divided all land on a reservation among the Indians living there when the president and two-thirds of the tribe agreed to do so. Although it passed in the Senate, it failed to pass in the House, perhaps because, as Henry Fritz suggested, western legislators found it too generous to Indians and opposed the bill.[10]

General allotment plans discussed in Congress in the late 1870s and early 1880s included provisions restricting the sale of land after allotment. Such provisions were the outgrowth of the experience of tribes allotted by treaty.

The Board of Indian Commissioners and congressional committees that investigated these allotted reservations concluded that, in most cases, Indians sold their land, either willingly or by coercion or fraud, once they had received an allotment. Reformers proposing allotment bills hoped that this problem would be avoided by forbidding alienation for a twenty-five-year trust period. Tribes that were allotted by special legislation in the 1880s received their allotments with twenty-five-year restrictions.[11]

The rejection of the Coke Bill came at a time of rising interest in Indian affairs. This growing interest in Indian affairs was reflected in the emergence of national groups organized to press for the reformation of Indian policy.

In 1879 women in Philadelphia who had worked on the Ponca removal case formed the Woman's National Indian Association. The Boston Indian Citizenship Committee was formed the same year, and in 1882 the Indian Rights Association was organized in Philadelphia. The Women's National Indian Association and the Indian Rights Association came to see allotment as the key to Indian policy reform and coordinated their efforts to work for an allotment bill. These organizations drew most of their original support east of the Alleghenies. Reformers and reform organizations were usually Protestant, and in Francis Prucha's words:

> The Protestantism of the friends of the Indian merged almost imperceptibly into Americanism. In a period when traditional values seemed threatened by hoards of immigrants coming to American shores—immigrants from eastern and southern Europe who seemed to fit only with difficulty into the accepted culture—the reformers insisted on the Americanization of all unfamiliar elements.[12]

Occasionally voices were raised against the idea of allotting land to Indians. Senator Teller of Colorado opposed allotment in congressional debates in the 1880s. He believed that Indians were not ready for white notions of property and that allotment would be a disaster. Similarly, a minority report of a House committee studying allotment in 1880 saw allotment as a pretext to ". . . get at Indian lands and open them to settlement. . . ."[13] The Indian Defense Association was the only Indian reform group to argue for allowing Indians to choose whether they wanted allotment of their lands. In general, reformers came to see allotment as the panacea for the problems of American Indians. The idea that individual ownership of property was the key to individual virtue and hard work was so widespread that it achieved virtually unquestioned acceptance. This prevailing faith in private property was translated into a widespread belief in allotment. Prucha noted that, in general, "So nearly universal was support of allotment of land in severalty that it is difficult to find statements opposing the proposal."[14] Of course, other motives, far less altruistic than those expressed by the reformers, prompted support for the passage of the allotment law. It is important, however, that the reformers set forth their arguments with such force and conviction that they dominated public utterances on the subject and that their arguments seemed reasonable to many people.

Although reformers saw the need to give Indians an individual title to their land, widespread sentiment also favored the opening of reservation lands to outside development. Reformers reconciled their interest in Indian advancement with the desire of many whites to open Indian lands for settlement. Some accepted the idea that land should be used and thought that protecting Indian ownership of unused land would encourage idleness. Others recognized the intense desire of white settlers to acquire Indian lands and hoped that allotting lands would guarantee that at least a part of the Indian reservations would remain in Indian hands. Some reformers, including Senator Dawes, were aware of the pressure by whites to acquire Indian lands.[15]

In 1883 a wealthy member of the Board of Indian Commissioners offered his resort hotel at Lake Mohonk, New York, as a meeting place for those interested in Indian reform. These yearly conferences brought together prominent individuals in and out of government to express opinions and arrive at common goals and plans for legislative action. Many of the individuals who attended were members of Indian reform groups, and the conferences were dominated by the Protestant "friends of the Indian" mentioned above. Senator Henry Dawes of Massachusetts, chairman of the Senate Indian Affairs Committee, attended these meetings.

Dawes introduced the bill that bears his name with the support of the groups represented at the Mohonk meetings. Senator Dawes told the Mohonk Conference that, "It should be called the Mohonk Bill . . . it is the inspiration of the people, you are responsible for it. . . ."[16] The Dawes Act generated little debate in either the House or the Senate. The added push of the Indian reform groups and the elimination of features that had been objectionable to western congressmen provided the cushion needed for passage.

Provisions of the Dawes Act

The General Allotment Act, or Dawes Act, of February 8, 1887, gave the president general authority to have a reservation allotted when he believed it was appropriate. Although the Dawes Act exempted some tribes from its provisions, including the Five Tribes and the Osage, most Indians living on reservations in the United States were potentially subject to allotment. The law provided that each head of a household was to receive a 160-acre tract of land, with single individuals over eighteen receiving an additional 80 acres and children under eighteen receiving allotments of 40 acres. On reservations with lands suited only for grazing, acreages were doubled. If land on a reservation was insufficient to allot each household 160 acres, allotments were prorated. Indians who were not residing on a reservation were eligible for allotments on land in the public domain. If an individual refused to choose an allotment within four years, one could be assigned to him.[17]

Allotted lands were placed in a trust for 25 years ". . . for the sole use and benefit of the Indian to whom such an allotment shall have been made."[18] While the land was in trust, an Indian could neither lease, sell, nor will the land. At the end of the trust period, an allottee was to receive a patent-in-fee, which gave him or her unrestricted title to the allotment (title in fee simple). At the time of allotment, an allottee also became a citizen of the United States.[19]

Unallotted lands not reserved for the use of the tribe were to be opened for sale to "actual settlers." The cession of surplus lands to the government was to be approved by the tribe, although in practice the government had a strong position in such negotiations. The role of the tribes was reduced further in 1903, when the courts held that tribal approval was not necessary for the disposal of surplus lands.[20] The proceeds from the land sales were held in trust for the tribe.

The Dawes Act was compulsory. A tribe could not elect to remain unallotted, and an individual could not refuse to accept an allotment. In a number of cases, tribes were asked to approve allotment agreements, but in the end, Congress had placed the weight of government and law behind the move to allot Indian lands, and Indians succumbed to the inevitable. Loring Priest concluded that the decision to allow the government to allot a reservation without the consent of the Indians, despite warnings about potential for abuses, reflected the unwillingness of reformers and Congress to tolerate opposition by Indians.[21] Implicit in the compulsory aspects of the Dawes Act was the notion that progress was something to be forced on Indians in their own best interest.

The Dawes Act opened the unallotted surplus to white settlement. Although reformers were aware of potential dangers in opening Indian lands to settlement, a number of reformers welcomed the entry of whites onto surplus lands as a way of integrating Indians and non-Indians. Others saw the opening of the surplus as a small price to pay for an allotment law. Of course, those congressmen who supported allotment primarily as a way of opening Indian lands to white settlement endorsed the compulsory aspects of the Dawes Act. Fritz concluded:

The individual allotment act which became law in February 1887, was dependent upon Western land hunger to carry it into effect. Western Congressmen were unwilling to vote for a land-in-severalty law as a straightforward humanitarian measure and until the Indian reform movement assumed national proportions, with its best support in Massachusetts, even Senator Dawes was skeptical of such a notion.[22]

The Administration of the Dawes Act to 1900

Congress underscored its endorsement of the allotment principle by passing a number of acts to reduce Indian holdings through cession and allotment. In 1889 the Great Sioux Reservation of North and South Dakota was reduced to six smaller reservations. The Sioux were pressured by federal agents to accept the treaty, which included provisions calling for the allotment of the diminished reservations.[23]

Another group singled out for special attention were the Chippewa of Minnesota. "An Act for the Relief and Civilization of the Chippewa Indians in the State of Minnesota" (the Nelson Act) was passed in 1889. It set up a mechanism whereby Chippewa Indians on a half dozen reservations ceded their lands to the government. Indian families were given the choice of accepting allotments either on their original reservation or on the White Earth Reservation. The ceded lands were sold to non-Indians with the proceeds held in trust for the tribe.[24]

Other special agreements in the 1890s called for land cessions by tribes in Montana, Idaho, and Washington. Otis cited a number of bills passed by Congress that allotted reservations in advance of the normal operation of the Dawes Act. Such agreements typically involved substantial cessions of surplus lands.[25] The operation of allotment and the related land cessions by Indians led to a rapid turnover in Indian property.

In his annual report for 1891, Commissioner Thomas Morgan noted that actual or potential land reductions in that year came to:

> . . . a grand total of 17,400,000 acres or about one-seventh of all Indian lands in the United States.
>
> This might seem like a somewhat rapid reduction of the land estate of the Indians, but when it is considered that for the most part the land relinquished was not being used for any purpose whatever, that scarcely any of it was in cultivation, that Indians did not need it and would not be likely to need it at any future time, and that they were, as it is believed, reasonably well paid for it, the matter assumes quite a different aspect. The sooner the tribal relations are broken up and the reservation system done away with, the better it will be for all concerned. If there were no other reason for this change, the fact that

individual ownership of property is the universal custom among civilized people of this country would be a sufficient reason for urging the handful of Indians to adopt it.[26]

Thus the commissioner of Indian Affairs in the early 1890s strongly endorsed the idea of allotment and the rapid reduction of Indian land that was occurring at the same time.

Not all Indian reservations were allotted immediately after the passage of the Dawes Act. Some reservations were allotted before the passage of the Dawes Act by legislation or treaty. Once the Dawes Act passed, the allotting of reservations continued throughout the half century the law was in force, and a number of important reservations were never allotted.

Allotted lands were originally placed in a twenty-five-year trust during which time they could be neither leased nor sold, but this policy was gradually modified. Senator Dawes introduced the first amendment to the Act. The amendment, passed in 1891, made two changes. It provided 80 acres for each adult rather than 160 acres for only the head of the household. This protected wives who were divorced by their husbands. More importantly, the amendment also stipulated that the secretary of the interior was to establish regulations for the leasing of allotments when an allottee "by reasons of age or other disability . . . could not personally and with benefit to himself occupy his allotment or any part thereof."[27]

It is curious that Senator Dawes was the author of this amendment, since the previous year, he had expressed fears that leasing would defeat the purpose of allotment. He reasoned that although:

There were instances of hardships under this inalienable allotment system, and instances of worthy young men who want to leave their allotment and go into some other business or get an education; and in an endeavor to . . . [correct this] . . . we are in danger of overthrowing the fundamental idea of the whole system. . . . In all this we forget that the Indian as a rule won't work if he can help it, and that the white man has never been known to take his foot off from an Indian's land when he once got it on.[28]

Despite these misgivings, Dawes followed the recommendations of the Lake Mohonk Conference and introduced a leasing bill. The amendment passed with little discussion. Wilcomb Washburn pictured Senator Dawes as a man of good intentions but little resolve. The sudden turnabout in the senator's position seems to have been in response to pressure from groups at Mohonk that favored allowing Indians to lease allotments.[29]

The standards established for leasing allotments initially were very severe but were relaxed over time. Authority for leasing was given to the secretary of the interior, but in practice it fell to the agent in the field to apply rules established in Washington. By the turn of the century, the leasing of allotted land was widely practiced on many reservations.[30]

Federal Indian Policy, 1900–1910

The next major legislative changes occurred in the first decade of the twentieth century. In 1901 the secretary of the interior was given authority to sell heirship allotments. *Heirship allotments* were those allotments still under trust status when the original allottee had died. An allottee was not allowed to will his allotment, so when he died, the land was divided among the heirs according to the state law in which the land was located. This led to situations where one small allotment had multiple owners, or one Indian owned small parts of more than one allotment. Such heirship allotments remain today a complicated and important problem in Indian land tenure.

In 1906 the Burke Act made important changes in the restrictions placed on Indian land holdings. Under the Burke Act, each allottee was to be dealt with on an individual basis. The act withheld citizenship from allottees until they were declared legally competent to manage their own affairs, and, more importantly, it provided that an individual could be declared competent to handle his or her own affairs in advance of the twenty-five-year trust period. Similarly, an individual could have the trust period extended past twenty-five years.[31] Being declared competent enabled an allottee to sell his land and made the land liable for state and local property taxes. A competent individual was issued a patent in fee that gave him a title to his land in fee simple and removed other restrictions on his property. The Office of Indian Affairs acknowledged that most applicants for such fee patents wanted to sell their land immediately. Francis Leupp, commissioner of Indian Affairs in 1906, greeted the Burke Act enthusiastically. He saw the discretionary authority of the act as nullifying ". . . the injustice which . . . a general provision [e.g., uniform twenty-five-year trust periods] might inflict on Indians capable of taking their places as citizens. . . ."[32] Another change came in 1907 when Congress granted the commissioner of Indian affairs power to sell the allotment of an Indian in trust status.

In this period, Congress passed legislation that further clarified its endorsement of the original allotment bill. The amendments to the Dawes Act fell within the original rationale of the allotment policy. The twenty-five-year trust period was seen as an intermediate stage in the move from tribal ownership of land and federal supervision to a state of complete freedom from restriction. Changes in the law preserved the idea of a transition period, but decisions about how long that transition period was to be were made on a case by case basis. Congress emphasized its continuing commitment to the philosophy of the Dawes Act by its passage of special acts to facilitate the allotment of lands. J. D. Kinney noted that Congress passed numerous allotment bills and related acts in the first decade of the new century.[33]

After 1890 a few individuals and groups expressed fears that allotment was being pushed too fast for the best interests of the Indian peoples. Few employees in the Office of Indian Affairs, however, expressed any doubt until much later. The united support of the Office of Indian Affairs and Congress swept along most individuals involved in the allotment process. Some objected that not all Indians were successful under allotment. But Commissioner William A. Jones replied to this objection in 1901 by bluntly stating " . . . that there will be many failures and much suffering is inevitable in the very nature of things, for it is only by sacrifice and suffering that the heights of civilization are reached."[34]

Oklahoma and the Indian Territory

The Five Civilized Tribes were the most prominent group exempted from the Dawes Act. By 1890 it was clear that the relative independence of the Indians would not be allowed to persist. At that date, only about 30 percent of the population of the Indian Territory was Indian, and the rest were white settlers or freed slaves.[35] The non-Indians were not necessarily citizens of the Indian nation in which they resided and were not provided with services by the tribal governments.

Legally, land in the Indian nations was held by the tribe with individual right of occupancy recognized and protected. If land were abandoned, it reverted to the tribe. It was a common practice to allow individual citizens from the tribe to fence in large tracts of unclaimed land and rent them from the tribe at a nominal fee. These lands could in turn be sublet to white farmers and cattlemen.[36] This system allowed some prominent families to amass great wealth.

In 1893 the recently retired Henry Dawes was appointed to head a commission to study the situation in the Indian Territory. The findings of the Dawes Commission were critical of the existing situation and pressed for the end of tribal government and the subsequent allotment of land. The Dawes Commission claimed that the mixed bloods and intermarried whites were exploiting the full bloods through their control of tribal politics. Angie Debo, among others, disagreed with the findings of the Dawes Commission. Debo argued that the termination of the tribal government of the Five Tribes was a gross injustice and concluded that the tribal governments served and protected the interests of full bloods in the Five Tribes.[37]

Under pressure from the Dawes Commission and Congress, the Chickasaw in 1896 agreed to terminate their tribal government and use the allotment process to divide tribal property among the enrolled members. Two years later, the Seminoles also agreed to abolish their tribal government. In 1897, impatient at delay, Congress passed the Curtis Bill, which provided for the ending of the tribal governments and the allotment of property if "voluntary" agreements could not be reached with each tribe. Spurred by this bill, all tribes came to terms with the federal government.

The terms of allotment varied among tribes but followed a similar pattern. First, a list of all enrolled members of the tribe was prepared. This list could include whites married to Indians and freed former slaves. Then, each individual was assigned an allotment. Since all land was owned by the Five Tribes, no surplus was available to be opened as it was under the Dawes Act. The allotments, however, consisted of two types of land: the homestead, which was subject to restrictions on its sale, and the surplus, which could be sold subject to fewer restrictions. In practice, full-blood Indians often received as their homesteads the land around their homes in the hills, and choice agricultural land in the flatlands was designated as surplus.[38] As was expected, the surplus was quickly sold to the influx of white settlers.

The movement from the passage of the Curtis Act to the dissolution of tribal governments was rapid. By 1906 the tribal governments were mere shells to manage remaining tribal affairs, with officials appointed by the president. The state of Oklahoma was formed from the Oklahoma Territory, the western part of the state, and the former Indian Territory, the eastern half. Once Oklahoma was admitted as a state, the state government and the state courts assumed an important role in supervising the property of members of the Five Tribes. The Indian wards in Oklahoma were too often the victims of frauds or other abuses.[39]

Federal Policy 1910–34

By the second decade of the twentieth century, a system had evolved whereby individual allottees were dealt with as individuals. Greater individual attention, however, did not necessarily mean that Indians in trust status had greater freedom of action. Money obtained from the lease or sale of allotted land could be controlled by the agent, and the assault by the agents on what they considered to be heathen practices continued. A somewhat silly example was Commissioner Jones's requirement that Indian males receiving government rations have short hair.[40] A result of the detailed regulation of Indian policy was an increase in the administrative costs of Indian affairs.[41]

The Office of Indian Affairs also tried other types of land-management policies on Indian reservations. Some tribes, notably the Menomenee and the Klamath, were allowed to operate their timber resources in common as a tribal forest. The Bureau of Reclamation began irrigation projects on a number of western reservations and interacted with the allotment program in influencing Indian land tenure. Mineral resources were extremely valuable on some reservations, and policies for the ownership and management of mineral resources were evolved in the post-1900 era.[42]

In 1917 Commissioner Cato Sells announced a major shift in the policies governing federal treatment of Indians in trust status. In the "new declaration of policy," Sells stated that the government intended to reduce the number of allottees in trust status. All individuals of greater than one-half Indian blood were immediately declared competent and given patents in fee. For the rest, competency commissions were established to decide each Indian's ability to handle his own affairs. This policy was in effect from 1917 to 1920, during which time more patents were issued than in the years from 1906 to 1916.

In 1920 Commissioner Charles Burke again tightened the rules for granting fee patents. By that time, public opinion was aroused by the rapid loss of Indian land. Later in the decade, the courts held that an individual could not be removed from trust status without his permission and lands that had not been lost or mortgaged could be returned to trust status.

Commissioner Burke served from 1921 to 1928, which were years of growing public dissatisfaction with federal Indian policy. John Collier, later to be commissioner of Indian affairs, achieved national attention for his work in support of legislation to protect Pueblo lands.[43]

Concern with the status of Indians in the 1920s led to the Institute of Governmental Research of the Brookings Institution to launch a massive investigation of the social and economic position of Indians in the United States. The study was conducted by an independent staff headed by Lewis Meriam, but with the cooperation of the Department of the Interior. The report was published in 1928 and was a watershed in the history of federal Indian policy.[44] It surveyed conditions among American Indians both on and off the reservations and made numerous recommendations for improving federal policy and improving its administration. Although the report was critical of Indian policy, the findings of the report were not challenged, and, indeed, the Office of Indian Affairs endorsed many of its recommendations.

The Meriam Commission painted a bleak picture of the economic position of most Indians. In essence, the commission thought the assistance given Indians in learning new occupations had been grossly inadequate. The Office of Indian Affairs was found to have been primarily concerned with

Indian property, not with teaching Indians to manage their own affairs. It also found that Indian health services and educational programs were grossly inadequate. The commission argued that the proper goal of the Indian service was to aid Indians through the provision of training and social and health services, while allowing them to choose how much or how little of white culture they would accept. As stated in the report:

> The fundamental requirement is the task of the Indian Service to be recognized as primarily educational in the broadest sense of the word, . . . devoting its main energies to the social and economical advancement of Indians, so that they may be absorbed into the prevailing civilization, or at least be fitted to live in the presence of that civilization at least in accordance with the minimum standard of health and decency.[45]

Although the Indian office endorsed many of the new proposals, Commissioner Burke remained committed to the philosophy of allotment. He attracted criticism from a rising Indian reform movement and was ultimately forced to resign amidst unproven charges of corruption. President Hoover's secretary of the interior, Ray Lynn Wilbur, appointed two Quaker philanthropists, John H. Rhoads and J. Henry Scattergood, to head the Indian bureau. Under their administration, cautious attempts were made to reform federal Indian policy. Although they endorsed the principle and proposals developed in the Meriam report, they were criticized by reformers for moving too slowly.

The bottom of the Great Depression brought the election of Franklin Roosevelt and, with it, the appointment of John Collier as commissioner of Indian affairs. In the first reform-minded year of the New Deal, Collier and his staff prepared a bill that completely overhauled Indian policy. The bill was introduced by Senator Wheeler and Representative Howard and endorsed by President Roosevelt. With some important modifications, it was passed in 1934.

The Indian Reorganization Act ended the allotment of Indian lands, although it applied only to those tribes that ratified it. The law provided that no tribally held land should be allotted in the future, and the secretary of the interior could, at his discretion, return *surplus* lands to a tribe that had been opened for homesteads but not yet entered. The law also authorized an annual appropriation of $2 million to purchase lands for Indians and a revolving credit fund of $10 million to make loans to incorporated tribes. The Secretary was also authorized to help Indian tribes adopt written constitutions and exercise other powers. Other provisions exempted Indians from civil service standards and gave them preference in employment in the Indian office, established loans for Indian students, and required that policies be established to conserve natural resources.[46] In all, 192 out of 262 tribes voted to accept the Indian Reorganization Act. Allotment, however, was ended even for those tribes that did not accept the Wheeler-Howard Act.

Allotment: Land Grab or Property Rights Reform?

The Dawes Act remained the cornerstone of federal Indian policy for nearly five decades. The recognized failure of the allotment policy raises a number of broad questions that in turn generate the more specific topics investigated in this study. The Dawes Act did indeed fail. As Commissioner of Indian Affairs John Collier wrote in 1933: "It is only recently that we have come fully to realize the magnitude of the disaster which the allotment law of 1887 has wrought upon the Indians."[47] By the early 1930s, the official position of the United States government was that allotment, and in particular the Dawes Act, had failed as a program to improve the economic and material position of American Indians. Historians have largely agreed with that conclusion. But in what sense was allotment a failure? Has allotment been viewed as a failure because it did not change Indians into "responsible, self-supporting citizens," or was it a "disaster" that actively worsened the lot of Indians in the United States?

Allotment was an assimilationist policy, designed to promote the economic development of Indians by encouraging integration with and assimilation into white society. Was such a policy simply misguided and doomed to failure due to a gross misunderstanding of the capabilities and wishes of the Indians? Or did it fail because it was badly implemented? The Meriam Commission, for example, accepted the principles of allotment but argued that federal officials had failed to give Indians proper aid and supervision. Could the Dawes Act have been made to work or at least to work better than it did, or was it so flawed that it was hopeless from the start?

Clearly, accepting the proposition that the Dawes Act was a failure does not close the door to further inquiry. In the following chapters, the questions outlined above and others are used as a starting point in examining the implementation of the Dawes Act and in assessing the effect of the allotment policy on Indians.

Despite the high hopes of the reformers, the Dawes Act led to one of the largest real estate transfers in history. As noted by Wilcomb Washburn, at the time of allotment, ". . . the Indian land base amounted to 138,000,000 acres. Between 1887 and 1934, about 60 percent of this land passed out of Indian hands."[48] Much of this land was transferred in ways that formally had little to do with the Dawes Act, but the point is still valid: an incredible amount of land passed from Indian hands in the forty-seven-year history of the Dawes Act.

Thus a crucial question is whether the Dawes Act should be viewed primarily as a thinly disguised device for expropriating Indian land. The incompetence and outright corruption that too often surrounded the administration of federal Indian policy and indeed land policy in general lend credence to this view. Students of federal Indian policy however, are unwilling to see the Dawes Act exclusively as a land grab.

For example, Harold Fey and D'Arcy McNickle concluded that:

> If the great expectation of the Allotment Act had been the complete separation of Indians from the land, then it came close to achieving that total purpose. However, that had never been the total purpose. Throughout all the discussions stress had been placed on the educational value of individualized ownership and the corollary value that would result from breaking up the solidarity of tribal existence.
>
> Any appraisement of the act therefore must be on the basis of what it proposed to accomplish; in that light, the act failed completely. The Indians did not become farmers; neither did they assume the habits of white people. Tribal existence became more difficult, as at Sisseton, but it persisted, old customs, old attitudes, old values persisted.[49]

Thus in evaluating the Dawes Act as a broad federal policy, it is necessary to consider both the fact that it led to a massive transfer of land holdings to whites and that it was a sincere attempt at land reform. It partook of both, and both elements need to be considered.

Historians and the Allotment Act

As stated above, historians have largely accepted the verdict that the allotment policy was a failure: it did not improve the welfare of Indians or succeed in making them into "self-supporting citizens." Most historical studies of allotment have considered one or more of four general issues.

The first issue treats the social and intellectual origins of the reformers and the reform movement that led to the passage of the Dawes Act. The second issue is a question of the overall result of allotment and the policy of forced assimilation of Indians into white society. The third issue, often contained as a part of tribal or reservation histories, investigates the ways in which particular Indian peoples reacted to life on the closed reservations and, later, to the allotment of their land and increased contact with whites. The fourth issue examines how Indian policy, as mandated by Congress and enforced by the executive branch, evolved over time.

Historians concerned with the movement that led to the passage of the Dawes Act have considered the intellectual origins of the allotment law, the social origins of the reformers and the history of the reform movement, why the policy of allotment came to be widely accepted, and how the Dawes Act became law.[50] Historians who have studied the battle for the passage of the Dawes Act make a convincing case that the motives of the reformers were sincere. Many of the individuals who gathered yearly at Lake Mohonk indeed considered themselves to be "friends of the American Indian" and were committed to the goal of assimilating Indians into the fabric of American society. As mentioned above, others were motivated by less altruistic goals.

Writers primarily concerned with assessing broad trends in Indian-white relations have often treated allotment as part of a larger movement to assimilate Indians into white society.[51] Such studies treat the conflicts between the values of white society, as expressed by the reformers and by Congress, on the one hand and those of the Indians on the other hand. These studies chronicle the ways in which the conflicts between federal policy and the desires of Indians were, or were not, resolved. For the period covered by the Dawes Act, many studies draw on the Meriam report as a major source of information and acute observation. The Meriam report itself was not a historical study. It assessed the problems of Indians, evaluated the nature and quality of programs to assist them, and proposed changes in the federal policy as of 1928.

Historians studying an individual tribe or reservation have been concerned with how the tribe reacted to the radical changes that followed the settlement of the tribe on a closed reservation and, later, the allotment and opening to whites of reservation lands. A number of historians have chosen to end their tribal histories with the allotment of the reservation or just before its allotment, leaving examination of the allotment era to persons concerned with the problems of assimilation and cultural change in the modern era. Some studies do, however, examine the problems of an individual tribe on a closed reservation through allotment and the opening of the reservation to white settlement, and these studies often provide valuable insights into how allotment affected different tribes.[52]

The last question is examined by works covering the history of federal Indian policy. This includes both the history of legislative and administrative actions concerning Indians and, in some studies, an assessment of how federal policies aided or failed to aid the health and welfare of American Indians.

Economists and the Allotment Act

In general, economists have not studied the Dawes Act or the policy of allotting land to American Indians. Nonetheless, interesting parallels can be drawn between the economic side of the arguments made by the reformers and the modern literature on the economics of property rights.[54] Although no modern economist would advocate the awkward, bureaucratically encumbered system of land ownership that allotment produced, the issue addressed and the logic of the arguments raised by reformers who advanced allotment do have common elements with the property-rights literature. Of course, reformers were not concerned with economic incentives alone. The reformers had an almost mystical faith in the power of private property to transform American Indians and assimilate them into hardworking farmers that transcended mere economic incentives.

In looking at property rights, economists have been concerned with how different types of rights to control property led to different economic incentives. In general, the economic literature on property rights has been primarily concerned with questions of efficiency, and questions of fairness and distribution have been given a secondary treatment. Often an implicit assumption is made that societies are composed of individuals with similar tastes, preferences, and opportunities. The question of the impact on different groups in society holding different amounts of wealth and different values has not been studied in detail. A key issue raised by the allotment policy, however, is whether the act of creating individual property rights in land benefited everyone, or whether it involved a redistribution of wealth with some groups gaining at the expense of others. The reformers believed that all Indians, or at least those willing to learn and work, would benefit by owning an individual property right in land as opposed to having all land owned by the tribes.

The property right created by the Dawes Act, however, was encumbered by restrictions about how and when an allottee could lease, sell, or mortgage his land. As we have seen, the Dawes Act has been judged by historians to have created a hardship for Indian allottees, and the loss in Indian land holdings that followed allotment has been sharply condemned. Did this loss of land, and the implied loss of welfare to American Indians, result from the creation of an individual property right for Indians? Or did it result from the fact that the property right given to Indians by the Dawes Act was so encumbered with restrictions that it was worthless? On a theoretical level, the issue is whether the creation of a new property right necessarily made everyone better off, especially in a case where the people receiving the property right had different cultural values. These issues are treated in the concluding chapter.

This study employs techniques that are in the spirit of the property-rights literature—an individual family's rights to the land, either for its own use or for sale, before and after allotment, are carefully examined. In examining the effect of allotment on Indian welfare, however, I consider a problem that is not normally addressed in the literature on property rights: how a system of property rights suited to one group in society affects another group with conflicting values.

Methodology and Outline of the Study

This study extends the methods of the so-called new economic history or cliometrics to the study of American Indian history. In practice, this means that secondary historical literature and primary materials have been combined with deductive reasoning to derive propositions about how the Dawes Act was implemented and how it affected allotted American Indians. These propositions are not treated as self-evident. The spirit of this study is behavioralist, and the ultimate test is whether these hypotheses are consistent with available evidence. Much of the evidence used in this study is quantitative; where possible I have also used secondary sources and contemporary accounts to get a fuller understanding of each of the questions examined below.

More traditional historical approaches are not dismissed as irrelevant. If correct, the hypotheses examined in this study could also be verified by traditional methods; for example, by a careful examination of documents and the accounts of contemporaries. Ideally, no cleavage exists between traditional, more qualitative approaches, and the deductive, quantitative approach taken here. The two approaches complement one another. Some questions can be approached only by traditional, qualitative methods, either because of limited data or the nature of the questions asked, and others can be examined fruitfully by supplementing traditional techniques with deductive reasoning, including economic theory, and quantitative evidence.[55]

In the following chapters, the Dawes Act is examined both as an important law that led to the transfer of a large amount of land from Indians to whites and as a serious attempt to induce social change by reforming Indian property rights. Part II of this study, chapters 2 and 3, investigates the way in which reservations were chosen for allotment.

Two models are formulated to facilitate the investigation of the factors that determine when a reservation was allotted. The first model formalizes the official position of the Office of Indian Affairs. According to this model, the Office of Indian Affairs acted in its role as guardian and delayed the allotment of a reservation until the Indians living there were ready for allotment. Such a model is analogous to modern theories of economic regulation that picture the government as acting to protect the public interest from private economic power. The second model holds that the Office of Indian Affairs acted in response to pressure from non-Indians who stood to gain from the allotment of a reservation, implying that allotment was carried out to reflect the benefits and costs of allotment to whites. Both models are tested using data for the entire United States. The empirical results support the view that the allotment of reservations reflected the economic interests of whites, not Indians. The view that reservations were allotted as Indians were ready for allotment is not supported by the data.

Chapter 3 looks at allotment on reservations in Nebraska and North and South Dakota. The history of allotment on individual reservations in the Northern Plains gives further insight into the allotment process. The timing of allotment of these reservations supports the view that non-Indians' economic interests shaped the course of allotment. The chapter concludes with an overview of the history of the allotment of Indian lands.

Part III of the study, which includes chapters 4, 5, and 6, looks at allotment as an important land reform. Chapter 4 examines allotment from a theoretical perspective. Discussions by reformers and others implied that before allotment, Indians held and worked their lands in common. In such a case, the allotment of a reservation would create a private property right where none had previously existed. The evidence, however, shows that individual Indians did have a recognized right to the land they cultivated. In such a case, allotment primarily made it easier to sell and lease land. The conclusion is that after allotment, a rational Indian farmer would devote fewer resources to his own farming. In general, the model concludes that, by itself, allotment would discourage Indian farmers.

Chapter 5 surveys Indian farming before allotment. The conclusions reached in chapter 4 rest on the proposition that Indians had a workable system of private property before allotment and were willing and able to be farmers. A survey of the histories of selected reservations shows that Indian farmers before allotment had workable systems of land tenure and were far more successful as farmers than the reformers had believed. This is confirmed by examining quantitative data on Indian farming before allotment.

Chapter 6 examines Indian farming after allotment. According to the model developed in chapter 4, Indian farming after allotment would have been expected to decline, and this did indeed occur. Indian farming and ranching on selected key reservations shows a marked decline following allotment —a decline that was tied to the lease and sale of allotted land. The quantitative data on Indian farming confirm this history of decline. In allotted states, fewer Indians were farming fewer acres after allotment than before. In general, Indians used fewer of all inputs than white farmers. The conclusion is that Indian farmers were further behind white farmers in 1930 than they had been in 1900 or 1910. This decline in Indian farming cannot be traced to a shift in other activities, for in 1930 allotted Indians remained a primarily rural people who depended upon agriculture to earn a living.

Part IV of the study, chapter 7, looks at the theoretical issues raised by the allotment policy. Chapter 7 summarizes the findings of this study and evaluates the successes and failures of the allotment policy from the perspectives of both the reformers and the Indians. Allotment is also discussed as an example of a change in property rights. As an exercise to gain an appreciation for the dilemmas faced by the reformers, a counterfactual alternative to allotment is proposed and analyzed.

Notes

1. For a discussion of possible alternatives to allotment, see Wilcomb E. Washburn, *The Assault on Indian Tribalism*.

2. William A. Brophy and Sophie D. Aberle, *The Indian: America's Unfinished Business*, pp. 72–73.

3. Laurence F. Schmeckebier, *The Office of Indian Affairs*, pp. 66–67.

4. Felix Cohen, *Handbook of Federal Indian Law*, p. 63.

5. Wilcomb E. Washburn, *The Indian in America*, p. 233.

6. Loring Benson Priest. *Uncle Sam's Stepchildren*, 6–14.

7. Henry E. Fritz, *The Movement for Indian Assimilation: 1860-1890*, p. 27.

8. Delos Sacket Otis, *The Dawes Act and the Allotment of Indian Lands*, pp. 4–5.

9. Cohen, *Handbook of Federal Indian Law*, pp. 66–67.

10. Fritz, *The Movement for Indian Assimilation*, p. 187.

11. Otis, *The Dawes Act*, p. 6.

12. Francis P. Prucha, ed., *Americanizing the American Indian*, p. 8.

13. House Committee on Indian Affairs, "Minority Report on Land in Severalty Bill," 1880, House Report No. 1576, 46th Cong., 2d sess. Serial 1938, reprinted in ibid., p. 128.

14. Prucha, *Americanizing the American Indian*, p. 122.

15. Otis, *The Dawes Act*, p. 14.

16. Ibid., p. 36.

17. The text of the Dawes Act is reprinted in Otis, *The Dawes Act*, pp. 177–84.

18. Otis, *The Dawes Act*, p. 180.

19. Legally, Indian tribes were "domestic dependent nations," and members of a tribe were not citizens. Before the Dawes Act, an Indian had to leave tribal status to be recognized as a citizen. A general citizenship bill for Indians was not passed until 1924.

20. Schmeckebier, *The Office of Indian Affairs*, p. 144.

21. Priest, *Uncle Sam's Stepchildren*, pp. 233–48.

22. Fritz, *The Movement for Indian Assimilation*, p. 211.

23. J. P. Kinney, *A Continent Lost—A Civilization Won*, p. 230.

24. Ibid., p. 229.

25. Otis, *The Dawes Act*, pp. 86–87.

26. *Annual Report of the Commissioner of Indian Affairs, 1891*, reprinted in Wilcomb E. Washburn, *The American Indian and the U.S.: A Documentary History*, 1: 454.

27. Otis, *The Dawes Act*, p. 187.

28. Cited in ibid., p. 109.

29. Washburn, *The Assault on Indian Tribalism*, pp. 24, 25.

30. Otis, *The Dawes Act*, p. 121.

31. Schmeckebier, *The Office of Indian Affairs*, p. 87.

32. *Annual Report of the Commissioner of Indian Affairs, 1906*, reprinted in

Washburn, *The American Indian and the U.S.*, 2: 757.

33. Kinney, *A Continent Lost—A Civilization Won*, 246–47.

34. Cited in Kinney, *A Continent Lost—A Civilization Won*, p. 232.

35. Schmeckebier, *The Office of Indian Affairs*, p. 127.

36. Ibid., pp. 127–28.

37. Angie Debo, *And Still the Waters Run*, chaps. 1, 5 passim.

38. Ibid., chap. 4.

39. Schmeckebier, *The Office of Indian Affairs*, pp. 135–42.

40. *Annual Report of the Commissioner of Indian Affairs, 1902*, reprinted in Washburn, *The American Indian and the U.S.*, 2: 715–16.

41. Harold E. Fey and D'Arcy McNickle, *Indians and Other Americans*, p. 85.

42. See Kinney, *A Continent Lost—A Civilization Won*, chap. 8.

43. Randolph C. Downes, "A Crusade for Indian Reform, 1922–1934," *The Mississippi Valley Historical Review* 32 (December 1945): 334–40.

44. Lewis Meriam and Associates, *The Problem of Indian Administration*.

45. Ibid., p. 21.

46. Fey and McNickle, *Indians and Other Americans*, pp. 111–12.

47. *Annual Report of the Commissioner of Indian Affairs, 1933*, reprinted in Washburn, *The American Indian and the U.S.*, 2: 907–8.

48. Wilcomb E. Washburn, *Red Man's Land—White Man's Law*, p. 145.

49. Fey and McNickle, *Indians and Other Americans*, pp. 88–89.

50. See, for example, Fritz, *The Movement of Indian Assimilation*; Priest, *Uncle Sam's Stepchildren*; Robert Mardock, *The Movement for Indian Reform*; Prucha, *Americanizing the American Indian* and *American Indian Policy in Crisis*; and Washburn, *The Assault on Indian Tribalism*.

51. See, for example, Washburn, *Red Man's Land—White Man's Law*, and *The Indian in America;* Edward H. Spicer, *A Short History of the Indians in the United States*, and Alvin M. Josephy, Jr., *The Indian Heritage of America*, chap. 27.

52. Some examples used in this study are Roy W. Meyer, *A History of the Santee Sioux*; John C. Ewers, *The Blackfeet: Raiders on the Northwestern Plains*; and William T. Hagan, *United States-Comanche Relations: The Reservation Years*.

53. See, for example, Scheckebier, *The Office of Indian Affairs*; Kinney, *A Continent Lost—A Civilization Won*; S. Lyman Tyler, *A History of Indian Policy*; and Meriam and Associates, *The Problem of Indian Administration*.

54. See Eirik Furubotn and Svetozar Pejovich, "Property Rights and Economic Theory: A Survey of Recent Literature," *Journal of Economic Literature* 10 (December 1972): 1137–62.

55. The dates used here are drawn from federal documents. Information on the progress of allotment and land transfers are taken from the *Annual Reports of the Commissioner of Indian Affairs*, 1875–1934. Data on the progress of Indian farming are taken from both the *Annual Reports of the Commissioner of Indian Affairs* and the *Census of the United States: Agriculture*, 1900–30. Before 1904 the *Annual Reports* included written commentaries by each agent and a statistical report on farming done by Indians on each reservation. For the period from 1900 to 1930, much useful data on both Indian farming and other economic activities of Indians are obtained for the census. For the late teens and 1920s, valuable accounts of the status of Indians can be found in the reports of individual commissioners in the *Annual Report of the Board of Indian Commissioners*.

PART TWO

Implementing the Act: A Policy in Practice

2

THE COURSE OF ALLOTMENT IN THEORY AND PRACTICE

The allotting of Indian reservations continued from the late 1860s until the Wheeler-Howard Act in 1934. Not surprisingly, most allotments were issued during the period the Dawes Act was in force. The factors that determined when reservations were allotted have largely been ignored in the literature on allotment policy. Yet understanding how allotment was implemented is an important part of the story of how the Dawes Act affected Indian peoples. The examination of these forces is the task of chapters 2 and 3.

Two hypotheses about how reservations were chosen for allotment are formulated to facilitate further exploration of these issues. The first hypothesis formalizes the official position of the Office of Indian Affairs and is referred to as the "guardianship model." This model depicts the Office of Indian Affairs as acting to protect Indian welfare by delaying allotment until the Indians living on a particular reservation were able to benefit from the allotment of their land. The second hypothesis is referred to as the "demand for allotment model." It construes the actions of the Office of Indian Affairs as those of a regulatory agency responding to pressures from non-Indian, economic interest groups. In this model, the choice of reservations for allotment is seen reflecting the interests of whites wanting to develop reservation lands.

It would be incorrect to dismiss the guardianship model as an uninteresting "straw man." Although no contemporary student of Indian affairs ascribes to the guardianship model, it does offer useful perspectives on allotment policy. The courts, for example, have rationalized the broad powers of the federal government over the lives and property of American Indians on the grounds that the federal government would be able to protect

Figure 2.1

NUMBER OF ALLOTMENTS ISSUED: BY YEARS

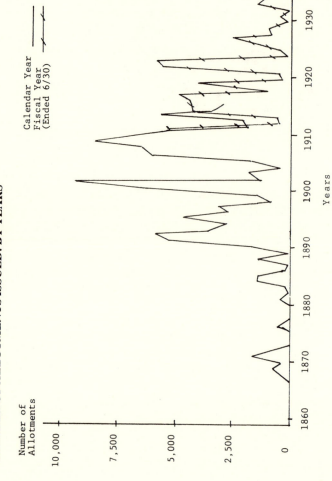

SOURCE: *Annual Reports of the Commissioner of Indian Affairs, 1916-1934.*

30

Figure 2.2
NUMBER OF ACRES ALLOTTED: BY YEARS

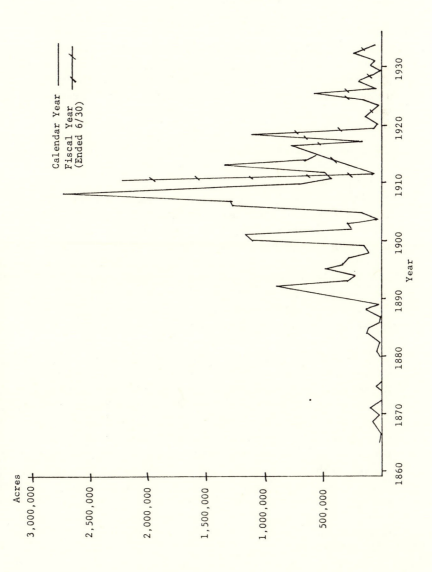

the interests of Indians who might otherwise be unable to protect themselves. Certainly, the reformers relied upon the federal government to guard the interests of Indians in trust status. More broadly, federal regulation of economic activity and federal regulations to protect consumers or groups with special interests are often predicated upon the assumption that the federal government will act as an impartial third party to protect the public interest from monopolies or defend the interests of the economically disadvantaged. If the government failed to protect the interests of allotted Indians, this failure has implications that extend beyond the allotment policy.

The Pace of Allotment Activity

A summary of the ebb and flow of allotment activity is presented by the graphs in figures 2.1. and 2.2. These figures, taken from the *Annual Reports of the Commissioner of Indian Affairs*, show yearly totals of acres allotted and the number of allotments issued.[1] Roughly speaking, the number of allotments recorded equals the number of individuals receiving allotments for the first time. Occasionally individuals already holding allotments received additional land to equalize the area of the holdings or for other administrative reasons. The number of acres per allotment could vary widely between reservations. Under the Dawes Act, Indians on reservations that were too small to permit 160-acre allotments received proportionally smaller parcels of land. In arid regions, allotments as a rule were larger—originally twice as large and later four times the size of allotments given on prime farm land.[2] The period of the Dawes Act has been regarded by historians as crucial in determining the subsequent pattern of Indian land holdings. Harold Fey and D'Arcy McNickle, for example, noted that the Indian land holdings after allotment left Indians with a poor base for future development. Their summary, in a broad sense, is apt enough: "As it happened, the lands that went first were the most valuable: agricultural lands in the river valleys, rich grasslands on the high plains, virgin forests in the Great Lake region. What remained [for the Indians] was desert or semidesert."[3] Yet they did not explain how or why this "happened." As shown in this chapter, a direct relationship exists between the eventual pattern of Indian land holding and the manner in which the allotment policy was implemented.

The question of why the allotment of Indian lands under the Dawes Act was drawn out to span nearly five decades has generally been neglected by historians. However, D. S. Otis and J. P. Kinney did discuss some factors that pushed forward the allotment of Indian lands in the first two decades the law was in force. Otis examined the haste with which the allotment policy was implemented in the early 1890s. He pointed to the steady

pressure from ". . . western land seekers and business promoters . . ." and
". . . the feverish hurry which a political administration feels when it has a
program to carry out."[4] Since the leaders of the allotment movement were
so firmly convinced of the ". . . almost automatic efficiency of
allotment. . . ," it was easy for governmental officials to yield to pressures
to hasten allotment with a clear conscience.[5] In a different vein, Kinney
argued that the allotment of Indian reservations was actively encouraged by
Congress as a way of ". . . hastening the day when the government would
no longer need to make large appropriations for the support, civilization,
and education of Indians."[6] The specific question examined below is what
led the Office of Indian Affairs to rush to allot some reservations while
others were allowed to remain unallotted for several decades or were never
allotted at all.

The Guardianship Model

Although idealized, the guardianship model is consistent with legal and
other statements about the proper role of the Office of Indian Affairs. As
noted above, a major legal and legislative justification for federal regulation of the lives and property of reservation Indians has been that the Office
of Indian Affairs would act as "guardian" of the interests of Indian
"wards" under federal supervision. For example, one major court decision
pictured the reservation as a kind of school in which ". . . Indians are
gathered . . . under the charge of an agent, for the purpose of acquiring the
habits, ideas and aspirations which distinguish civilized from uncivilized
man."[7] In practice, of course, the federal government had to reconcile the
interests of Indians with the demands of other groups, especially western
settlers and taxpayers, for federal funds and access to federal lands. The
Office of Indian Affairs was clearly the agency to which Congress assigned
the task of protecting and expressing the interests of American Indians. The
guardianship model is analogous to public-interest theories of regulation
where the government is pictured as acting to prevent business firms from
exploiting consumers through the use of potential monopoly power.[8]

If the federal government had tried to act as a guardian of Indian property,
a rational course of action would have been to delay the allotment of those
reservations where Indians were unprepared to benefit from allotment.
Thus if the guardianship model is substantially valid, the order in which
reservations were chosen for allotment would have been a function of the
level of economic development of each reservation. Some of the more ar-
ticulate commissioners of Indian affairs expressed such a view of the best
way to implement the allotment policy. One outstanding example was
General Thomas J. Morgan, who served as commissioner from 1889 to
1893, crucial early years of the allotment program. Morgan was a staunch

assimilationist, and his appointment as commissioner of Indian affairs was opposed by some westerners who regarded him as an "eastern crank," that is, too idealistic and concerned with Indian welfare. Wilcomb Washburn noted that "rarely has a Commissioner of Indian Affairs shown the earnestness and dedication of Commissioner Morgan."[9]

Morgan firmly believed in the wisdom of allotting Indian reservations. He wrote that, "I have no doubt as to the wisdom of this policy [allotment], and believe it ought to be pursued vigorously and intelligently until every Indian shall be brought under its operation, so that the relation of all shall be changed from that of wards to that of citizens."[10]

By 1892, however, Morgan admitted that not all Indians were ready to benefit from allotment. In his annual report for that year, he presented the following discussion:

Undoubtedly discretion should be used so as not to allot lands to tribes who are manifestly unfit for citizenship, or who are not soon likely to become so, and it is probable that in some instances mistakes have already been made in this respect. I am convinced that time should be given, so that the Indians to whom allotments are to be made may become familiar with the idea and all that it involves, and may thus be, in some degree, prepared in mind for the great change that must come to them when they are taken from under the protecting care of the agent and the Indian Bureau and are made independent citizens, dependent alone upon their own exertions and subject to the ordinary laws and processes of civilization. The change is a monumentous one, and involves a reconstruction in many cases of all their fundamental conceptions of life and a radical change in their relations. It ought not, therefore, to be expected that they will easily and intelligently adapt themselves to the revolution even when they have time for its consideration.[11]

Similarly, he wrote that, ". . . I cannot too strongly express my earnest conviction that the work of education should keep far ahead even of that of allotting lands, lest the allotment of lands and the conferring of citizenship prove not only a detriment to the Indians themselves, but, in some cases, at least, work to harm the community."[12] Thus Morgan was defending the view that reservations should be chosen for allotment only when the inhabitants were ready to accept the opportunities conferred by allotment. A strong element of paternalism was evident in Morgan's statements. He expected Indians to oppose allotment and believed it was up to the government to implement the policy when it deemed them ready. Despite the misgivings about the possible detrimental effects of premature allotment, Morgan allowed the allotment of reservations and opening of the surplus to proceed rapidly.

Later commissioners made no explicit statements about how reservations were chosen for allotment, but most expressed their support for the principles of the allotment policy and the idea that the Office of Indian Affairs had an obligation to protect the interests and property of allotted Indians.[13] It was not until 1933 that Commissioner John Collier denounced the policy of allotting Indian lands.[14]

If correct, the guardianship model generates testable propositions about how reservations would have been chosen for allotment. However, ample reasons, both theoretical and empirical, lead one to question the accuracy of the guardianship hypothesis. In particular, the model omits any explicit accounting of any direct or indirect impact of allotment on non-Indian interests.

The Demand for Allotment Model

Allotting land to Indians opened this land for lease or sale to whites, thereby benefiting non-Indian farmers and merchants. An increasingly accepted view in economics and other disciplines is that regulatory agencies have often come to reflect the interests of the regulated group. This view of regulation is known to economists as the "capture model" of regulation. The capture model has in turn stimulated further research and development of more sophisticated models that view regulation as part of a more complicated process in which a regulatory agency balances the interests of a number of groups, not just the regulated industry. The capture model, however, remains an important case that is valid for a number of examples of regulation. Modified to fit the unique circumstances presented by the Dawes Act, the model provides the starting point for the analysis that follows.

A regulatory commission is often legally a quasi-independent agency, assigned the task of balancing the general public welfare against the legitimate claims of the regulated industry. Since the public at large has a relatively small stake in actions of the regulatory agency, a free-rider problem is created. Each individual's stake is so small and the number of interested parties so large that group action is limited by costs of organization and information, and each individual consumer is content to let others act in his interest.

The regulated industry, however, is concerned with the decisions of the regulatory agency. Thus trade associations will lobby before the regulatory commission, and each of the regulated firms will spend a lot of time and money to influence the opinion of the commission. This can occur directly through the presentation of data, lobbying, and argument or indirectly through the intercession of members of Congress. In addition, personal and professional ties between the regulated industry and the regulatory commission are often very close. An agency that fails to serve the interests of its client group may find that, among other things, it has little political influence and few friends to protect its interests, or its budget, in Congress.

The outcome is that the regulatory commission often acts in a way that aids the interests of the industry at the expense of the public at large. Prices are higher, existing firms are protected, and the competition from new firms or firms in other industries is discouraged.[15]

The Office of Indian Affairs, however, was different from other regulatory agencies, since the strongly assimilationist nature of its policies and programs led the agency to oppose actions on the part of Indians through the tribe. In principal, it served the individual Indian, but Indians as individuals were permitted little opportunity to influence its policies. Indeed, unallotted Indians could not even vote before 1924. In this situation, the Office of Indian Affairs was not "captured" by Indian tribes and its policies did not systematically reflect the wishes of Indians. The Office of Indian Affairs, however, could be "captured" by other groups that gained or lost as a result of its policies. Ideally, any group that was pro-assimilationist and anti-tribe might be able to align its interests with those of the Office of Indian Affairs. Some groups in white society potentially stood to benefit from the allotment of Indian lands and were willing to endorse the assimilationist and anti-tribe values of the Office of Indian Affairs.

The demand for allotment model proposes that the Office of Indian Affairs chose reservations for allotment in a manner that served the interests of non-Indians who stood to benefit from allotment. The hypothesis has two parts. The first part is that some benefits accrued to non-Indians from the allotting of Indian reservations and these potential benefits were perceived by non-Indians. The second part is that groups that stood to benefit from the opening of an Indian reservation were able to influence policy sufficiently to have a reservation more desirable to them chosen for allotment ahead of reservations where the value of benefits to non-Indians was less. The demand for allotment model does not picture allotment as a process whereby a strong majority—whites—exploited a weak minority—Indians. Most whites had little direct stake in the allotment of an individual reservation. Rather, the model concludes that it would have been rational for the Office of Indian Affairs to have allotted reservations to satisfy the letter of the law and the interests of those whites who stood to benefit directly from allotment. It does not necessarily follow that because a reservation was opened to satisfy the interests of white settlers, Indians necessarily suffered. The effect of allotment on the welfare of allotted Indians is discussed in Part 3.

A white settler or land speculator could acquire reservation land after allotment in three major ways: purchasing surplus land at a low fixed price, leasing allotted lands, and purchasing allotments once restrictions on alienation were removed. Indian lands constituted a significant addition to the public domain when unsettled land was increasingly scarce.

The most straightforward source of potential benefit to non-Indians was from the purchase of surplus, that is, unallotted lands opened for non-

Indian development. The Dawes Act provided that surplus lands were to be opened in 160-acre parcels "to . . . secure homes for actual settlers."[16] In practice, the surplus lands were disposed of in a variety of ways. Until 1900 the federal government typically purchased the land from the tribe at a fixed price and then opened it for sale in a manner similar to the Homestead Laws. After 1900 surplus land was held by the federal government and sold for the tribe by the General Land Office under general or special laws. Most surplus land sold by the General Land Office was disposed of much like other lands in the public domain. Provisions of land entry that established a low, uniform purchase price for broad classes of land meant that the potential gain per acre was greater the higher the value of the land. In the early years, right of entry was given to the first person on a site. Later, the rights to file claims were assigned by lottery.[17] Although settlement was limited to "actual settlers," the literature on the opening of the public domain suggests that land speculators were often successful in circumventing restrictions on who could enter public lands.[18]

Shortly after its passage, the Dawes Act was amended to allow for the leasing of allotments where an allottee was incapable of farming his own land. In practice, this meant that the agents were in charge of enforcing rules for leasing allotted lands. Leases came to be granted more and more freely, and by the turn of the century, the leasing of allotments was relatively common. Leasing spread even as commissioners of Indian affairs warned of the dangers of issuing leases for allottees who should have been encouraged to farm their own land. The agents in the field were under strong pressures from both whites and Indians to be liberal in approving leases. Commissioner Jones, in the annual report for 1900, complained that the leasing privilege was being abused and noted that ". . . on some reservations leasing is the rule and not the exception, while on others the practice is growing."[19] The agent for the Omaha and Winnebago reservations in 1895 was faced with both legal hurdles and the threat of armed resistance to his attempts to remove illegal leasors from the reservation.[20]

By the mid-1890s it was reasonable to anticipate being able to lease allotted lands. Leasing Indian land was attractive to nearby whites and this gave further incentive to have a reservation opened via allotment. Unlike the opening of the surplus, the price at which lands were leased was a function of land quality. It is plausible, however, to argue that the fact that leases were entered into indicates that some consumer surplus was captured by white leasees, even if lease prices were competitive ones. There are transactions costs in making a lease and employing leased land, and it is probable that a higher proportion of land would have been leased, the more valuable the land, *ceteris paribus*. It is reasonable to think that demand was more inelastic and consumer surplus per acre was greater for good land than for poor land.

The third way of entering Indian land was to buy an original allotment.

Initially, the Dawes Act forbade the sale of allotted lands during a twenty-five-year trust period. But after 1901, it was possible to purchase inherited lands, and by 1907, all allotted lands were potentially available for purchase if the government issued a fee patent or if the agent deemed such a purchase to be in an allottee's interest.[21]

The amount of land opened up to white settlement by the allotment of Indian reservations was extensive. According to the U.S. National Land Planning Committee in 1935, a total of 22.7 million acres of land were sold as surplus during the allotment era. Another 23.2 million acres of land allotted to Indians under the Dawes Act or by special agreements with the Five Civilized Tribes were later removed from trust status and *hence* available to be purchased by whites. These figures are reported in the Appendix A, Table A.26.

The gains from leasing or purchasing an Indian allotment would naturally have been greater if the land were leased or purchased at a below market price. The evidence suggests that this sometimes occurred. In his report for 1910, Commissioner Valentine reported on fraudulent land sales on the Kickapoo Reservation in Oklahoma and the White Earth Reservation in Minnesota.[22] With respect to the situation at White Earth, he commented that, "It is the same old story of the robbery of Indian lands and the dirty work that goes with it."[23] Leasing presented much the same problems. Leases were negotiated for the Indians by the agent, and the revenues were under the supervision of the agent. Donald Berthrong reported that on the Cheyenne Reservation, in many cases, the courts were reluctant to enforce decisions involving Indian claims against whites, and as a result, white lessors broke agreements with impunity.[24] A persistent problem for the agent was "informal leases" through which an Indian received direct payments without the knowledge of the agent. According to Berthrong, such arrangements were sometimes for less than full market value. The sheer number and complexity of lease agreements might well have led even a conscientious agent to lease land out at less than its full market price.

Another group that stood to gain from the opening of reservation lands were merchants and others who did business with either Indians or whites near a reservation. Merchants with an established trade with Indians could expect increased sales after the opening of a reservation. Allotment was sometimes accompanied by cash settlements of outstanding claims by Indians against the government. Sales of surplus land also led to an accumulation of tribal funds that were often released to members of the tribe. Other merchants stood to gain from the development of Indian land by white settlers who would be potential customers. As discussed below, Montana merchants sought to have Indian reservations opened as a means of increasing their markets.

But opposed to the non-Indians who stood to gain from allotment were others with an interest in maintaining the closed reservation. White cattlemen sometimes grazed cattle on open reservation land. This was occasionally done without the formality of lease, but it was also done with legal leasing agreements. Those who were illegally occupying Indian lands might also want to delay the opening of the reservation. From the point of view of non-Indians, a reservation ideally suited to allotment would have been a small reservation, lying in fertile soils with little unusable land, and having a high proportion of the total area available for disposal as surplus. This ideal reservation would have been in a relatively developed region near transportation facilities and other improvements. The least desirable reservation for allotment would have been a large reservation in an arid region far from transportation and markets, since such lands were of relatively little value to farmers.

The above sketch suggests possible ways in which white economic interests were affected by allotment. The discussion so far has deliberately avoided the Five Civilized Tribes of eastern Oklahoma. As mentioned in chapter 1, the Five Tribes were exempted from the Dawes Act and in many ways constituted a unique case. At the time of the passage of the Dawes Act, Indians were already a minority in eastern Oklahoma, and whites and Indians were arrayed on both sides of the allotment question.

The structure of government, and the Office of Indian Affairs in particular, makes it likely that organized interests were able to influence the course of Indian policy. The discussion that follows is not meant to test the model but to suggest how Indian policy could have been influenced. This study takes a behavioralist position: the ultimate test will be to examine what actually occurred in the alloting of reservation lands, not what people said they were doing or intended to achieve. If the model tested here with quantitative data is correct, more traditional approaches should reveal corroborating evidence and add useful insights.

One force shaping the formation of Indian policy was Congress. Although the actual allotment of Indian lands was in the hands of the executive branch, Congress was actively involved in allotment through its appropriations for the allotment of individual reservations. If the constituents of a senator or congressman were actively seeking the allotment of an Indian reservation, it is likely that Congress would respond to those interests. An interesting case is Congressman and later Senator from Montana Joseph M. Dixon, an influential figure in Montana history. Congressman Dixon set out in 1904 to prove to his constituents that he could act effectively in their interests. According to his biographer, Jules Karlin, Congressman Dixon regarded the opening of the Crow and Flathead reservations among his most important legislative objectives. Merchants in Billings had lobbied for nearly a decade to have the nearby Crow Reservation allotted, to trade with new settlers. A variety of factors thwarted this goal: less than adequate representation in Congress, the opposition of some eastern groups opposed to further land losses by Indians, and a reluctance on the part of Congress to appropriate funds to compensate the Crow for claims against the government. Aided by the energetic efforts of Dixon, in April 1904 a bill to allot the Crow reservation passed Congress. After his success with the Crow Bill, Dixon turned his attention to the Flathead Reservation.[25]

The allotment of the Flathead Reservation, which was rich in both timber and land suited to agriculture, promised to be a more difficult task. Dixon was aware that it generally took a few years of agitation and sometimes the consent of the Indians involved to breach a treaty agreement. Also, eastern "sentimentalists" were reported in opposition to allotment without the consent of the Flathead. This consent was not forthcoming, and the leaders of the Flathead refused even to answer Dixon's letters. On the other hand, Missoula merchants wanted the reserve opened for settlement to "stimulate business" in western Montana. Armed with provisions from the 1855 treaty with the Flathead, which allowed the allotment of the reservation, Dixon was able to secure passage of a bill allotting the Flathead Reservation. It should be noted that Congress legally had the right to pass allotment bills without Indian approval. In acting to secure allotment of two large reservations, Dixon won support from influential merchants in both eastern and western Montana. Despite opposition by the Flathead, their reservation was allotted.[26]

Outsiders could have influenced the allotment of Indian lands in other ways too. Living in relatively isolated surroundings, employees of the Office of Indian Affairs undoubtedly gave a sympathetic hearing to the neighbors who formed most of their social contacts. As discussed below, allotting agents received subtle and direct pressures from neighboring whites to allot poorer lands to Indians and leave better lands for sale as surplus.

The Office of Indian Affairs was a division in the Department of the Interior that also had responsibility for the sale and leasing of the public domain. The established position of the Interior department was to open land for settlement on relatively favorable terms and not to keep land closed. It is likely that people interested in having lands allotted would have received a sympathetic hearing in other branches of the department.

Further, out-and-out corruption also may have played a role in influencing federal policies. The poor record of employees in the Office of Indian Affairs in the 1870s and 1880s lend credence to this possibility. In the 1870s, for example, two commissioners of Indian affairs were forced to resign under suspicion of corruption.[27]

In this model, the preferences of American Indians are assigned a secondary role in determining whether a reservation was allotted. Agents believed their task was not to listen to Indian opinions on the subject but to convince or coerce members of the tribe into accepting allotment. According to Otis, ". . . there is evidence which suggests that the high pressure campaigns which were carried on by officials were designed primarily at achieving results [e.g., the acceptance of allotment]."[28]

In some cases, this pressure came in the face of strong objections to allotment by tribes or actions within tribes. According to Otis, some tribes ". . . were opposed to allotment because they feared white cultural penetration."[29] Reformers assumed that the individuals engaged in market activities would favor allotment. It is reported, however, that other individuals favored allotment because of the cash payments that accompanied the opening of the reservation. Senator Dawes himself stated that some Indians were ". . . crazy to have allotment, because along with it comes the provision that they may sell to the government the balance of their land."[30] The prospect of being able to lease or sell allotted lands could have the same effect. For persons who did not anticipate farming or ranching in the immediate future, allotment was a means of getting a cash return to an otherwise idle asset. This attitude would be reinforced if they feared that their land might be taken later, perhaps without compensation.

The arguments discussed here about factors influencing the attitudes of different groups within tribes will be important later in assessing the impact of allotment. In the demand for allotment model, however, the impact of a tribe's opposition to allotment is assumed to have been small. Although a tribe might succeed in delaying the beginning of allotment or delaying its completion by a few years, the amount of resistance that would be tolerated was limited. The Yankton agent in 1888 induced cooperation by calling in two companies of soldiers.[31] This, however, appears to have been an exception. Otis and Kinney reported that most tribes seem to have cooperated with allotment, because they either supported it or believed it was inevitable.[32] Evidence on Indian attitudes is fragmentary at best. Although votes were held on some reservations, the agent typically worked to induce a tribe to accept allotment. The Dawes Act did not require that Indians consent to be allotted, and any referendum would have been conducted with the knowledge that the government would ultimately prevail.

Resources available for allotment were limited. Each year the Office of Indian Affairs had to decide which reservations to begin allotting. In 1913 Commissioner Sells reported that the cost of allotting the 34 million acres assigned up to that point, including the Five Civilized Tribes, had been $4.5 million.[33] If special congressional legislation were needed to facilitate allotment, an additional expense was added. The costs of allotment reported by Commissioner Sells appear to have been mainly for surveying the land, handling the administrative procedures of assigning allotments to each individual, recording the patent for the land in Washington, and opening the reservation. Since allotment was not free and budgets were limited, the Office of Indian Affairs had to decide which reservations would be allotted and which would, for that year at least, remain closed.

The Allotment Process

Under the Dawes Act, special agents were appointed to supervise the allotment of each reservation. Previously, allotments had been handled by the agent on the reservation. The allotting agent was expected to assign an allotment to each individual, including in the allotment if possible, any land upon which he had already made improvements. In the 1890s, allotting agents were sometimes given the task of negotiating the purchase of the surplus land, but after 1903 it was ruled that the government did not have to negotiate for the purchase of surplus land.[34] In practice, the special agents were in a very advantageous position to conclude such agreements. The Yankton agent commented unfavorably upon the tactics used by the special agent in negotiating and then winning approval of an agreement for the sale of the surplus.[35]

Lands were sometimes declared to be surplus before the allotment of the whole reservation. This seemed to occur in cases where the land was sparsely settled and Indians living there could be either issued allotments or easily relocated on the rest of the reservation. On the Fort Hall Reservation in Idaho, seventy-nine allotments were issued in connection with the opening of part of the reservation in 1902, and the rest of the reservation was opened and most of the population allotted in 1914.[36] This procedure was relatively expensive, since it involved special allotment bills and special procedures for either allotting or relocating Indians living on the ceded lands.

The opening of a reservation legally referred to the removal of restrictions on non-Indians settling within the boundary of the reservation and usually followed closely the beginning of allotment. On many reservations, all allotments were issued at one time, and on others, the allotment of lands dragged on for years.

The work of the allotting agents has been severely criticized. For example, the Meriam report in 1928 found that:

> The original allotments of land to the Indians were generally made more or less mechanically. Some Indians exercised their privilege of making their own selections; others failing to exercise this right were assigned land. Often Indians who exercised their privilege made selections on the basis of the utility of the land as a means of continuing their primitive mode of existence. Nearness to the customary domestic water supply, availability of firewood, or the presence of some native wild food were common motives. Few were sufficiently farsighted to select land on the basis of its productivity when used as the white

man used it. The Indians were not sufficiently advanced generally to make their selections on this basis, and the allotting work was done too fast and on too wholesale a basis for the representatives of the government to advise and lead them to sound selections . . . the objective apparently was to get the allotment work done rather than to give each Indian a piece of property which if effectively used would furnish the basis of support according to sound standards.[37]

Otis reported that pressure was placed upon the agents assigning allotments to Indians. He cited General Wittlesey of the Board of Indian Commissioners, who noted that, "Another hindrance is the influence brought to bear by surrounding white settlers who are waiting to get possession of the lands that may be reserved after allotments are completed. If there are valuable tracts of land, they try to prevent those from being allotted, and to prevent Indians from selecting them, by bribery and by other means."[38] Similarly, Alice C. Fletcher, an early anthropologist and an enthusiastic supporter of allotment, who served as an allotting agent, complained of being followed constantly by neighboring whites who tried to discourage her from assigning good lands to Indians.[39] Berthrong reported that newspapers in the Oklahoma Territory demanded that some of the more fertile areas of the Cheyenne and Arapaho reservations be reserved for white settlers. Pressure was also exerted to speed up the allotment process to hasten the opening of the reservation for settlement.[40] An allotting agent was apparently judged by his superiors according to how rapidly he completed the task and by neighboring whites according to how much he looked after their interests. The interests of the allotted Indians appear to have suffered as a result.

The Demand for Allotment: A Formal Model

The demand for allotment model assumes that reservations were chosen for allotment based on the potential benefits to non-Indian settlers, speculators, and merchants. The more desirable a reservation was to outsiders, the more pressure they would have placed on the Office of Indian Affairs and the more likely that it would have been allotted sooner. It is also assumed that the crucial date was the year in which the allotment of a reservation began, since the opening of a reservation allowed non-Indians access to reservation land.

Costs as well as benefits resulted from the allotment of Indian lands. Most of the direct costs to the Office of Indian Affairs were a function of the number of acres allotted: surveying and the administrative expenses of issuing allotments. Expenses were also connected with allotment that continued after a reservation was allotted. Once an Indian was allotted, the Office of

Indian Affairs had to supervise his or her property individually. One sign of these increased administrative costs was the rapid growth of the number of clerks needed in Washington. From 1900 to 1920, the number of employees in the Office of Indian Affairs in Washington increased from 101 to 262.[41] For simplicity, it is assumed below that costs per acre were constant in allotting Indian lands.

The decision facing the Office of Indian Affairs was which reservation to allot next. The model of how this decision was made is presented in figure 2.3. On the horizontal axis, reservations are ranked from left to right according to the dollar benefits per acre, with the most valuable on the left. It is assumed that the costs per acre are constant for all reservations. At a given moment, all reservations to the left of point A would be sufficiently attractive to justify their being allotted, and reservations to the right of point A would not justify the expenditure.

Two factors could lead to allotment of additional reservations. First, the costs per acre of allotting reservation lands could decline, leading to the allotment of reservations that had previously seemed unattractive. The passage of the Dawes Act made the process of having a reservation allotted a far less time-consuming and costly affair to arrange and implement and consequently shifted the MC (costs per acre) function downward. Second, function B (which measures benefits per acre) could shift up to the right because of higher agricultural prices, improvements in transportation, improvements in facilities, increased settlements, or changes in technology. In terms of figure 2.3, the B function shifts upward to B', leading to the allotment of the reservations representing the land from A to A'.

The model can be interpreted in a dynamic context as well. Changes in the economic environment led to changes in the expected benefits from the allotment of Indian lands. At some point, a threshold of allotment is reached, and the pressure for allotment is sufficient to justify the costs and the allotment process begins. The model allows room to account for the desires of Indians to accelerate or retard the date of allotment. Nevertheless, in the empirical tests that follow, no variable reflecting the interest of Indians is included.

It is important to clarify what the model does not imply. The notion that the implementation of the program of allotting lands in severalty was shaped by non-Indian interests does not necessarily mean that the policy was a thinly disguised scheme for expropriating Indian lands, although it in fact did lead to a large transfer of land from Indians to non-Indians. The argument is that the general program of allotting land in severalty was bent, pulled, and shaped by non-Indian economic interests. It is plausible to attribute the best of intentions for Indians on the part of reformers and the administrators in the Office of Indian Affairs who planned and instituted the allotment of Indian lands.

Figure 2.3
THE DEMAND FOR ALLOTMENT MODEL

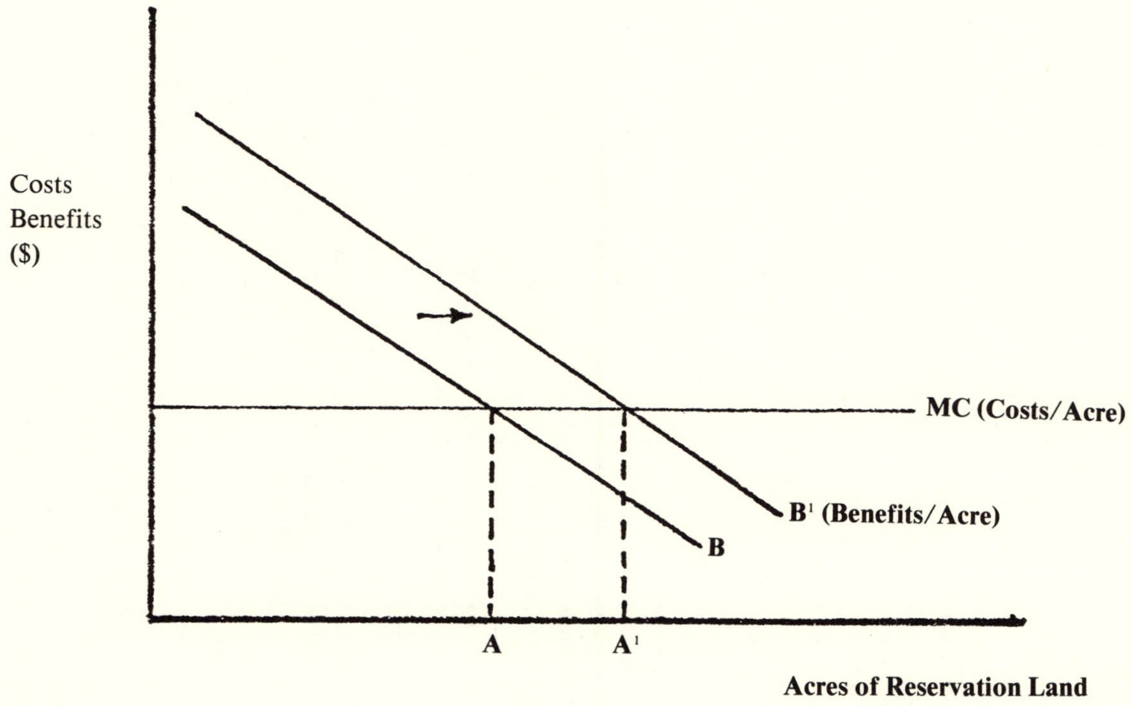

Costs
Benefits
($)

MC (Costs/Acre)

B¹ (Benefits/Acre)

B

A¹   A

Acres of Reservation Land

Empirical Results: The Aggregate View

In testing the demand for allotment model, the data are examined to determine if the timing and pattern of allotment of different reservations corresponds to the predictions of the model. Looked at in its broad outlines, other explanations could account for the observed pattern of allotment activity as well. These explanations are discussed in chapter 3, where the examination of allotment is carried to a more disaggregate level by considering allotment within a three state region: Nebraska, North Dakota, and South Dakota.

In the discussion below, the phrase "date of allotment" is used. To use this term unambiguously for every reservation in the sample, it is defined as the date by which 10 percent of the acres ever allotted on the reservation had been allotted. Allotment was not an instantaneous process. Some reservations had all allotments issued in one year; others could be spread out over two or three decades. Figures are taken from the *Annual Reports of the Commissioner of Indian Affairs*.

The sample used in the statistical analysis includes only reservations on which more than 100 allotments were issued and 10,000 acres allotted. This includes some reservations allotted before the passage of the Dawes Act and included by the Office of Indian Affairs in its statistical tables. Jurisdictions listed by the Office of Indian Affairs as separate reservations in the *Annual Report of the Commissioner of Indian Affairs, 1915* are treated as reservations.[42] As noted above, the Five Tribes of eastern Oklahoma are omitted from the sample.

The major statistical test of the demand for allotment model uses regression analysis to examine the relationship between the date when a reservation was allotted and the attractiveness of that reservation. It is hypothesized that the most attractive reservations were the first to be allotted, and the least attractive reservations were the last chosen for allotment.

Two strong assumptions are made in estimating the model. The first is that the land in the state is homogeneous, except for rainfall, which is measured for each reservation. Intrastate variations in land quality are assumed to be captured in the stochastic term. The second assumption is that data from 1910 are a good proxy for the relative attractiveness of land at the time the allotment decision was made. The year 1910 is used because by that time, no state had a substantial proportion of its area still in Indian hands (except for Arizona, where the huge Navajo Reservation and other important reservations were never allotted). Sixty-four of the eighty-one reservations included in the sample were allotted between 1888 and 1913.

The regression model assumes that a negative linear relationship exists between the date of allotment and the level of development of a state in 1910.

The estimated model is:

$$Y = B_0 + B_1X_1 + B_2X_2 + B_3X_3 + B_4X_4 + B_5X_5 + \in$$

where:

Y : The date at which a reservation had 10 percent of total allotment approved.

X_1: A dummy variable for rainfall. 0 is a reservation in a region of greater than 20 inches of rainfall, 1 if less than 20 inches of rainfall.

X_2: Percent of land in the state that was improved land as reported in the 1910 census.

X_3: Population density of the state in which the reservation is located.

X_4: A dummy variable for Oklahoma; 1 in Oklahoma, 0 otherwise.

X_5: A dummy variable for Minnesota; 1 in Minnesota, 0 otherwise.

It is hypothesized that B_1 is positive, B_2 is negative, B_3 is negative, B_4 is positive, and B_5 is positive.

A dummy variable is used for rainfall to measure whether a reservation was in an area suitable for farming without irrigation or in a region more suited for grazing, dry farming, or irrigated agriculture. Rainfall was chosen as the most important single index of the type of agriculture that could be conducted.[43] The choice of 20 inches was dictated in part by convenience, but few reservations would change their classification for reasonable alternative cutoff points. This is the only variable in the model that measures intrastate variations in the attractiveness of reservation land. Data are taken from the *Yearbook of Agriculture, 1941: Climate and Man* and refer to average annual precipitation, 1899–1939.[44]

The next two variables are measures of the development and potential pressure for allotment within a given state. The percentage of land improved is an index of the average suitability of land for commercial use in farming. The population density is a proxy for potential political pressure and closeness of overhead improvements.

A dummy variable for Oklahoma is included to reflect the unique status of reservations in western Oklahoma and the Indian Territory. Before 1890 settlement and development of western Oklahoma was restricted, since much of the state was within the borders of Indian reservations. Although many whites lived in Oklahoma, pressure for allotment was inhibited by restrictions on white settlement, the lack of internal improvements and services, the increased costs of allotting such a large mass of land, and perhaps the more effective opposition to allotment by Indians united by common interests and physical proximity. Once opened for non-Indian settlement, Oklahoma developed rapidly.

Minnesota is another case where it is expected that allotment would have been delayed. Reservations in Minnesota were allotted under the Nelson Act of 1889. This act gave Indians in Minnesota the choice of accepting allotments on their original reservation or being relocated to the White Earth Reservation and allotted there. This law concentrated Minnesota's Chippewa on one reservation and undoubtedly reflected white economic interests. It also, however, made allotment more costly and time-consuming to implement.

As in other tests, the sample included all reservations having more than 10,000 acres allotted or more than 100 allotments. The sample includes reservations allotted by treaty before 1887 but omits the Five Civilized Tribes. The results of the regression are as follows:

$$Y = 1899.8 + 12.3X_1 - 0.133X_2 - 0.296X_3 + 11.2X_4 + 13.1X_5$$
$$(5.28)\quad (2.88)\quad\;\;\; (3.08)\quad\;\;\; (4.79)\quad\;\; (4.01)$$

$R^2 = 0.647$

$F = 27.2$

$N = 80$

Values in parentheses are t ratios.

All coefficients are significant at the 1 percent level, and all have the predicted sign. Over 64 percent of the variation in the dates of allotment between 1869 and 1932 is explained in the model.

The coefficients have straightforward interpretations. A reservation in a region with less than 20 inches of rainfall per year was allotted 12.3 years later than a reservation located in the same state having more than 20 inches of rainfall. As predicted, reservations in Oklahoma and Minnesota were allotted later than reservations in other states by 11.2 and 13.1 years respectively.

The main explanatory variables are percentage of land improved and the population density per square mile. For the sample, the mean percentage of land improved was 43.44 percent, ranging from 1.7 percent in Arizona to 78.6 percent in Nebraska. The model predicts that everything else being equal, a reservation in a state like Arizona would be allotted 10.2 years later than a reservation in a state like Nebraska. The population density had a mean of 16.25, with a range from 1.5 in Wyoming to 48.9 in Michigan. The model predicts that a reservation in Michigan would be allotted 14.0 years earlier than a reservation in Wyoming.

An analysis of the residuals indicates that the model has a problem explaining very early and very late allotments. Twelve reservations were allotted before 1887. Of these reservations, eight were allotted two or more years earlier than the model predicted. Only the earliest two deviated by more than ten years from the date predicted by the model. These two are the Potowatomie Reservation in Kansas and the Winnebago Reservation in Nebraska, allotted in 1868 and 1871 respectively. They were both allotted under special circumstances. The Potowatomie were relocated from Wisconsin and Illinois, and allotment was done by treaty in conjunction with the sale of part of the reservation and removal of part of the tribe to Oklahoma.[45] The Winnebago allotment was something of an experiment with most allotment not being issued until 1893.

On the other end of the scale, the model predicts "early" for the last reservations allotted. The latest estimated date of allotment for any reservation is 1911. Although the Fort Belknap and the Northern Cheyenne reservations in Montana were allotted in 1925 and 1932 respectively, the estimated date for each was 1910. Both reservations are in the relatively dry eastern half of the state, and their allotment coincides with a renewed interest in dry farming in the western Dakotas and eastern Montana.[46]

In addition to the four reservations mentioned above, only seven other reservations have deviations from the predicted value that are larger than ten years.

It is to be expected that a number of reservations would deviate from the regression line, since the aggregate variables used do not capture special cases with any precision; for example, a reservation in a particularly attractive or unattractive location within a state.

The regression results presented above are consistent with the demand for allotment model. The reservations that were allotted first were those in states that had been developed and settled by 1910. As noted above, although these results are consistent with the demand for allotment model, they might also be consistent with other explanations as well. Nonetheless, the existence of a model that explains the pattern of allotment of Indian reservations without referring to the preparedness of Indian peoples for allotment necessarily calls into question the guardianship model.

Although the Five Tribes are not included in the sample used to estimate the equation on page 48, the estimated equation can be used to examine an interesting counterfactual proposition. If the values of the independent variable for each of the Five Tribes are substituted into the equation, the resulting values can be interpreted as the "predicted" dates at which the Five Tribes would have been allotted had they been included in the Dawes Act. The predicted value determined in this manner is 1895 (due to the way in which the values of the independent variables are assigned, the date is the same in all five tribes). In fact, the date predicted in this way corresponds closely to the actual dissolution of the governments of the Five Tribes. The Dawes Commission of 1893 was appointed to negotiate agreements to the tribal governments and allot all tribal lands. The first tribe to agree to allotment and the dissolution of the tribal government was the Chickasaw in 1896. The Curtis Act of 1898 threatened an imposed settlement on any tribal government that refused to reach a "voluntary" agreement with the federal government. Faced with this deadline, the last of the Five Tribes came to terms, and tribal lands were divided shortly thereafter. Although this analysis is admittedly crude, and not to be taken too seriously, it points out that, although the Five Tribes were relatively well organized and lobbied to protest their interests in Congress, in the long run, they were no more able to resist internal and external pressures for allotment than other tribes.

In addition to the regression analysis explained in detail above, the demand for allotment model was tested using nonparametric statistical tests. The relationship tested is that between the rank order of allotment of different reservations and four proxies for attractiveness of land in each state. The null hypothesis is that the variables were independent. The variables used in these tests are the percentage of land in improved acres in the state or territory in 1890, the percentage of the state that was either cropland or plowable pasture in 1930, the rural population density in 1910, and the value per acre of land in farms in 1910. All data are taken from the census. The three census years are at the beginning, middle, and end of the allotment era.

In all four cases, a statistically significant relationship existed between the order of allotment and the proxy for the level of development in the state. These tests offer additional support for the demand of allotment model and are reported in the appendix.[47]

An important part of the story of how Indian land holdings changed during the era of land allotment was the amount of tribal land left in Indian hands, including reservations that were never allotted. When allotment was stopped in 1934, Indians were left with differing amounts of tribal land, and some important reservations were never allotted. The largest of the unallotted reservations was the huge Navajo Reservation in Arizona and New Mexico.[48]

Table 2.1 shows the relationship between the ratio of tribal land remaining in Indian hands to total acres allotted, including reservations that were never allotted, and the percentage of the land in the state that was in cropland or plowable pasture in 1929. The null hypothesis of no relationship can be rejected at the 0.1 percent level. Indian reservations that were not allotted or left with large amounts of tribally held land were in states that had a low proportion of the total area developed for farming. Typically, such states were relatively arid.

Although it is not a direct test of the demand for allotment model, the fact that a statistically significant relationship exists between the amount of

TABLE 2.1

Ratio of Tribal Land, 1940 , to Total Acres Allotted: Percentage of Land in the State in Cropland and Plowable Pasture, 1929

Ratio of Tribal to Allotted Land	Percentage of the State in Cropland and Plowable Pasture	
0.00 to 0.10	9	41
0.101 to 1.00	9	6
1.01 to 100.0	14	11
Unallotted	16	3

N = 99
X² (3 d.f.) = 40.1
Significant at 0.1% level

SOURCES: Annual Reports of the commissioners of Indian Affairs, 1916-34; Fifteenth Census of the United States, 1930, Vol. V: Agriculture, pp. 44-45.

land in a state that was improved and the amount of land in tribal hands is consistent with the demand for allotment model.

Indirect support for the demand for allotment model is provided by the way in which the Office of Indian Affairs used its authority to issue patents in fee. As discussed in chapter 1, the Burke Act of 1906 gave the Office of Indian Affairs the authority to issue patents in fee to Indians deemed ready to manage their own affairs. From 1907 to 1916, the Office of Indian Affairs issued 9,894 patents. Beginning in 1917, Commissioner Cato Sells declared a "new policy" that encouraged the issuing of such patents. All Indians of less than one-half Indian blood were automatically issued patents, and commissions were set up to evaluate the competency of Indians who still had their lands held in trust. From 1917 to 1920, 17,376 patents were issued, many with only a cursory examination of the qualifications of the allotted. Beginning in 1921, a more conservative policy was adopted and far fewer patents were awarded. In all, 5,972 patents were issued from 1921 until 1934. The abandonment of the liberal policy of issuing patents in 1920 was due in part to concern that many Indians sold their allotments as soon as they were issued patents.[49]

The last years of World War I were marked by high agricultural prices and a speculative demand for land that led to a boom in land prices. It is consistent with the demand for allotment model that, in this period of high prices and increased demand for land, the Office of Indian Affairs yielded to white pressure and relaxed the rules surrounding the issue of patents. The tightening of the rules after 1920 is coincident with a sharp decline in land values and agricultural prices and a corresponding fall in the demand for agricultural land. It also apparently reflected a genuine concern that too many Indians had lost their land and turned once again to the federal government for assistance.

Allotment and the Guardianship Model

The findings reported above have used the demand for allotment model to examine the pattern of allotting reservations. This model of how reservations were chosen for allotment explains important patterns in the allotment of Indian lands. Nonetheless, the guardianship model of how reservations were chosen for allotment has not yet been tested.

The guardianship model supposes that the factors that determined whether a tribe was ready for allotment were internal to the tribe. Allotment was to allow Indians to benefit from the opportunities and incentives of a market economy. Tribes that had more experience in market-oriented activities, therefore, should have been the first allotted, and those that were largely dependent upon the federal government or traditional activities (such as hunting) for support should have had allotment delayed until they had acquired more experience with commercial affairs.

The first test of the guardianship model examines the relationship of the order in which reservations were allotted and the agent's estimate of the percentage of tribal income earned in what were called "civilized pursuits." Each agent was asked to estimate for the people under his supervision the percentage of subsistence earned in each of three categories: "civilized pursuits," "hunting, fishing, and root gathering," and "issue of government

TABLE 2.2
Agents' Estimates of Percentage of
Support from "Civilized Pursuits" for 1892:
Order of Allotment

	OBSERVATIONS	
CATEGORIES	ALL RESERVATIONS	AFTER 1887
0-25%	14	14
26-50%	15	12
51-75%	10	9
76-100%	30	24

ALL RESERVATIONS

$N = 69$
H (distributed X^2, 3 d.f.) = 14.78
Significant at 1% level

AFTER 1887

$N = 59$
H (distributed X^2, 3 d.f.) = 13.07
Significant at 1% level

SOURCES: *Annual Report of the Commissioner of Indian Affairs, 1892,* 784-801; also *Annual Reports,* 1916 to 1934.

NOTE: See table A.22, appendix A.

rations.'' A test of the relationship between the agents' estimate of percentage of income earned in civilized pursuits in 1892 and the order in which reservations were allotted yields a statistically significant relationship. The confidence level is lower than for those tests reported in the previous section, but it does offer some support for the guardianship model. This test is shown in table 2.2.

A more valid test of the guardianship model would be to examine whether reservations were allotted after the level of self-support by Indians had increased to some threshold level of self-sufficiency or at least showed substantial improvement. If Indians on reservations allotted late remained at the same level of self-support that they had achieved at an earlier date, the guardianship hypothesis would be called into question. The changes in self-sufficiency of reservations allotted relatively late are examined in chapter 3.

Using the demand for allotment model, it is also possible to explain the positive relationship between allotment and income earned in civilized pursuits. Reservations allotted early were typically in states well suited for farming, with Indian populations that had been adjusting to reservation life for a relatively long time. Reservations allotted late were often in arid regions where the land was best suited to cattle raising, and often the tribes had been settled for a shorter time. It is not surprising that Indians on the first reservations allotted were relatively more often engaged in market activities than Indians on reservations allotted relatively late.

TABLE 2.3
Ratio of Acres Cultivated in 1892 to Total Acres Allotted:
Order of Allotment

| | Observations | |
CATEGORIES	ALL RESERVATIONS	AFTER 1887
Less than 0.009	24	22
0.01-0.025	17	15
0.026-0.05	10	7
Greater than 0.051	10	7

ALL RESERVATIONS

N = 61
H (distribution X^2, 3 d.f.) = 11.97
Significant at 1% level

AFTER 1887

N = 48
H (distribution X^2, 3 d.f.) = 14.2
Significant at 1% level

SOURCES: Annual Report of the Commissioner of Indian Affairs, 1892, pp. 802-817; *Annual Reports*, 1916 to 1934.

NOTE: See table A.22, Appendix A.

A second test of the guardianship model used, shown in table 2.3, is a cruder measure of self-sufficiency among Indian farmers: the ratio of acres cultivated to total acres allotted. Since allotments on reservations suited to grazing were relatively large, and farming activities were limited, the low ratio of acres cultivated to acres allotted could be a measure of reservations containing land suited to grazing rather than farming and not a measure of readiness for allotment. Large reservations in cattle country were typically allotted relatively late. The null hypothesis of no relationship can be rejected at the 1 percent level. Again, a better test of the guardianship hypothesis would examine whether reservations allotted late showed substantial improvement in acres cultivated before allotment was initiated by federal agents.

The statistical tests and literary evidence presented thus far support the demand for allotment model, which is based on the assumption that the Office of Indian Affairs was captured by whites with a direct interest in the allotment of Indian lands. Unfortunately, these aggregate tests can be given more than one interpretation, and the quantitative results need to be supplemented by more traditional evidencce.

Notes

1. These figures do not include lands allotted Indians from the public domain.

2. The cyclical movement of the number of allotments and the acres allotted are analyzed again at the end of chapter 3.

3. Harold E. Fey and D'Arcy McNickle, *Indians and Other Americans*, p. 85.

4. Delos Sacket Otis, *The Dawes Act and the Allotment of Indian Lands*, pp. 82–83.

5. Ibid., p. 83.

6. J. P. Kinney, *A Continent Lost—A Civilization Won*, p. 247.

7. Cited in Monroe Price, *Law and the American Indian*, p. 88.

8. See Richard Posner, "Economic Theories of Regulation," *the Bell Journal of Economics* 5 (Autumn 1974): 335–53, for a critical view of the public interest theory of regulation.

9. Wilcomb E. Washburn, *The American Indian and the U.S.*, 1: 574.

10. *Annual Report of the Commissioner of Indian Affairs, 1892*, reprinted in Wilcomb E. Washburn, *The American Indian and the U.S.*, 1: 575.

11. Ibid., p. 575.

12. Ibid., p. 578.

13. An easily accessible source for the opinions of the commissioners of Indian affairs is provided by Washburn, *The American Indian and the U.S.* For an example of a commissioner supporting the view that the Office of Indian Affairs had an obligation to protect and supervise Indians, see Commissioner W. O. Jones in the *Annual Report of the Commissioner of Indian Affairs, 1900*, reprinted in Washburn, *The American Indian and the U.S.*, 2: 700.

14. *Annual Report of the Commissioner of Indian Affairs, 1933*, reprinted in Washburn, *The American Indian and the U.S.*, 2: 966.

15. The capture model of regulation is put forth by economist George Stigler, in "The Economic Theory of Regulation," *The Bell Journal of Economics and Management Science* 2 (Spring 1970): 3-21. The capture model is explained in Posner, "Economic Theories of Regulation" and Bruce Owen and Ronald Braeutigam, *The Regulation Game: Strategic Uses of the Administrative Process*, chap. 1. Political scientists and historians have long considered such a view of regulation. See Grant McConnell, *Private Power and American Democracy* (New York: Alfred A. Knopf, 1966): and Gabriel Kolko, *Railroads and Regulation, 1877-1916* (New York: W. W. Norton and Co., 1965).

More recent work that presents more sophisticated views building on the capture model can be found in Sam Peltzman, "Towards a More General Theory of Regulation," *Journal of Law and Economic* 19, no. 2 (August 1976): 211-40; and Owen and Braeutigam, *The Regulation Game*. Examples of the application of a capture model include Paul W. MacAvoy, *The Economic Effects of Regulation, the Trunkline Railroad Cartels and the Interstate Commerce Commission Before 1900* (Cambridge: the MIT Press, 1965); and Jonathan Pincus, "A Positive Theory of Tariff Formation Applied to the Nineteenth Century United States" (Ph.D. diss., Stanford University, 1972), and "Pressure Groups and the Pattern of Tariffs, *Journal of Political Economy* 83 (August 1975): 757-78.

16. The text of the Dawes Act is reprinted in Otis, *The Dawes Act*, pp. 177-84.

17. See Lawrence F. Schmeckebier, *The Office of Indian Affairs*, pp. 165-66.

18. See Paul Gates, *The Farmer's Age: Agriculture 1815-1860* (New York: Holt, Rinehart and Winston, 1960), chaps. 3, 4; Fred A. Shannon, *The Farmer's Last Frontier 1860-1897* (New York: Holt, Rinehart and Winston, 1945), chaps. 2, 3; and Roy Robbins, *Our Landed Heritage: The Public Domain, 1776-1936* (Princeton, N.J.: Princeton University Press, 1942, reprinted in paperback, Lincoln: University of Nebraska Press, 1962), passim.

19. *Annual Report of the Commissioner of Indian Affairs, 1900*, reprinted in Washburn, *The American Indian and the U.S.*, 2: 701.

20. *Annual Report of the Commissioner of Indian Affairs, 1895*, pp. 37-41.

21. See chapter 1.

22. *Annual Report of the Commissioner of Indian Affairs, 1910*, reprinted in Washburn, *The American Indian in the U.S.*, 2: 808-9.

23. Ibid., p. 808.

24. Donald Berthrong, "Federal Indian Policy and the Southern Cheyenne and Arapahoes—1887-1907," in *The Western-American Indian* ed. Richard N. Ellis (Lincoln: University of Nebraska Press, 1972), p. 139, originally published in *Ethnohistory* 3 (Spring 1956): 138-48. See also his *The Cheyenne and Arapaho Ordeal* (Norman: University of Oklahoma Press, 1976) and "Legacies of the Dawes Act: Bureaucrats and Land Thieves at the Cheyenne-Arapaho Agencies of Oklahoma," *Arizona and the West* (Winter 1979): 335-54.

25. Jules Karlin, *Joseph M. Dixon of Montana, Part I: Senator and Bull Moose Manager, 1867-1917*, p. 56.

26. Ibid., pp. 57-58.

27. See Henry E. Fritz, *The Movement for Indian Assimilation, 1860-1890*, chap. 1.

28. Otis, *The Dawes Act*, pp. 89-90.

29. Ibid., p. 93.

30. Quoted in ibid., p. 91.

31. Ibid., p. 96.

32. See Otis, *The Dawes Act*, pp. 90–97, and Kinney, *A Continent Lost—A Civilization Won*, p. 247.

33. Washburn, *The American Indian and the U.S.*, 2: 823.

34. Schmeckebier, *The Office of Indian Affairs*, p. 144.

35. *Annual Report of the Commissioner of Indian Affairs, 1893*, pp. 310–11.

36. *Annual Report of the Commissioner of Indian Affairs, 1915*, p. 83.

37. Lewis Meriam and Associates, *The Problem of Indian Administration*, p. 470.

38. Otis, *The Dawes Act*, p. 145.

39. Ibid.

40. Berthrong, "Federal Indian Policy and the Southern Cheyenne and Arapahoes—1887-1907," pp. 136–37.

41. *Annual Report of the Commissioner of Indian Affairs, 1920*.

42. *Annual Report of the Commissioner of Indian Affairs, 1915*, pp. 82–89. Data are taken from the *Annual Reports*, 1915-34.

43. Mary Hargreaves uses 15 inches as the point at which it becomes necessary to depend on dry farming. Twenty inches was used to insure the exclusion of marginal reservations and for ease of measurement. See Mary Wilma H. Hargreaves, *Dry Farming in the Northern Great Plains*, p. 8.

44. U.S. Department of Agriculture, *Yearbook of Agriculture, 1941: Climate and Man,* pp. 751-1201, passim.

45. See Grant Foreman, *The Last Trek of the Indians,* pp. 218ff, and Edward H. Spicer, *A Short History of the Indians of the United States*, pp. 77ff.

46. See Hargreaves, *Dry Farming*, p. 20.

47. See appendix A, tables A.22 to A.25.

48. Some Navajos living off the reservation were allotted land from the public domain in New Mexico. See Lawrence C. Kelly, *The Navajo Indians and Federal Indian Policy, 1900-1935*, pp. 23-28.

49. Figures taken from *Annual Reports of the Commissioner of Indian Affairs*, 1920-34.

3

GUARDIANSHIP, LANDHUNGER, AND THE NORTHERN PLAINS RESERVATIONS

In contrast to chapter 2, which examined allotment on an aggregate level, this chapter looks at allotment in a single region comprising the states of Nebraska, North Dakota, and South Dakota. A large number of Indian peoples lived in this area, and all of the reservations there were allotted. Geographically, the three states are part of the Northern Plains region and have interesting topographical and climatological features, which shaped the timing and pattern of settlement of the region. The hypotheses developed and tested on an aggregate level in chapter 2 are tested here against the experience of Indians in Nebraska, North Dakota, and South Dakota. Of course, caution must be used in generalizing conclusions derived from one region to the whole country.

The Geography of the Northern Plains

Although many factors determine the usefulness of the land in agriculture in the Northern Plains, rainfall is the most important determinant of the type of farming best suited for a region in the plains. Mary Hargreaves noted that it is difficult to raise crops in regions with less than 15 inches of rainfall.[1] The nature of the soils and patterns of drought and humidity are also very important. The map of rainfall in figure 3.1 shows that average rainfall in the Northern Plains declines as one moves from east to west.

Obviously changes in climate and other factors are also evident as one moves from south to north. West of the region where rainfall is sufficient for standard farming techniques is an area where grain can be grown using a variety of techniques usually classified as dry farming. Dry farming entails using large fields to compensate for low yields per acre. In general, dry farming is practiced in the western parts of these three states.

The Indian reservations of Nebraska are located in the eastern half of the state. That region contains rich soil well suited to the growing of corn and winter wheat.[2] Thus the Indian lands are located in a prime agricultural region. Reservations in South Dakota are scattered throughout the state according to the U.S. Department of Agriculture, *Yearbook of Agriculture, 1941: Climate and Man*:

> . . . The eastern half of the state is practically all arable and fertile land, suitable for growing crops, but the western half, because of limited moisture and more rugged terrain, is best suited for stock grazing, although other forms of agriculture are profitable in years of ample moisture. . . .[3]

North Dakota contains three entire reservations in separate parts of the state and portions of two other reservations. *Climate and Man* describes North Dakota as follows:

> Most of the eastern part has fine agricultural lands, the soil consisting of a black loam of varying depth, underlaid with a subsoil of clay. The west is gently rolling, with soil ranging from poor in the Badlands to excellent in some other sections. Cereal are grown in large quantities and diversified farming is universal.[4]

These capsule descriptions of the three states are consistent with the proposition that the attractiveness of the land for agriculture in the Northern Plains declines as one moves from east to west. These descriptions of the region are essentially static. To have a more complete picture for the story developed here, it is necessary to examine the way in which settlement and development occurred.

Settlement in the Northern Plains

Not surprisingly, the first parts of each of these three states to be settled were in the eastern half of each state. The areas settled first were both closest to older settlements and well suited to agriculture and are still among the most densely settled regions in the plains.

Nebraska, the first state of the three to be settled by whites, was already a state in 1870, at which time it had a population of 122,993, with 1.3 percent of its total land area classed as farmland. By 1880 the population had risen to 452,402, with 11.3 percent of the area improved, and by 1890 the population was over 1 million, with 31 percent of the land area improved.[5]

Figure 3.1
RAINFALL IN THE NORTHERN PLAINS

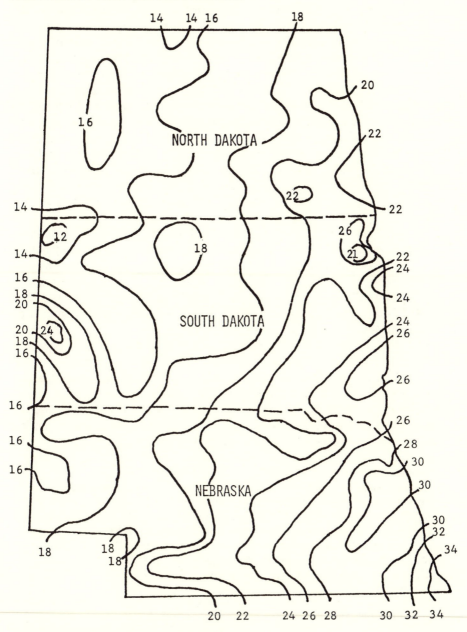

Average Precipitation (inches), 1899-1939.

SOURCE: Yearbook of Agriculture, 1941: Climate and Man.

Generally, settlement in Nebraska moved from east to west, and within the settled region, the most densely settled areas were in the southeast.

The Dakotas were only sparsely settled in 1870. By 1880 the population of that part of the Dakota Territory that was to become the state of South Dakota was 96,268, with 1.8 percent of the total area improved farmland. The future state of North Dakota had a population of 36,909, with 0.6 percent of the area improved land. By 1890 both had been admitted as states, and South Dakota's population had grown to 348,600, with 14.1 percent of the total area improved land, and North Dakota had 190,983 people, with 10.4 percent of its land improved.[6] The pattern of settlement in the Northern Plains is reflected in the map in figure 3.2, which shows the counties that had been settled by 1890. The unshaded area is the unsettled region. Clearly, by 1890, given current technology, transportation, and factory prices, land east of the settlement line was more attractive than land west of that line.

The demand for allotment model predicts that the pressure for allotment became greater as the value of the land on a reservation increased. Allotment would occur when the benefits from allotment were sufficient to warrant the costs of allotting the reservation. In general, it is to be expected that the "threshold" where it becomes profitable to allot a reservation would be crossed about the time adjacent lands of similar quality had become sufficiently attractive to warrant development.

The idea of a threshold of allotment focuses attention upon the pace and pattern of settlement, which in turn reflect relative prices, the quality of the land, and the availability of transportation. After 1897 agricultural prices began a gradual increase that lasted over two decades. This rise in prices induced a movement into previously uncultivated western lands and also induced experimentation with new types of farming. Land prices in settled regions rose to new heights. Mary Hargreaves noted that:

> Home-seekers who could not make a heavy capital outlay [to buy a farm in a settled region] were forced to look further west. Viewing the semi-arid region in those years of plentiful rainfall, they were encouraged to expand the agricultural frontier from the valleys and fringes of the Plains far back over the uplands. The development of dry farming in eastern Montana and the western Dakotas—combined with the revival of earlier efforts to establish such enterprise in the central Plains—afforded the largest additions to cultivated acreage made in the United States after 1900.[7]

Allotment in the Northern Plains

This chapter so far has explored the settlement of the Northern Plains by whites. If the demand for allotment model is correct, a direct relationship

Figure 3.2

SETTLEMENT IN THE NORTHERN PLAINS

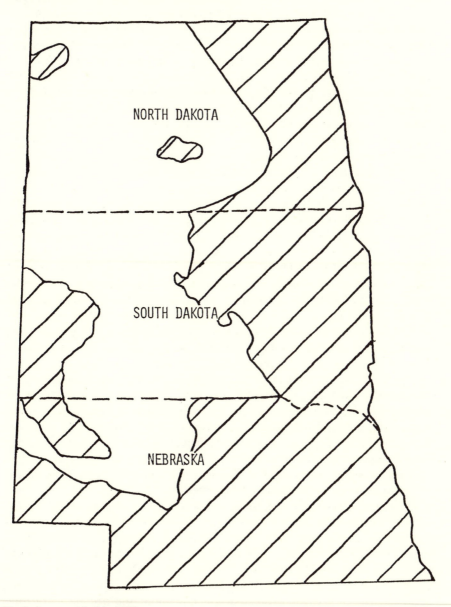

NORTH DAKOTA

SOUTH DAKOTA

NEBRASKA

Shaded area settled in 1890.

SOURCE: Eleventh Census of the United States, 1890, Vol. V: Agriculture, plate 5.

should exist between allotment and the settlement of the region. Figure 3.3 presents a map of the region showing major Indian reservations in the three states. The dates in parentheses refer to the dates by which 10 and 90 percent of allotment were completed. This map shows a consistent pattern of eastern reservations being allotted before the reservations farther west.

It should be noted in comparing the maps in figures 3.2 and 3.3 that all reservations allotted before 1889 lie to the east of the 1890 line of settlement, which refers to the border between settled and unsettled areas, as defined in the 1890 census with one exception discussed below. Reservations allotted in 1900 or later lie to the west of the line of settlement. This is consistent with the demand for allotment model. In terms of the model, the rise in land prices accompanying the rise in agricultural prices after 1897 led to increased pressure for the allotment of the previously unallotted reservations in the western Dakotas.

All reservations in these three states were allotted between 1870 and 1910. We can usefully divide these years into three periods: the pre-Dawes Act period to 1887, 1887–99, and post-1900. The only reservations allotted before the passage of the Dawes Act were in Nebraska. Allotment began on three of the four reservations in Nebraska—the Omaha, Winnebago, and Santee reservations—before the passage of the Dawes Act. The fourth reservation in Nebraska, the Ponca, was allotted in the first wave after the passage of the Dawes Act. Nebraska was the first state settled of the three examined here, and hence it is consistent with the demand for allotment model that reservations in Nebraska were the first allotted. All four reservations in the state lie in the region settled by 1890.

The first reservation in Nebraska to be allotted was the Winnebago. The Winnebago Indians were originally inhabitants of the Old Northwest and were one of the tribes moved several times as settlement pushed west.[8] In the mid-1860s, the tribe was moved from land in Wisconsin to lands purchased from the Omaha tribe. Allotment work began under the original treaty, and the 10 percent level was reached in 1871. A majority of the acres were not allotted, however, until 1893, and it was not until 1901 that 90 percent of the total allotments ever granted had been issued.

The neighboring Omaha Reservation was the site of a major experiment with allotment often cited by reformers. Some members of the tribe petitioned Congress in the 1880s requesting that the reservation be allotted, a move D. S. Otis interpreted as a desire to forestall removal to Oklahoma.[9] Despite some questions about the readiness of the Omaha for allotment, in 1884, 963 individuals were allotted roughly 78,000 acres. Interestingly, agents in the mid-1890s expressed concern about the decline in farming among the Omaha and the large number of leases of allotted lands that had been approved.[10]

Figure 3.3
ALLOTMENT IN THE NORTHERN PLAINS

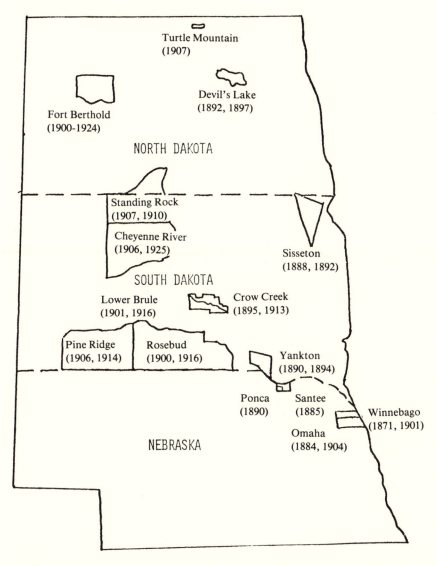

Turtle Mountain
(1907)

Devil's Lake
(1892, 1897)

Fort Berthold
(1900-1924)

NORTH DAKOTA

Standing Rock
(1907, 1910)

Cheyenne River
(1906, 1925)

Sisseton
(1888, 1892)

SOUTH DAKOTA

Lower Brule
(1901, 1916)

Crow Creek
(1895, 1913)

Pine Ridge
(1906, 1914)

Rosebud
(1900, 1916)

Yankton
(1890, 1894)

Ponca
(1890)

Santee
(1885)

Winnebago
(1871, 1901)

Omaha
(1884, 1904)

NEBRASKA

NOTE: Outlined areas are Indian reservations. First date in brackets is the date by which 10 percent of total allotments were issued; second date is date by which 90 percent were issued.

SOURCE: Date on Allotments from *Annual Reports of the Commissioner of Indian Affairs 1916-1934*.

63

The third reservation allotted before the passage of the Dawes Act was the Santee, allotted in 1885. It is on the border of South Dakota, in a less attractive region than either the Omaha or Winnebago reservations.

The passage of the Dawes Act lowered the cost of allotment. In terms of the model, the marginal cost of allotting Indian lands shifted downward.[11] Between 1890 and 1895, five reservations were allotted (dates in parentheses are dates of allotment): the Ponca Reservation in Nebraska (1890), the Yankton Reservation in South Dakota (1890), the Crow Creek Reservation in South Dakota (1895), the Sisseton Reservation in South Dakota and North Dakota (1888), and the Devil's Lake Reservation in North Dakota (1892). All five were within the region that was settled by 1890. Thus five of the six reservations that should be considered prime candidates for allotment in the demand for allotment model were allotted shortly after the passage of the Dawes Act. The sixth, the Turtle Mountain Reservation, is a special case discussed below.

These reservations were already being considered for allotment before the Dawes Act. Indeed, allotments were being assigned on the Sisseton Reservation when the Dawes Act was passed, and the work was revised in accordance with the act's provisions.[12] Whether or not the Indian peoples on these reservations wanted allotment had little effect on whether a reservation was allotted. Informal allotments assigned by the agent on the Crow Creek Reservation had been accepted in 1881, while, as indicated above, on the Yankton Reservation, a faction opposed allotment and harassed the surveyors until two companies of soldiers were summoned to the reservation.[13] Yet the Yankton Indians, in a more desirable region, were allotted five years sooner than the Crow Creek Indians.

Reservations Allotted after 1900

Reservations allotted after 1900 were typically large reservations in the more arid western Dakotas: the Lower Brule (1901), Pine Ridge (1900), Rosebud (1900), and Cheyenne River (1906) reservations in South Dakota; the Standing Rock (1907) Reservation in North and South Dakota, and the Fort Berthold (1900) and Turtle Mountain (1907) reservations in North Dakota. Interest in allotting the western reservations corresponded to the movement of population into the western Dakotas and the increased practice of dry farming.

The Great Sioux Reservation provides an interesting example of how allotment was implemented. In 1889 the reservation was reduced by legislation and divided into six smaller reservations: Pine Ridge, Rosebud, Cheyenne River, Standing Rock, Lower Brule, and Crow Creek. The law reducing the area of the reservation included provisions calling for the allotment of the six reservations. Mary Johnston noted that:

The Government was slow in applying allotment to the Great Sioux although the agents of Rosebud, Pine Ridge, Cheyenne River, Standing Rock, Crow Creek and Lower Brule had instructions, soon after the passage of the Dawes Act, to do all in their power to induce allotment at those five agencies [Crow Creek and Lower Brule were under the same agency]. They had endeavored to carry out their instructions . . . [but they were limited by a lack of funds]. . . .[14]

Near the end of 1889 the Commissioner of Indian Affairs reported to the Secretary [of the Interior] that the Indians of the Sioux reservation were urging the Department to have their land surveyed so they could receive allotments before the land was opened to *white settlers who would not respect their rights and would force them from their lands.* The Commissioner agreed that their apprehensions, in light of past experiences, were well founded, but without sufficient appropriations the land could not be surveyed.[15] (Emphasis added)

Despite the willingness of the Office of Indian Affairs and expressions from the agents that the Sioux at the various agencies were willing to cooperate with allotment, Congress was unwilling to appropriate the necessary funds to begin allotment. In terms of the demand for allotment model, little pressure was exerted to open lands in addition to those ceded in 1889. The 1889 cessions had opened some land near the edge of settled areas that was being sought for development.

The troubles with the Messiah cult in 1890 and 1891 ultimately led to the massacre at Wounded Knee in 1891.[16] The most immediate result of this atrocity was that it prodded Congress to appropriate needed relief money for the Sioux.

When allotment began on the former Great Sioux Reservation, a definite east to west movement was occurring in the order reservations were allotted. This is clear on the map in figure 3.3. Such an east to west pattern, is, again, consistent with the demand for allotment model.

The Turtle Mountain Reservation is the exception to the statement that all reservations allotted after 1900 were west of the 1890 settlement line. But it is an exception consistent with the argument developed here. The Turtle Mountain Reservation presented peculiar legal and administrative problems for the federal government: by administrative oversight, the land in the vicinity of the Turtle Mountain Reservation had never formally been ceded to the United States. The people on the reservation were Chippewa, a tribe with bands in both Canada and the United States; the proximity of the reservation to the Canadian border meant that some of the full- and mixed-blood Indians in the neighborhood of the reservation were legally Canadians. Other problems were created by whites married to Indians.

In the mid-1880s, a reservation was organized from a part of the unceded region. In 1907 the reservation was allotted as part of an agreement approved in 1904, which in turn was a modified version of an agreement originally negotiated in 1892. It called for a cash settlement of $1 million for the ceded lands and allowed members of the tribe who were unable to obtain allotments to be allotted lands from the public domain. Congress' unwillingness to ratify this agreement delayed the allotment of the reservation. In terms of the demand for allotment model the increased expense of allotting the Turtle Mountain Reservation led to its being allotted at a later date.

The agent for 1904 reported that, "This tribe [the Turtle Mountain Chippewa] includes all degrees of blood and civilization, from whites to full-bloods and from highly cultivated civilization to the most benighted of the uncivilized."[17] Apart from the tone of the agent's remarks, which illustrate some of the ethnocentric self-confidence so characteristic of writings from this period, his comments point out that widely divergent levels of acculturation existed among these Indians. Where possible, the least acculturated full-blood Indians were given allotments on the reservation itself, and the more acculturated Indians received allotments from the public domain in Montana, North Dakota, and South Dakota. In all, 326 individuals received allotments totaling 43,829 acres on the reservation, and 2,691 allotments were issued for 399,817 acres on the public domain.[18]

It is interesting to speculate that the pattern of having allotments from the public domain go to relatively acculturated individuals might be general. As discussed below, a steady stream of allotments from public lands occurred throughout the forty-seven years the Dawes Act was in force. The Dawes Act gave members of bands not on reservations a means of creating a property right for themselves. It seems likely that the more acculturated an individual was, the more likely he would be to take advantage of this opportunity, but little information is available about who received public domain allotments.

Up to this point, the guardianship model has been ignored in the discussion of the allotment of reservations in these three Plains states. Tables 3.1 and 3.2 give a variety of data on agricultural activity taken from the *Annual Reports of the Commissioner of Indian Affairs*. Table 3.1 gives data for reservations allotted before 1900. It should be recalled that the Winnebago, Omaha, and Santee reservations were allotted before the passage of the Dawes Act.

In the last column in table 3.1, "Percent of Income Earned in Civilized Pursuits," the three reservations allotted before 1887 all reported a high percentage of income earned in civilized pursuits. In terms of acres cultivated, they are less clearly superior. A comparison of all reservations allotted after 1900, in table 3.2, with those allotted before 1900, in table 3.1, reveals that the reservations allotted before 1900 had populations more oriented to "civilized pursuits," which usually meant farming.[19]

TABLE 3.1
Nebraska, North and South Dakota:
Reservations Allotted Before 1900

Reservation (Date Allotted)	Date	Population	Acres Cultivated	Output (Corn Equivalent, BU.)	Number of Cattle	Percentage of Subsistence in "Civilized Occupations"
Omaha, Neb. (1884)	1890	1,173	1,380	121,553	638	100%
	1900	1,182	13,000	94,227	700	30
Ponca, Neb. (1890)	1890	217	455	11,978	308	95
	1900	828	3,500	8,289	150	50
Santee, Neb. (1885)	1890	868	3,991	14,537	280	95
	1900	1,019	6,439	29,858	105	50
Winnebago, Neb. (1871)	1890	1,212	4,165	56,656	462	95
	1900	1,124	5,000	40,868	150	20
Crow Creek, S.D. (1895)	1890	1,058	2,823	3,255	1,441	50
	1900	1,047	960	4,632	650	35
Sisseton, S.D. (1888)	1890	1,509	3,152	6,574	299	100
	1900	1,840	4,000	50,073	185	70
Yankton, S.D. (1890)	1890	1,725	4,050	30,509	926	50
	1900	1,700	11,000	81,473	1,000	70
Devil's Lake, N.D. (1892)	1890	1,041	2,372	7,339	249	100
	1900	1,041	5,853	21,033	134	70

SOURCE: *Annual Reports of the Commissioner of Indian Affairs, 1884-1900.*

Thus on first examination, some support is evident for the guardianship model. Carried one step further, however, the data lead to another interpretation. As discussed in chapter 2, the guardianship model of allotment implies that reservations were held back from allotment until they had crossed some threshold of readiness for allotment or showed signs of improvement. But in Table 3.2, no support is given for the hypothesis that Indians on reservations allotted after 1900 had reached a threshold of readiness for allotment. In terms of income from "civilized pursuits," three reservations show a substantial reported *decline,* and only one shows an increase of more than 5 percent. The only substantial sign of progress was the increase in the head of cattle on reservations in the western plains. Allotment, however, was designed to promote farming and was not well suited to promote cattle ranching, a point developed further in chapter 6.

The higher percentages of self-sufficiency for the reservations allotted before 1900 reflect the fact that they were in regions more suited to farming and closer to markets and outside employment. The very high percentages of income from civilized pursuits reported for the Omaha and Winnebago in 1890 (100 and 95 percent respectively) are suspicious in light of the rapid fall by 1900 (down to 30 and 20 percent respectively). As shown in table 3.2, this rapid decline in percentage of income earned in "civilized pursuits" was not accompanied by declines in agricultural activity. It is likely that what was reported in 1890 was income from the leasing of allotments and tribal lands. Lease income accounted for most of the earnings of these tribes in 1900, by which time it was reported as a separate category. By 1894, 223 leases had been approved on the Omaha and Winnebago reservations. The rapidity with which licit leasing was introduced and spread leads to the suspicion that informal and illicit leasing of allotted and tribal lands was already practiced before 1894.

Thus the hypothesis that the pattern of allotment was determined by the Office of Indian Affairs acting in the capacity of a guardian is not a good explanation of the observed behavior. Certainly, little evidence appears to support the view that reservations allotted later had crossed a threshold of self-sufficiency and hence were ready for allotment.

The reservations in the western Dakotas were both the last and the largest reservations allotted. They took an average of fourteen years to go from having 10 percent of the total acres allotted to having 90 percent allotted; smaller reservations allotted after the Dawes Act lying east of the 1890 settlement line took an average of less than six years to allot. Although the longer time to allot the western reservations may be attributable to the larger size of these reservations, it is also reasonable to expect that portions of these large reservations were less desirable and left as tribal lands until a later date.

TABLE 3.2

Nebraska, North and South Dakota:

Reservations Allotted After 1900

Reservation (Date Allotted)	Date	Population	Acres Cultivated	Output (Corn Equivalent, BU.)	Number of Cattle	Percentage of Subsistence in "Civilized Occupations"
Cheyenne River, S.D.	1890	2,823	2,160	1,149	9,000	50%
(1906)	1900	2,550	1,000	1,314	20,387	50
Lower Brule, S.D.	1890	1,026	1,485	7,043	1,197	34
(1901)	1900	475	500	3,251	1,511	20
Pine Ridge, S.D.	1890	5,701	3,375	2,340	8,610	33
(1906)	1900	6,619	1,425	2,139	41,936	35
Rosebud, S.D.	1890	5,345	4,322	9,462	3,695	25
(1900)	1900	4,931	1,665	8,991	16,200	20
Fort Berthold, N.D.	1890	1,183	890	9,984	160	70
(1900)	1900	1,098	1,690	1,636	3,809	35
Standing Rock, N.D.	1890	4,096	5,000	19,925	4,560	30
(1907)	1900	3,588	3,306	25,876	21,799	50
Turtle Mountain, N.D.	1890	1,439	2,372	18,197	666	65
(1907)	1900	2,429	8,350	15,211	637	55

SOURCE: Annual Reports of the Commissioner of Indian Affairs, 1884-1900.

Again we find the idea that tribal lands were retained in areas that were the least desirable is valid for the Dakotas and Nebraska. As reported in table 3.3, only two reservations in the Northern Plains had a ratio of tribal to allotted lands greater than 0.10: Cheyenne River and Pine Ridge. Along with the Fort Berthold and Standing Rock reservations, they are the westernmost reservations in these states and are located in relatively arid country. Both reservations had more than 100,000 acres of tribal land in 1940.[20]

The Allotment of the Rosebud Reservation

A revealing case study of how the allotment was carried out is given by Carl Eicher in his 1960 study of the Rosebud Reservation. Eicher investigated how the pattern of land ownership he observed in 1960 came into being. He drew on agency sources to report that between 72 and 100 percent of the three western counties on the reservation—Todd, Mellette, and Tripp—were allotted to Indians, and only 9 and 4 percent respectively of Gregory and Lyman, the two most eastern counties on the reservation, were allotted to Indians. Eicher described Todd and Mellette counties as arid, but he reported that, "Land in the eastern half [Tripp, Gregory, and Lyman counties] of the reservation . . . [had] . . . ample rainfall for reasonably successful general farming of wheat, hay and corn. . . ."[21]

By historical chance, the agency was located in the western portion of the reservation, and allotment work began near the agency. The first allotments were approved in 1898. By 1900, 10 percent of the total allotments ever issued had been assigned, and 50 percent had been assigned by 1902. Two-thirds of the total had been allotted by 1907, and the 90 percent level was reached in 1916. With this in mind, it is interesting to note that:

> In 1904, the Rosebud people relinquished all unallotted land in Gregory County [the most eastern of the five counties on the reservation] for $2.50 per acre. The relinquished lands were thrown open to homesteading and any citizen of the U.S. was permitted to register. A total of 106,269 persons made registrations for the 2,400 homesteads available. In 1907, the Rosebud Indians, by an agreement with the government, relinquished all unallotted land in Tripp County. A total of 114,769 persons registered for a chance to draw one of the 4,000 available homesteads. In 1910, Rosebud people relinquished all unallotted lands in Mellette County, and these lands were opened for homestead.[22]

By 1904 the allotment of the reservation was little more than 60 percent completed. Allotments were again issued in 1907, after most of the land in the most desirable part of the reservation, Gregory and Tripp counties, had been opened to non-Indians. Thus while lands in the western part of the

TABLE 3.3
Reservations in the Northern Plains: Land Areas

Reservation	Area 1890[a]	Total Acres Allotted	Tribal Land 1940	Surplus[b]	Surplus Land Total Allotted	Tribal Land Total Allotted
Omaha, Neb.	65,191[c]	130,522	4,486	—	—	0.03
Ponca, Neb.	96,000	27,236	836	—	2.5	0.03
Santee, Neb.	1,311[c]	73,373	2,774	—	—	0.04
Winnebago, Neb.	14,612[c]	122,333	3,432	—	—	0.03
Fort Berthold, N.D.	2,912,000	601,013	23,192	2,287,786	3.8	0.04
Devil's Lake, N.D.	230,400	137,301	0	93,099	0.67	0
Standing Rock, N.D.	2,672,640	1,401,022	128,216	1,143,402	0.81	0.09
Turtle Mountain, N.D.	46,080	43,820	0	2,260	0.09	0
Cheyenne River, S.D.	2,867,810	1,292,225	637,849	937,849	0.73	0.49
Crow Creek, S.D.	203,397	280,123	878	—	—	0.003
Lower Brule, S.D.	472,550	224,715	18,865	228,970	1.01	0.08
Pine Ridge, S.D.	3,155,200	2,365,253	244,090	545,857	0.23	0.10
Rosebud, S.D.	3,228,480	1,862,676	18,346	1,347,458	0.72	0.01
Sisseton, S.D.	780,893	308,838	0	472,055	1.53	0
Yankton, S.D.	430,405	268,383	3,252	158,769	0.59	0.01

SOURCES: *Annual Reports of the Commissioner of Indian Affairs*, 1890, 1916-1934; ''Statistical Supplement to the Annual Report of the Commissioner of Indian Affairs for the Fiscal Year ended June 30, 1940,'' pp. 30-36.

[a]Unallotted land on the reservation.
[b]Surplus area 1890—total allotted—tribal land.
[c]Allotted before 1890.

reservation were still in the process of being allotted, some of the best land on the reservation had been relinquished.

As a guardian, the Office of Indian Affairs was acting in a peculiar manner. It made little effort to preserve the best lands for the Rosebud Indians in the face of a strong non-Indian demand for land on the reservation, indicated by the massive overapplication for the available homesteads. No direct evidence of wrongdoing on the part of the allotting agent can be found, but whatever his motivation, his actions benefited white settlers at the expense of the Rosebud Indians. Of course, the fact that prime eastern lands were being sold to non-Indians as allotment was proceeding in the drier western counties is consistent with the demand for allotment model.

Evaluating Alternative Hypotheses of the Allotment of Indian Lands

On both the aggregate and disaggregate level, the demand for allotment model offers a simple, workable explanation of how reservations were chosen for allotment. On the macrolevel, statistically significant relationships exist between the dates when reservations were allotted and the level of development in the state. On the microlevel, the allotment of reservations in Nebraska, North Dakota, and South Dakota closely followed the settlement of those states.

The guardianship hypothesis does not work well in explaining the pattern of allotment. Although some relationship exists between the percentage of income earned in "civilized pursuits" and the date of allotment, no support is evident for the view that the Office of Indian Affairs delayed allotment until the Indians living on different reservations had become more self-sufficient.

Nonetheless, any hypothesis that concludes that reservations would have been allotted as the surrounding community was developed, or as the land became more attractive, would also be consistent with the data. Thus it might be possible to rehabilitate the guardianship hypothesis by arguing that delaying allotment until the surrounding community had developed was in the interest of Indian allottees. If, for example, allotment was timed to coincide with increased access to markets to buy or sell crops, it would explain the observed course of allotment. Such a policy, however, would have been in direct conflict with the main features of federal Indian policy. The Office of Indian Affairs was trying to encourage Indians to become subsistence farmers. The twenty-five-year trust period on allotted lands was designed to encourage Indians to stay and farm reservation lands. As late as 1928, the prestigious Meriam Commission endorsed a program of helping Indians learn to operate small general farms, geared to home consumption.[23] As shown in chapter 5, most Indian farms were small and grew crops for their own use, so little reason was found to delay allotment until the introduction of markets near the reservation.

Alternatively, it could be postulated that allotment was delayed to increase the value of the surplus lands sold to whites or the value of the allotments that were leased or sold. Some may have thought, for example, that funds from the sale of surplus land or perhaps the leasing of allotments were necessary to give Indians sufficient working capital to succeed as farmers. But again, this line of reasoning is inconsistent with the rest of federal policy. Typically, little was done with the proceeds of the sale. Often the government distributed it to individual members of the tribe on a per capita basis or kept it in tribal accounts for use at a later date. If widespread and systematic plans had existed for the use of surplus funds, such as a loan program to allow Indians to buy equipment, it might be possible to assign a crucial role to money received from the sale of the surplus lands. This, however, was not the case. The small per capita payments issued from tribal funds were often either wasted or too small to aid Indian farmers in buying major purchases of equipment.

Thus the Indian office had no reason to wait for an influx of white settlers and an increase in land prices to allot an Indian reservation. The guardianship hypothesis cannot be rehabilitated by pointing to the benefits that accrued to Indians who received allotments in relatively developed regions. Also, the Indian office did not depend upon the development of the local community to implement its programs: Indians were encouraged to become subsistence, general farmers and not market-oriented specialists, and no systematic programs were using funds from the sale of Indian surplus or allotted land.

Patterns in the Allotment of Reservations

The demand for allotment model has been used to explain a variety of allotment programs. Returning to figures 2.1 and 2.2, it is possible to discuss some of the broad patterns in the implementation of allotment. The whole allotment era can be divided into subperiods: before 1887, 1888-99, 1900 to June 30, 1916, and July 1, 1916 to 1934. These subperiods were chosen because they refect different levels of allotment activity. Allotment activity in each period is presented in table 3.4.

Before the passage of the Dawes act, just under 600,000 acres were allotted. From 1881 to 1887, roughly 490 allotments were issued per year. In terms of the demand for allotment model, it was relatively expensive to allot a reservation before the passage of the Dawes Act. The reservations allotted in these years were in Kansas, Nebraska, Michigan, Wisconsin, and western Washington. They were relatively small reservations in attractive locations.

TABLE 3.4
Allotment Activity

Period	Total Allotments	Allotments per Year	Acres Allotted	Acres per Year
Before 1887	7,493		586,805	
1881-87[a]	3,429	490	296,467	42,352
1888-99[a]	32,791	2,733	3,724,031	310,336
1900-6/30 1916[b]	72,844	4,415	14,739,323	893,323
7/1 1916-1933[c]	28,404	1,578	5,408,280	318,134
Public Domain				
To 1915[a]	7,520		1,083,944	
1912-23[c]	3,243	270	532,344	44,362
1924-33[c]	1,315	132	182,140	18,214

SOURCE: Annual Reports of the Commissioner of Indian Affairs, 1916-1934.

[a]Calendar year ended 12/31.
[b]Data linked (fiscal year and calendar year); therefore small errors may appear in the totals.
[c]Fiscal year ended 6/30.

Immediately following the passage of the Dawes Act, allotment activity picked up to a level of over 2,700 per year. A large number of the reservations allotted were in Oklahoma. In addition, numerous allotments were issued for lands in Oregon, eastern Washington, Idaho, the eastern Dakotas, and Minnesota. Such reservations can be thought of as being prime targets for allotment once the Dawes Act lowered the administrative costs of having such lands allotted.

The third period marked the peak of the allotment activity. An average of 4,420 allotments a year were issued, and a total of 14,739,823 acres were allotted. Allotment work continued in many of the same regions affected during the 1890s, especially Oklahoma and Minnesota. In addition, the large reservations of the plains states were also allotted. The allotment of reservations in these more arid regions corresponds to the development of dry farming in the central plains, as discussed by Hargreaves.

After 1916 the level of allotment activity declined markedly. Most reservations had already been allotted or were in the process of being finished by 1916. Only nine reservations were allotted after 1910 and only four after 1916. The reservations that began allotment were in dry areas: southern Idaho, eastern Montana, Arizona, and southern California. Most of the acres allotted were in Idaho and Montana. This flurry of allotment activity corresponded to renewed interest in dry farming. Hargreaves noted that, "With relatively favorable weather conditions from 1920 to 1928, grain growers in the semi-arid regions readjusted their operations to overcome the problem of demand. . . . With such innovations [e.g., mechanized equipment and improved credit facilities] in the early twenties, dry farmers undertook to maximize low acreage income by a vast expansion of the area in cultivation."[24] Montana had 17.2 percent of all land in crops and plowable pasture by 1929 relative to 11.8 percent improved in 1919. It was in this region of expanding acreage that the last reservations were allotted. Again, allotment activity can be seen as related to new lands becoming profitable for development.

Allotment came to an end in 1934. During the more than five decades that reservations were allotted, a vast amount of Indian land was deeded to individual Indians or opened to white settlers. As reported in appendix A, table A.2, 26.12 million acres were allotted to Indians under the Dawes Act, and by special legislation, another 15.79 million acres were divided among members of the Five Tribes. The pattern in which reservations were allotted was not a random event. Allotment was used as a means to open Indian lands to development, and thus the patterns of land holding on Indian reservations that evolved by 1934 and can be observed today were in part a function of the way in which the reservations were allotted.

Establishing the point that allotment was carried out in response to the pressure of market forces, of course, does not imply that it was harmful to Indians. Other theoretical and empirical questions must be examined before the broad outlines of how allotment affected the welfare of American Indians and society at large can be evaluated. Nonetheless, the way in which official programs were shaped by the profitability of certain policies for non-Indians raises questions about the effective motives underlying the design and implementation of federal policies touching upon Indian affairs.

Notes

1. Mary Wilma H. Hargreaves, *Dry Farming in the Northern Great Plains*, p. 8.
2. U.S. Department of Agriculture, *Yearbook of Agriculture, 1941: Climate and Man*, p. 977.
3. Ibid., p. 1117.
4. Ibid., p. 1053.
5. U.S. Department of the Interior, Bureau of the Census, *Thirteenth Census of the United States, 1910, Vol. V: Agriculture*, pp. 40, 45.
6. Ibid.
7. Hargreaves, *Dry Farming*, p. 16.
8. See Grant Foreman, *The Last Trek of the Indians*, pp. 218ff.
9. Delos Sacket Otis, *The Dawes Act and the Allotment of Indian Lands*, p. 14.
10. Ibid., pp. 128-31.
11. See chapter 2.
12. Roy W. Meyer, *A History of the Santee Sioux*, pp. 215-16.
13. *Annual Report of the Commissioner of Indian Affairs, 1881*, pp. 85-87; and the *Annual Report of the Commissioner of Indian Affairs, 1888*, p. 65.

14. Mary Johnston, *Federal Relations with the Great Sioux Indians of South Dakota, 1887-1933*, p. 8.

15. Ibid., p. 82.

16. The Messiah cult was a religious movement that prophesied a return of the buffalo and the good times for Plains Indians as well as a return to old values. A band of Sioux followers of this movement were surrounded and partially disarmed by the seventh cavalry in 1891 near Wounded Knee Creek when a fight broke out. At least 153 Indians died, with some estimates placing the number of dead as over 300 men, women, and children, along with 25 soldiers, many hit by their own fire. See Dee Brown, *Bury My Heart at Wounded Knee*, chap. 19, for a popularized account; Edward H. Spicer, *A Short History of the Indians of the United States*, pp. 92, 120, places the indicent and the reactions of the Plains Indians in a larger context.

17. *Annual Report of the Commissioner of Indian Affairs, 1904, Part I*, p. 269.

18. *Annual Report of the Commissioner of Indian Affairs, 1915*, p. 98.

19. See chapter 5 for a discussion of farming and ranching on many of these reservations.

20. See table 3.3.

21. Carl K. Eicher, "Constraints on Economic Progress on the Rosebud Sioux Indian Reservation" (Ph.D. diss., Harvard University, 1960), p. 89.

22. Ibid.

23. Lewis Meriam and Associates, *The Problem of Indian Administration*, pp. 490-91.

24. Hargreaves, *Dry Farming*, p. 20.

PART THREE
Allotment's Impact on Indian Farming

4

REFORMER'S GOALS AND THEORETICAL EXPECTATIONS

In evaluating allotment, we are faced with the difficulty that the reformers did not accept the usual criteria used by economists in making statements about welfare. At the heart of welfare economics is the idea that an individual is the ultimate judge of his or her well being. Hence an individual's assessment of his or her own preference is accepted as valid. The reformers, however, were not concerned with what Indians wanted or what they might think about allotment. An Indian who resisted assimilation into white society was wrong, and hence his or her preferences could be disregarded. If necessary, the reformers were willing to use coercion to bring about what they viewed as socially beneficial results.

For now, the split between what the reformers wanted to accomplish by allotting Indian lands and what the Indians may have wanted is accepted. The goals of the reformers are used below as the starting point for an examination of the efficacy of the Dawes Act. Some aspects of how Indians may have viewed allotment are discussed in this chapter and in chapter 7.

The reformers hoped the Dawes Act would accomplish at least six things: break up the tribe as a social unit, encourage individual initiative, further the progress of Indian farmers, reduce the cost of Indian administration, secure at least part of the reservation as Indian land, and open unused lands to white settlers. This discussion of the impact of allotment on Indians focuses on the first three points; the remaining questions are considered in the concluding chapter.

Reformers were determined to weaken the tribe as a social unit. They saw the tribe as a highly cohesive group in which hereditary chiefs and rigid traditions exercised great authority over the actions of members of the tribe.

It was this rigid control of an individual's activities that was seen as critically hindering economic advancement. An important feature in this stereotyped picture of Indian life, since the reformers were not careful in drawing distinctions between different tribes and cultures, was the sharing of property. The chiefs were seen as having great power to redistribute wealth and as being opposed to any change that would weaken their authority.

The reformers made numerous references to factionalism in different tribes. This factionalism was seen as a split between the "progressives," typically young, and the "conservatives," typically old. It was hoped that allotment would break the hold of the conservative older chiefs and allow the progressive younger Indians to advance more rapidly. Defenders of allotment made no clear distinction between acculturation and economic advancement. The goal of reformers was the acculturation of Indians into white society, and that included a wide range of behavior. The focus of this study on the economic aspects of allotment would have made no sense to a reformer, who saw economic change as a part of, and dependent upon, a wholesale acceptance of white culture by Indians.

Not surprisingly, the reformers adamantly rejected the tribe as a means to promote economic development by Indians. Many reformers saw social change as evolutionary and occurring in distinct stages. Since Indians were at an earlier, more primitive communal stage, these reformers were interested in hastening the day when Indians would act as civilized individualists and abandon the tribe as an outmoded social institution.[1]

The driving force of change was to be the enlightened self-interest of the individual Indian. Freed from the binds of tribal customs and authoritarian chiefs, the individual would soon want to accumulate wealth and property and, as he progressed economically, would acquire the habits and customs of Christian society. The key was to be private property: an Indian who held individual title to his land would feel that his property was secure from both Indians and whites. The reformers had an almost mystical view of the power of allotment to transform Indians into hardworking individualists. The idea of private property was closely linked in their minds to Protestant Christian virtues, and they were convinced that private property by itself would transform the Indians. Individual ownership of land was intended to give Indians more economic incentives to become hardworking farmers, but to the reformers, these incentives were only one part of the broader transformation that allotment was designed to promote.

Senator Dawes expressed some of the reformers' aversion to the way in which Indians held land when he commented on the Five Civilized Tribes' practice of having land legally owned by the tribe:

> Yet the defect of the system was apparent. They have got as far as they can go, because they own their land in common. It is Henry George's system, and

under that there is no enterprise to make your home any better than that of your neighbors. There is no selfishness, which is at the bottom of civilization. Till this people will consent to give up their lands, and divide them among their citizens so that each can own the land he cultivates, they will not make much progress.[2]

Even those reformers who were less confident about the prospective course of allotment thought that by giving Indians a title to their land equal in law to that held by whites, their land would be made safe from pressure for its cession by whites or by corporations such as the railroads.

Pride of ownership and the returns from selling the fruits of one's own labor were to be the carrots to induce economic development. The stick was the prospect that if one failed, neither the government nor the tribe would provide a comfortable cushion. A strong element of Social Darwinism permeated the reformer's thoughts. Those who failed to learn the lessons of thrift and industry were to learn the price of improvidence. Although it was regretable that some must fail, this was seen as the inevitable price of civilization.

The reformers did not clearly indicate how all of these changes were to be brought about. Discussions of educational policy focused primarily on preparing Indians for citizenship. This meant teaching Indians a wide range of white culture and values and preparing them to be active and patriotic participants in local and national affairs. Vocational skills were taught in the schools but only as a part of the larger program of assimilating Indians into white culture. Indeed, the policy of locating boarding schools off the reservation was in conflict with the plan to teach Indians to farm. The climate and the crops at these boarding schools were often very different from those of the students' homes. The weaknesses of educational programs for Indians in the 1890s and later have been criticized in great detail.[4] These reports stress the lack of programs to help Indians learn commercial agriculture and the lack of adult vocational education.

One basic program to assist adults in becoming farmers was to employ white agency farmers to help and supervise the work of Indians. The effectiveness of this assistance varied widely. By the time of the Meriam report, the agency farmers were often little more than clerks preoccupied with the paper work generated by allotment.[5] In general, the government provided no large-scale capital assistance, although it was expected that Indians would spend the annuity and other payments they received on agricultural implements. The government expected Indians to become farmers in a gradual transition from small plots to subsistence farming to commercial agriculture. Experience had taught both reformers and government agents that this transition might take more than one generation. The twenty-five-year trust provisions in the Dawes Act were rationalized as allowing the next generation of Indian farmers to have time to learn farming before restrictions were removed. In the short run, the government attempted to promote small-scale subsistence farming among Indians as a transition to large-scale commercial agriculture. In general, however, the reformers were vague about how Indians were to learn to farm. Great hopes were placed on the benefits of having whites move onto and near Indian reservations. They expected whites settling upon the surplus to serve as models of industry and temperance for their Indian neighbors. The reformers also expected Indian interests to be served by local politicians who would need to compete for the votes of the newly allotted Indians.

In the decades that followed the passage of the Dawes Act, officials of the Bureau of Indian Affairs (BIA) and observers outside of government were forced to admit that Indians had neither prospered as farmers nor retained ownership of their allotted lands. This was contrary to deeply held beliefs and puzzled those concerned with Indian policy. Their explanations for the failure of Indian farmers included complaints about misguided or paternalistic programs, policies that made it far too easy to lease or sell allotted land, and the actions of crooked merchants and land speculators. Some also pointed to a lack of industry among Indians. In this view, Indians were apparently content to live off relatives, government subsidies, or lease payments rather than work for themselves. Thus officials such as Commissioner of Indian Affairs W. A. Jones believed that Indians needed to be forced to stand on their own feet.[6] Such a view provided a convenient rationale for allowing continued sales of land from Indians to whites. In the words of one Indian office official, if Indians lost their land, they would be forced ". . . to earn their bread by their labor."[7] Of course, a number of conscientious agents agonized about the loss of Indian land, but as long as they were convinced of the efficacy of allotment, they were caught on the horns of a dilemma.

Not surprisingly, contemporary historians have rejected explanations of the failure of Indian farming that allege Indian laziness or backwardness. At the turn of the century, it was commonly believed by social scientists and government officials alike that Indian cultures would quickly disappear. The persistence of these cultures and the increased respect of modern social scientists for Indian values have led to a different interpretation of the failure of allotment. The BIA is taken to task for not respecting the strength of Indian traditions and hence not realizing that Indians were unwilling to abandon their traditional ways to become farmers. The BIA is also criticized for woefully insufficient programs to aid Indians in adapting to the modern world. Indian poverty is seen as an understandable response to misguided efforts to push Indians into white society. Donald Berthrong, for example, concluded that on the Cheyenne-Arapaho Reservation, "Misguided idealism, crippling legislation, destructive Indian policy and BIA regulations, hostile courts or indifferent courts, and white greed sapped the economic vitality from the Cheyenne and the Arapaho peoples.''[8] Although the reformers were ready to criticize Indians for their lack of progress, Berthrong expressed admiration for the ability of the Cheyenne and Arapahoe to maintain their culture and identity despite these obstacles. Until Indians had made the transition to settled agriculture, many concluded that the Bureau of Indian Affairs should have guarded the land base of Indian tribes for the future.[9]

The analysis developed in this book does not challenge the view that Indian farmers faced an immense array of economic and cultural difficulties in becoming farmers. It does conclude, however, that given the appropriate incentives, Indians made progress as farmers before allotment.

The Tribe as an Aid to Development

Reformers vigorously and firmly rejected the tribe as a positive force either in Indian culture or in the development of reservation resources. Interdependent elements may have been involved in the development of a reservation. But if such interdependencies did exist, a development program that tried to focus on the individual and neglected these external effects would have been less successful than it otherwise would have been. Several examples show how interdependence provided advantages:

Learning effects: The reformers pictured Indians as learning to farm by copying their white neighbors. It is probable that, at least in some cases, Indians learned farming more easily from other Indians than from whites. If so, a successful Indian farmer would have been able to share knowledge and serve as a model for other Indians. External benefits would have been part of having one Indian learn farming, and in such an ''infant industry'' situation, a valid case can be made for encouraging Indian farmers through subsidies or other means.

Mutually agreed upon adjustments: The reformers presented farming and indeed all market-oriented activities as a package that was in opposition to all that was ''Indian''. Yet in some cases, it was possible to reconcile traditional culture and the changes of modern economic life to minimize this hostility. Having one's neighbors and other peers share in these adjustments eases the transition. On the Blackfeet Reservation, John C. Ewers reported that in the early 1920s, Agent Campbell introduced a significant change:

> Prior to Campbell's superintendency, the tribal sun dance encampment had occupied a full month of the Indian's time at a crucial period in early summer when they should have been home tending their crops or livestock. Campbell was sympathetic toward the Indians' religious traditions, but he was also a practical man. He and the Indians worked out a compromise. Instead of a

single tribal sun dance there would be three of them in three districts of the reservation. Each family would attend the one nearest to its home. The encampment would be a single week's duration.[10]

Such an adjustment in a common activity requires common consent. One individual acting alone could not have changed the time and location of the Sun Dance. In this case and in others, the tribe could have served as a unit to reduce the costs of these adjustments.

The tribe as a device for disseminating information and capturing economies of scale: The tribe was in an excellent position to provide services especially suited to Indian needs in cases where economies of scale were evident. For example, the tribe could have served as a financial intermediary on loans to remedy the absence of a mechanism to finance Indian farming. An individual with a patent in fee could mortgage the land, but that was not possible for a person with a trust patent. Similarly, it might be possible for the tribe to have served as a marketing cooperative or cooperative for the purchase of tools. In so doing, the effects of discrimination could have been reduced, especially those associated with "market signaling."[11]

The reformer's dogmatic rejection of collective action through the tribe thus may have been in conflict with the goal of promoting the development of Indian farming. Of course, in allowing the tribe to act as corporate unit, the government would have created a possible conflict between the policies of the tribe and the wishes of an individual or group. That is a very real concern in a situation where the tribe can exercise broad authority. The role of the tribe as a vehicle to aid economic development is considered below.

Pre-Allotment Land Tenure

As discussed in chapter 1, the pro-allotment rationale has many elements in common with the literature on the economic role of property rights. The approach of the property-rights literature is to assume that individuals act to set marginal private benefit (including nonpecuniary factors) equal to marginal private cost, thereby maximizing their individual welfare. The key in this approach lies in specifying how property-rights systems affect the benefits and costs facing economic decision makers. In its economic dimension, allotment was an attempt by reformers to establish a more efficient system of land tenure. The discussion of the impact of allotment on land tenure in this chapter is used to suggest how allotment might have affected Indian farming. The predictions that follow from this analysis are then used in studying the actual experience of Indian farmers and ranchers before and after the allotment of reservation land.

Surprisingly, the reformers themselves paid very little attention to actual land arrangements existing on Indian reservations in the 1880s. D. S. Otis observed that:

> . . . friends and enemies of allotment showed no clear understanding of Indian agricultural economy. Both were prone to use the word "communism" in a loose sense in describing Indian enterprise. It was in the main an inaccurate term. General O. O. Howard told the Lake Mohawk Conference in 1889 about a band of Spokane Indians who worked their lands in common in the later part of the 1870s, but certainly in the vast majority of cases Indian economic pursuits were carried on *directly with individual rewards in view.* This was primarily true of even such essentially group activities as the Omahas' annual buffalo hunt. Agriculture was certainly but rarely a communal undertaking. The Pueblos, who had probably the oldest and most established agricultural economy, were individualistic in farming and pooled their efforts only in the care of the irrigation system. What the allotment debaters meant by communism was that title to the land was dependent on its use and occupancy. They also meant vaguely the cooperativeness and clannishness—the strong communal sense—of barbaric life, which allotment was calculated to disrupt.[12]

A modern reader following the discussions of the reformers might easily conclude that Indians were practicing some form of common field farming. As noted by Otis, that was not the case. Common field farming requires extensive centralized direction, either through tradition or by a centralized leadership. No such agricultural traditions existed in most tribes, at least not for full-time, settled agriculture by men, and traditional, strong, central authority among Indians was uncommon.

The only example of common field farming cited in the article "Agriculture on Indian Reservations" in the 1900 *Census of Agriculture* was on the Crow Reservation.[13] On that reservation, one large agency farm was worked by Indians supervised by the agent and his assistants. Often reservation farms were started by the agent as a preliminary step to establishing Indian farmers on their own. Such ventures were short-lived and depended upon the cooperation of the agent.

Ewers reported one attempt by the government to introduce common property in animals on the Blackfeet Reservation between 1910 and 1920:

> To encourage the able bodied men in this later group [full-bloods who were not ranching] to raise cattle on their own land, the government purchased 1,888 head of cattle to form a tribal herd. But the full-bloods, who had always considered livestock in terms of individual possessions, showed little interest in the tribal herd. They acted as if it belonged to someone else. As an object lesson in stock raising among the less ambitious full-bloods, this experiment was a failure. . . .[14]

Another example of common property among Indian farmers was the pooling of farm tools, again under the supervision of the agent or the agency farmers. References to such practices occur periodically in the reports from different reservations, accompanied in some cases by complaints that the system was not working.

If Indians were not farming their land in common, what form of land tenure was practiced? It seems that on most reservations, possession of the land depended upon its actual occupancy, and if abandoned, the land reverted to common ownership. An Indian family was able to stake out a claim that was then recognized as its own property. In some cases, the agent appears to have played a direct role in the survey and assignment of claims. Practices on many reservations seem to follow a similar pattern. These common patterns of land tenure on reservations inhabited by Indian peoples with different cultural backgrounds may have been the result of the common experiences with white forms of land tenure, economic expediency, and similar pressures from the agents.

Most evidence is consistent with the view that Indian farming was carried out on individual plots with possession of the land by each family recognized by the tribe and the agent. Secondary works that touch on pre-allotment land tenure suggest that it was a satisfactory land-tenure system. James Fitch stated that ". . . the Yakimas had made quite remarkable progress in farming without fixed individual tenure. Unofficial assignments of plots to individual families had initially been made by Agent Wilbur, and these apparently served satisfactorily without generating land use or inheritance problems."[15] Similarly, Ronald Trosper found that a workable system of individual tenure was operating on the Flathead Reservation before allotment.[16]

Not surprisingly, informal techniques for establishing claims at times lead to problems. Meyer discussed some of the problems that arose on the Sisseton Reservation from too haphazard an assignment of land:

> Although the Sissetons had begun locating on farms during Thompson's term as agent, no thorough going survey of the reservation was made at that time. Consequently people had settled pretty much as they pleased, without regard to whether their farms were subject to description in the customary surveyors terms. By 1874, "all sorts of difficulties had grown out of local contentions about timber, land, etc.," as Adams commented. The next year C. C. Royce was sent out by the Interior Department to survey the Indian's claims preparatory to issuing certificates of allotment. Royce also found "numerous and very vexious diputes" among the Indians as to boundaries of their claims. In many cases they had settled too close together to permit the assignment of 160 acre tracts to each family without requiring some to move.[17]

The Yankton Reservation in southeastern South Dakota provides a good example of the evolution of a pre-allotment land-tenure system. According to the agents, the reservation had lands suited both to grazing and to the farming of vegetables and grains. In the 1860s, shortly after the founding of the reservation, the agents established a so-called agency farm. The agent and hired white farmers aided and supervised the Indian employees working on the farm. The land was broken by outside contractors, as was the custom with white settlers.[18] By 1874 Agent Gasman reported that:

> About 2000 acres were planted this last spring entirely by Indians and half-breeds—a good proportion by agency employed Indians, the rest by those who owned the fields and had teams to plow with. Owing to the fact that many are without oxen, I am compelled to hire a large amount of plowing; this however is all done by Indians and half-breeds.

Indian farming had evolved from a completely surpervised activity into one in which individual initiative played a greater role.

Four years later, Agent Douglas reported that:

> Indian farming, *each man to himself and on his own plot of ground,* is increasing every year. Their wheat fields average from 5 to 15 acres each. A good breadth of corn was planted, and looks unusually promising and they will have more than their usual supply of vegetables including potatoes, onions, turnips, pumpkins, etc. Those with wheat fields have shown a good deal of pluck in harvesting their crop endangered by excessive rainfall, cutting it with mowers and scythes and stacking it without any help from the farmers.[20] (Emphasis added)

The Indians had progressed toward the goal of individual farming, although agent and white assistant farmers still played a prominent role. The government provided seed, farm implements, and some animals. In addition, the more reluctant among the Yankton were pushed into farming.

Agent Ridpath, in 1883, began allotting lands to those who would voluntarily accept them. He reported that:

> Some of the older people of the tribe opposed it, and a council was held, at which time I explained to them the object, and that it was the work of the government. This satisfied them and now the majority of men are anxious to take allotments.[21]

Allotment in this context I take to mean a formally surveyed plot that was assigned to each family regardless of whether or not all of it was farmed. Since by the 1880s the agents were working to have the Indians in their charge accept allotment, it is not clear how eager the Yankton were for allotment or how much pressure was applied to gain their consent at that time. Nonetheless, opposition among the Yankton seems to have been to the actual legal allotment of land and not to individual rights to use the land.

The system of recognizing individual property in land had already been established as a long tradition and accepted before the formal allotment of land. Commenting on the handling of the survey and assignment of allotments in 1888, Agent Kinney reported:

> Much dissatisfaction was openly expressed by the Indians having small strips of timber of their *claims* by the instructions of the special agents not to allot any timber. They claimed that it was an injustice to them after having taken claims embracing small patches of timber bordering on a small water course and protecting it for *twenty years*, that such patches should be denied them and left in common for all Indians, who at once availed themselves of the privilege by cutting it and hauling it to the settlements for sale. I did not agree with the special agent in these instructions to the surveyors. The Timber along the banks of the Mississippi River, it was understood, should be free to all the Indians to use for fuel and other useful purposes, but to appropriate the timber on an Indian claim for common use I considered not only unjust, but in violation of the spirit of the law and the instructions governing allotments.[22] (Emphasis added)

The above quotation suggests that individual ownership of improvements was recognized and respected. Only when the allotting agent declared the timber to be public property was it cut down and sold.

I have found no discussions of how disputes over land, water, and grazing rights were settled. The agent and the agency farmer could have easily adjudicated disputes using common sense and their own experience with land tenure among whites. Similarly, the courts of Indian offenses, established in the 1880s, could have handled such cases.

The system of land tenure on the closed reservation is called here a "system of use rights." What economic behavior is encouraged by such a system? In agriculture the establishment of a claim to land by its settlement and cultivation would have encouraged land-intensive techniques. The price of raw land was essentially zero, and it would have been to the advantage of each farmer to bring as much raw land as possible into cultivation. Such a system might have brought chaos where land was very scarce, but where land was plentiful and the goal was to encourage Indians to become farmers on an ever-increasing scale, such a system would be very sensible. In keeping with the behavioralist orientation of this study, the ultimate test of the success of the system is how well it allowed Indian farmers to develop as farmers and ranchers.

An important question in evaluating pre-allotment land tenure is the security of the improvements in the land made by an individual. Uncertainty about one's claim in the future to long-lived investments could easily discourage needed investment. It is interesting that Trosper cited a settlement in the early 1880s in which the Flathead Indians granted a railroad right of way across the reservation, and thirty individuals were compensated for losses due to the proposed route passing through their improved land.[23]

Obviously, even if the rights of an Indian to his land and improvements were recognized as salable, Indian families on a closed reservation would have been limited to selling their rights to Indians. Such a restriction would limit the market and, *ceteris paribus*, limit the value of the investment.

Allotment as a Change in Land Tenure

If Indians had a recognized right to the land they were farming before allotment, how did formal allotment change the situation? For a family that operated a small subsistence farm before allotment, formalizing its land holding would have brought few changes. If the family were allowed to keep the land it had been farming, its allotted land was probably larger than the area it had occupied. The family may have received a cash settlement in connection with the sale of the surplus lands, which could have affected its farming. Ideally, from the reformer's point of view, the family would have used the money to improve its farm.

It is possible that an allotted family might have felt more secure in the possession of its land. It is also possible, however, that it felt less secure, since many Indians distrusted any action by the government—a state of mind not without warrant in many cases. The problem of heirship lands introduced a needless and expensive uncertainty in Indian land tenure. Complex inheritance procedures meant that an allotment might be split among so many heirs that it was unworkable.

Allotment gave Indians a greatly encumbered property right. Under the original provisions of the Dawes Act, allotted land could be neither leased nor sold nor willed to the owners' heirs. However, as noted above, these provisions were soon modified to allow lease or sale when approved by the agents. The restriction on the sale of Indian lands was included in the Dawes Act as a result of the bitter experiences of Indians in the 1850s and 1860s who had typically sold their allotments (often at a below-market price), had quickly spent the proceeds, and had been left destitute.[24] Since the argument of the modern property-rights literature is based on the advantage of having resources readily transferable between uses and users, much of the force of the modern case for individual property is lost if the land cannot be transferred.

The restrictions on the use an Indian could make of his or her allotment highlight a fundamental contradiction in the Dawes Act. If Indians were ready to handle their own affairs, why should their property be restricted? If a legitimate need for a trusteeship existed, why create such a cumbersome and inflexible way of administering it?

Although an allotted Indian had a restricted property right, allotment made it easier to transfer land to whites. Allotment, however, made it harder for an Indian to transfer land to another Indian and made it more difficult for the agent to reorganize Indian land holding to increase economic efficiency. By and large, Indians did not have enough cash to buy out another Indian, and most Indians had no access to credit. Before allotment, unoccupied land could be claimed by any individual who wanted to employ it for an economically attractive purpose. After allotment, the land would have had to be purchased or leased. If Indian land was divided into uneconomically small or fragmented units, it could be difficult to reorganize land tenure. Ranching, for example, required large tracts of land. If a reservation retained substantial tribal lands, it was possible to operate it as an open range and take advantage of economies of scale ranching. But if the allotments were scattered and the surplus lands opened to whites, reorganizing land holdings for ranching could be virtually impossible.

Meyer reported that on the Santee reservation:

> The fact was, though the Indian Bureau refused to admit it, that the Santee Reservation (what was left of it) was incapable of supporting the number of people living on it, given the climatic conditions of the region. The land was better suited to the range cattle industry, but allotment in severalty had so broken up the Indians's holdings that cattle could not run over large expanses of territory.[25]

On balance, allotment seems to have made it easier to transfer land to whites and harder to transfer it to Indians. The allottee's actual possession of land may well have been made more insecure, given the prospect of one being declared competent and having to pay taxes or of the land being hopelessly subdivided among the heirs after the death of the original allottee. In addition, reorganization of land tenure became virtually impossible due to the expense of extinguishing title to the land.

In analyzing the allotment of Indian land as a change in property rights, a number of questions arise that are not typically considered in the literature on property rights. Indians were and are a minority group whose customs and traditions differed from those of the majority of people in the United States. These differences are important in considering the effect of integrating Indians into white society and white institutions.

Placing Indians in the legal and institutional arrangements of the rest of society restricted their ability to form organizations to reflect their special interests. In particular, tribal governments were suppressed during the period the Dawes Act was in force. It is common in historical and sociological studies to conclude that different types of institutions are appropriate in a functional sense for different stages of social development. In economic terms, the benefits and costs of a specific institutional arrangement are different at different levels of economic development. It is possible that Indians wanted and would have benefited from the use of the tribal governments to provide certain services and to capture economies of scale in some activities. The question of how tribal or group action might have aided Indians is discussed below.

Another problem arose when Indians and whites were treated differently by white-dominated institutions. Before 1906 an allottee automatically became a citizen. Yet this did not guarantee that he would receive equal treatment from governmental institutions. Meyer reported that on the Santee reservations the county government refused to maintain the roads on the grounds that Indians did not pay taxes. Whiskey sellers on the same reservations were typically given one-dollar fines. In Oklahoma Indian minors were all too often victimized by state-appointed guardians. Donald Berthrong cited instances where individuals were able to defraud Indians of their land on the Cheyenne-Arapaho Reservation, only to escape legal action.[26]

Indians were and are a minority group subject to discrimination. Discrimination against Indians has taken various forms. The model best known to economists is that where members of the majority exercise their "taste" for discrimination by refusing to associate with members of the minority unless they receive monetary compensation. This is the model developed by Gary Becker. A second type of discrimination arises when Indians are assumed as a group to be more "unreliable" than whites in the market transactions characteristic of white society. It is possible that on the average this assertion is true due to cultural differences and different experiences. In such a case, perfectly capable Indians may be tarred with the same brush and hence systematically denied opportunities open to others of equivalent ability. The analysis of such circumstances has been developed by A. Michael Spence as an aspect of the theory of "market signaling." A third type of discrimination arises from the self-interest of the discriminating group that violates the rights of the minority groups and thereby increases its own wealth. This model is used by Trosper and others. The integration of Indians into white society increases discrimination and the harmful effects of discrimination. Thus allotment made Indians even more vulnerable to discrimination than they were on the closed reservation.[27]

Reformers believed that opening Indian reservations to white institutions would hasten the assimilation of Indians into white society. It is possible that in most cases, the benefits of integration were overestimated. White settlers in the vicinity of Indian reservations were at times hostile to Indians and Indian interests. Misunderstanding between Indians and whites who lived in close proximity to one another appear to have been common in the 1890s. It is not clear whether proximity necessarily encouraged favorable exchanges of ideas between Indians and whites.

Writers on the social role of property rights have not considered the possibility that different groups in a society may have different tastes or may be treated differently under the same system of property rights. It is important to consider these factors in examining the situation faced by Indians as the result of allotment.

A Model of Indian Economic Activity

If allotment acted primarily to make land easier to sell to white farmers, what does economic theory ʀ   ict about the impact of allotment? The model developed below is a version of the standard allocation of time model. Such models have been used to study household behavior and peasant agriculture.[28] Below, the basic unit of analysis is the individual Indian household, not the tribe. In the period considered here, the authority of tribal leaders was undermined and the agent was instructed to encourage individuals to act independently of the tribe.

Assume that the household gets satisfaction from two types of goods: traditional goods (T) and market goods (M). Traditional goods are assumed to be produced only by the household itself and cannot be obtained in the market. Traditional activities include hunting, participation in group activities and ceremonies, leisure, crafts, and similar types of activities. Market goods are those that can be purchased from or sold to members of the majority community. It is assumed that T goods and M goods are not perfect substitutes.

It is also assumed that two factors of production are owned by Indians: land or resources (N) and labor (L). The total amounts of both factors owned by the family are N and L.

Traditional goods are produced by the household using land and labor at home. The amount of traditional goods produced depends upon the amount of labor, L_1, and resources, N_1, used to produce traditional goods. It is also assumed that no market exists for traditional goods. Formally this becomes:

$$T = T(L_1, N_1)$$

Market goods are acquired by Indians either by selling resources (exporting) or by home production. *Home production* means that the Indian family uses its resources in farming or ranching for itself. *Exporting resources* means leasing or selling resources or hiring out one's labor to white entrepreneurs.

The following notation is used:

P is the price received by the Indian household for home production of market goods.

r is the price received for selling resources by individuals to the outside economy, after allotment.

w is the wage received for working off the reservation or for non-Indians.

N_1 is resources used in the production of traditional goods.

L_1 is the labor used in the production of traditional goods.

N_2 is the resources used in the production of market goods at home.

L_2 is labor used in market goods production at home.

N_3 is resources leased or sold (exported) from the reservation after allotment.

L_3 is labor time employed outside the reservation.

N is the total amount of resources (raw land) available to the family.

L is the total amount of labor time available to the family.

The formal model is solved below for two cases. In the first case, it is assumed that the amount of resources available to the household is unlimited and that the market price of resources is zero. This corresponds to a pre-allotment reservation where additional undeveloped land was available to the household for free. Thus before allotment, the resource constraint was not binding, and $N > N_1 + N_2 + N_3$. After allotment (case 2), a family could only use or lease land on its allotment, and the resource constraint was binding, that is, $N = N_1 + N_2 + N_3$. The changes in the conditions for a maximum from the pre-allotment (case 1) to the post-allotment (case 2) are pointed out below.

The amount of market goods produced at home is given by $H(N_2, L_2)$. The total amount of market goods available to the household before allotment is given by:

$$M = P \bullet H(L_2, N_2) + wL_3$$

and after allotment by:

$$M = P \bullet H(L_2, N_2) + wL_3 + rN_3$$

Trade in factors between Indians is treated as being negligible, and hence all exported resources are employed by non-Indians. The sale of traditional goods, such as handicrafts, is also assumed to have been negligible. In the model, the household derives satisfaction only from the amounts of T and

M goods that it consumes. The problem is formally one of maximizing satisfaction subject to budget constraints. Before allotment, market goods can be acquired by working for wage w.

Formally, this becomes:

$$\text{Max } U = U(M, T)$$

subject to

$$T = T(L_1, N_1)$$
$$M = P \bullet H(L_2, N_2) + wL_3$$
$$L = L_1 + L_2 + L_3$$

Using the LaGrange multipliers, this becomes maximized:

$$G = U(M, T) + \lambda_1(T - T(L_1, N_1)) + \lambda_2(M - P \bullet H(L_2, N_2) - wL_3)$$

The first order conditions for a maximum are:

(1) $\partial G/\partial T = \partial U/\partial T + \lambda_1 = 0$

(2) $\partial G/\partial M = \partial U/\partial M + \lambda_2 = 0$

(3) $\partial G/\partial L_1 = \lambda_1 \partial T/\partial L_1 + \lambda_2 w = 0$

(4) $\partial G/\partial N_1 = \lambda_1 \partial T/\partial N_1 = 0$

(5) $\partial G/\partial L_2 = \lambda_2 (\partial H/\partial L_2 + w) = 0$

(6) $\partial G/\partial N_2 = \lambda_1 (-p(H/N_2)) = 0$

(7) $\partial G/\partial \lambda_2 = T - T(L_1, N_1) = 0$

(8) $\partial G/\partial \lambda_1 = M - P \bullet H(L_2, N_2) - w(L - L_1 - L_2) = 0$

In case 2, after allotment, resources could be sold off the reservation (e.g., land could be leased to white farmers), and an individual family's access to resources was limited to what it owned.

$$\text{Maximize } U = U(M, T)$$

subject to

$$T = T(L_1, N_1)$$
$$M = P \bullet H(L_2, N_2) + wL_3 + rN_3$$

$$L = L_1 + L_2 + L_3$$
$$N = N_1 + N_2 + N_3$$

Using the LaGrange multipliers, this becomes:

$$\text{Max } G^1 = U(T, M) + \lambda_1(T - T(L_1, N_1))$$

$$+ \lambda_2(P \bullet H(L_2, N_2) - w(L - L_1 - L_2) - r(N - N_1 - N_2))$$

The first-order conditions for a maximum are the same as case 1, except equations 4, 6, and 8 are replaced by 4a, 6a, and 8a respectively.

(4a) $\partial G^1/\partial N_1 = \lambda_1 \ T/ \ N_1 + \lambda_2 r = 0$

(6a) $\partial G^1/ \partial N_2 = \lambda_1 (P \partial H/\partial N_2 + r) = 0$

(8a) $\partial G^1/\lambda_2 = M - P \bullet H(L_2, N_2) - w(L - L_1, L_2) - r(N - N_1 - N_2)$

If the production functions for traditional production and home production of modern goods are subject to diminishing returns and exhibit properties normally associated with production functions, the second-order conditions for a maximum are fulfilled.[29]

Solving equations 1 through 8 and 4a, 6a, and 8a gives the following results:

(9) $\partial U/\partial T = \lambda_1$

(10) $\partial U/\partial M = \lambda_2$

(11) $\partial U/\partial T \bullet \partial T/\partial L_1 = \partial U/\partial M \bullet w$

(12) $P \bullet (\partial H/\partial L_1) = w$

(13a) $\partial U/\partial T \bullet \partial T/\partial N_1 = \partial U/\partial M \bullet r$

(14a) $P(\partial H/\partial N_1) = r$

(15a) $\dfrac{\partial T/\partial L_1}{\partial T/\partial N_1} = w/r = \dfrac{\partial H/\partial L_2}{\partial H/\partial N_2}$

The intuitive interpretations that follow from the first-order conditions are straightforward. Equations 9 and 10 give intuitive interpretations for the LaGrange multipliers. The multiplier λ_1 is the marginal utility from a unit of traditional goods, and λ_2 is the marginal utility of a unit of market goods. Equation 11 shows that before and after allotment, an hour of labor time will yield equal marginal utility either in production of traditional goods at home or by working for wage w to buy market goods. Equation 11 also yields an acceptance wage. An Indian will not enter the labor force unless the marginal utility of income equals the marginal utility of spending time in traditional pursuits (including leisure). Equation 12 shows that the marginal revenue generated by producing market goods at home will equal the wage rate.

Equation 13a shows that after allotment an additional unit of resources to produce either market or traditional goods will yield equal satisfaction (utility). Equation 14a shows that the marginal revenue product of a unit of resources used in producing market goods will equal the rental price of resources. It follows that the marginal rate of technical substitution between labor and resources in both market production and traditional production will equal the ratio of the market prices of the two factors (see equation 15a).

Graphically, the model can be represented as follows. The household maximizes its welfare by choosing the best combination of traditional and market goods that it can obtain subject to its limited amount of labor and (after allotment) resources. Traditional goods are produced at home, and market goods can be either produced at home or obtained by selling labor (working for non-Indians) before allotment or by selling labor or resources after allotment. The production possibilities curve for producing either modern or traditional goods at home is shown in figure 4.1a. Being able to buy market goods by selling labor in the market expands the production possibilities set to include points along line *a,b,* where the household obtains market goods both by producing them at home and by working for wage *w.* This is shown in figure 4.1b. Welfare maximization occurs at point *Y,* where the family's indifference curve is tangent to the expanded production-possibilities set.[30]

After allotment, the production set is increased by being able to rent resources to non-Indians at price *r.* The new production-possibilities curve is shown in figure 4.2. The consumption possibilities set shifts to *a'b'* and a new equilibrium is reached at *Y'* by selling both resources and labor to non-Indians and reducing the amount used in the home production of market goods. This point is clarified further below. As long as the family is using both labor and resources to produce market goods and traditional goods at home and is exporting both factors, the amount of home production of market goods depends only on the market prices of labor and resources.[31]

The discussion so far has rested on the assumption that an Indian household acted to maximize its own welfare or utility. The conclusions

Figure 4.1
PRODUCTION-CONSUMPTION FRONTIER BEFORE ALLOTMENT

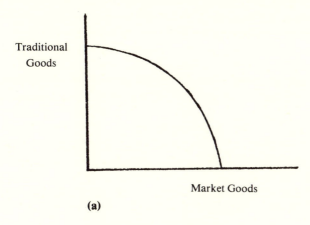

(a)

Home Production Frontier

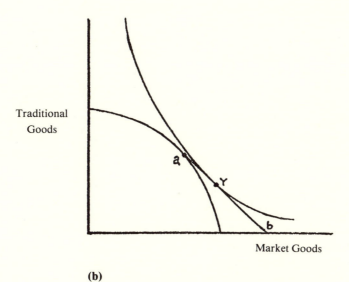

(b)

Trade Expanded Production-Consumption Frontier

about how the average household will behave after allotment are more general and do not require the assumption that the household was maximizing a utility function. For example, assume the allocation of labor and resources among traditional production, home production of market goods, and market goods obtained through trade was done on a stochastic basis, perhaps through trial and error, along the budget constraints. Allotment shifted the consumption opportunities of the household making the export of resources easier, and it can be shown that the average Indian household would end up using fewer resources in producing market goods at home.[32]

It was stated above that a household would reduce the amount of labor and resources devoted to the production of market goods at home. In acquiring market goods, an Indian family had the choice of working at home or outside the home and using its resources at home or selling or leasing them to outsiders (exporting them). Before allotment, the family could sell its labor or engage in home production of market goods or both. After allotment, it could use both land and labor at home or export them. A utility-maximizing Indian household would employ labor and capital at home in producing market goods up to the point where the marginal revenue from using labor at home (MRP) equals the market price of labor and capital. Before allotment, the outside price of resources is zero, and the family would use land and other resources until its MRP declined to zero. See equations 4, 6, 4a, 6a, 12, and 13a. Graphically, the model is presented in figure 4.3. The problem is to represent the impact of allotment on Indian economic activities. The question is simplified since we are interested in the impact of allotment on the production of market goods at home by Indians, that is, on Indian farming. The goal of the reformers was to encourage Indians to become self-sufficient farmers through a gradual progression from subsistence farming to commercial agriculture. This was to be done by encouraging Indians to farm their own land. Allotment made it possible for an Indian family to sell resources to non-Indians. Being able to sell resources is represented in this model by offering Indians a positive price for the sale of resources to non-Indians. That price is r.

As shown above, before allotment, undeveloped land was employed until its marginal product was zero. After allotment, the amount of land employed by Indian farmers would be reduced to the point where its marginal revenue product in producing market goods at home equaled the return from leasing (see equation 4a). Assuming that land and labor are complements, a reduction in the amount of land employed causes a reduction in the marginal revenue product of labor at home, leading to a reduced amount of labor employed there as well. The net effect is shown in figure 4.4. Allowing Indians to sell resources for price r leads the amount of resources used at home to fall from N_2 to N'_2 and the amount of labor to

Figure 4.2

PRODUCTION-CONSUMPTION FRONTIER AFTER ALLOTMENT

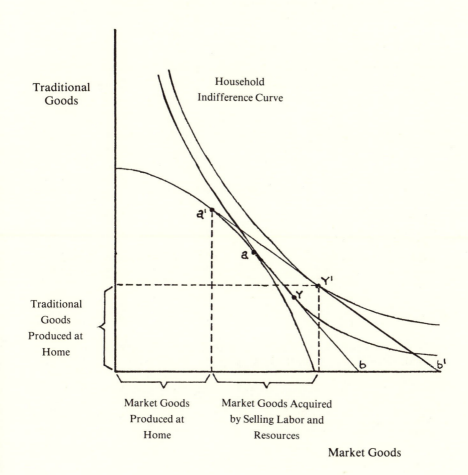

Traditional
Goods

Household
Indifference Curve

a'

a

Y'

Y

b

b'

Traditional
Goods
Produced at
Home

Market Goods
Produced at
Home

Market Goods Acquired
by Selling Labor and
Resources

Market Goods

Figure 4.3

LABOR AND RESOURCES EMPLOYED IN THE PRODUCTION OF MARKET GOODS BEFORE ALLOTMENT

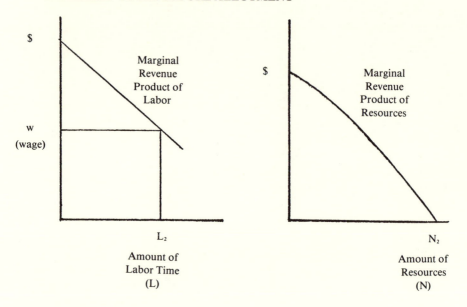

Figure 4.4

LABOR AND RESOURCES EMPLOYED IN THE PRODUCTION OF MARKET GOODS AFTER ALLOTMENT

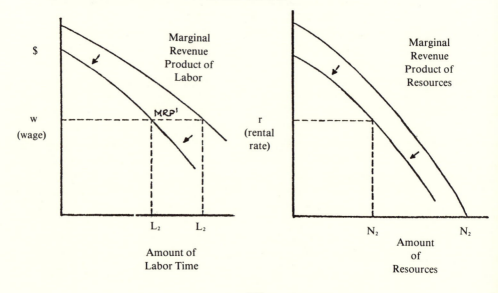

100

fall from L_2 to L'_2. As long as the family engages in both home production of market goods and the export of resources, the result is independent of the amount of traditional goods consumed by the family. If the legal or illegal sale of resources occurred before allotment and the net effect of allotment were to increase the return to selling resources, the results would not change.

Paradoxically, the amount of labor sold off the reservation does not necessarily increase. If the traditional goods are normal goods, both income and substitution effects in consumption must be considered as well as the substitution of labor for resources in traditional activities. If, for example, the income effect exceeds the substitution effect, Indians will spend more time and/or resources in traditional activities. If the amount of increased labor in producing traditional goods exceeds the amount of labor time withdrawn from home production of market goods, the net effect may be less labor sold off the reservation.

Extensions of the Model

Up to now the model has examined a family's decision as to how to allocate labor and resources in a single period; for example, one planting season. This example, however, omits a key aspect of the problem. Farming required a wide variety of skills and habits that could best be learned or, in some cases, could only be learned by an Indian family if it actually farmed its land. The skills learned in previous years were an important factor in determining the productivity of a family in any one year. It is assumed here that the greater the level of output in a given year, the greater the level of skills gained in that year through on-the-job training. Such experience raised the marginal and intramarginal products of both capital and labor.

Formally, the household-production function, $H = H(L_2, N_2)$, can be replaced by a dynamic production function that includes a measure of skills (human capital). One such production function is $H_t = H_t(L_{2t}, N_{2t}, H_{t-1}, H_{t-2}, H_{t-3} \ldots)$. Experience in each previous year is entered separately, since members of the household grow older and are replaced by the younger generation, and hence the value of experience acquired in the past declines. It is also assumed that it is qualitatively different to have farmed a given amount in one period than to spread the same amount of farming over a period of two or more years. Thus each year's experience is entered separately, with a declining value placed on experience acquired in the more distant past.

A family's decision of how much to produce at home in period t not only affected the consumption in period t, but the level of production and consumption in later years as well. A household invested in human capital through home production. Using the revised version of the model, allotment again can be seen as discouraging Indian farming. In the first year after allotment, call it year t, a family was encouraged, *ceteris paribus*, to reduce the level of home production relative to what would have occurred without allotment. Home production in year $t + 1$ would be discouraged still further by the reduction in the level of human capital available to the family relative to that which would have been available had the land not been allotted. In each successive year, the home production of market goods is reduced both through the attraction of leasing land or hiring out as laborers to non-Indians and by the reduced productivity of land and labor at home through the decrease in skills and experience of Indian farmers.

A second way in which a reduction in farming in period t could affect the amount of farming done by an Indian family in succeeding years was through a reduction in investment in physical capital. Physical capital includes buildings, equipment, fences, and improvements in the land. Although the formal analysis of a single period does not include investment, it is clearly important in explaining the productivity of Indian farmers. The larger the stock of nonhuman capital, the greater the marginal product of labor and resources. The amount that a family would want to invest in equipment and improvements in their farm is a function of the expected rate of return on each of the possible investments. If equipment and improvements in the land are made more productive when a family has more training (human capital), a decline in the rate at which Indians learned farming would have reduced the return on investments in equipment and improvements (physical capital). Other things being equal, this would have reduced the rate of investment by Indians in physical capital and further retarded Indian farming.

Another feature of allotment was the sale of the surplus lands. The proceeds from the sale were held by the agent until distributed to the members of the tribe, used for tribal purposes, or used to pay off claims and expenses of the tribe. In many cases, the funds were distributed on a per capita basis, increasing the liquid wealth of members of the tribe. Selling the surplus did not help Indians learn to farm. At best it may have helped a family acquire capital for further improvements in the land, or the lessor may have improved the land. Allotment was a strange way to ease the capital constraint faced by Indian farmers. However, it is possible that Indians could and did learn valuable skills from selling labor to white neighbors. It is likely, however, that much of the labor performed by Indians was harvest labor or some other type of unskilled work from which they were likely to learn few useful skills.

Allotment and Cultural Change

Allotment was seen by the reformers as a means of removing those aspects of Indian culture that they considered "uncivilized." Such a goal was tied to the rigid Protestant values of the reformers and raises the question of how allotment affected customs and practices the reformers and Indian agents saw as inhibiting economic development. First, it is not necessarily true that trying to preserve traditional values made an Indian opposed to economic development; second, many Indian customs objected to by the agents were unlikely to be affected by allotment.

Clearly, the customs of many Indian peoples were incompatible with the requirements of settled agriculture. People who had lived a nomadic life and had adopted customs and values suited to it found the demands of the new ways of making a living foreign and difficult. It does not follow, however, that Indians were unwilling to compromise and adapt to new circumstances. It is more reasonable to conclude that Indian peoples at the time of allotment were facing a difficult period of adjustment and tried to reconcile new ways of earning a living with traditional values. In a number of tribes, a split occurred between a traditional or full-blood faction and a progressive or mixed-blood faction, reflecting different degrees of acculturation into white society.[33] The agents and the reformers often spoke as if it were axiomatic that the more traditional Indians would oppose adopting new ways of making a living. However, people who wanted to maintain a traditional existence would place a high value on economic independence. Certainly, those with more exposure to white customs might be better able to learn new job skills, but this is not the same as saying that full bloods automatically opposed learning new ways of earning a living.

At least in some instances, a desire to preserve traditional values was combined with a willingness to adapt to agriculture. On the Blackfeet Reservation, Ewers found that when a program of assisting small-scale farmers was introduced in the 1920s:

> The five-year program achieved its greatest success among the older and middle-aged fullbloods who took pride in being able to feed themselves and their families through their own labors in small-scale farming operations. The modest accomplishments of some of them were widely publicized.[34]

In this case, at least, traditional values were an aid to success in subsistence agriculture.

Similarly, on the Sisseton Reservation, some of the respected men in the tribe attempted to combine success in farming with the preservation of many traditional values. This emerges in Meyer's account of a conflict between Gabriel Renville, a chief of the Sisseton Indians, and the agent.

> The conflict was between the "church party," made up of those Indians who had been most strongly under missionary influence on the reservation and who had often surpassed their teachers in moralistic rigidity, and the "scout party," headed by Gabriel Renville, who preserved many of the "heathen"

customs, such as polygamy and dancing, and paid little attention to Christian observances. The dichotomy was not simply between civilization and anti-civilization factions, for *Renville and some of his followers were among the progressive farmers on the reservation*, and they accused some of the ministers belonging to the other group of devoting so much time to their spiritual duties that they neglected their farms. Generally, however, the least progressive members of the tribe sided with Renville in his disputes with the agent, with the result he was tarred with the same brush so far as Adams was concerned. (Emphasis added)[35]

Indians were faced with a choice between spending time in traditional activities that had value and spending time in modern activities that also had value. It is not surprising that attempts were made to have some of both worlds. As explained earlier, the agent for the Blackfeet worked out a compromise whereby the traditional Sun Dance was only held for one week. Ewers reported that, "Even then, Big Lodge Pole insisted on bringing his cow, chickens and pigs to the 1923 encampment in his district, saying that he did not want to neglect his stock, but he did not want to miss the Sun Dance either. Every evening he sent one of his sons on horseback to make sure that his crops were doing all right back home."[36]

The agents and the reformers reported a number of instances among Indians where the demands of farming conflicted with Indian customs. The key question is whether those practices were likely to be changed by allotment. Although reformers pictured the influence and coercive power of the chiefs as an obstacle to progress, many of the instances they cited did not depend on the power of the chiefs but rather reflected the preferences of the Indians themselves. Customs that rested on the desires of each family or group of families would not be directly affected by allotment.

Further, it is likely that the Indian agents probably overestimated the barrier to development that the traditional cultures presented. Meyer stated that although the survival of older ways did "constitute hindrances to the drive to make the Santee self-sufficient . . . the problems arising from the survival of the older culture were not so serious as the agents thought they were. . . ."[37]

A common criticism was well expressed by the Meriam report.

> The Indian tendency is to lock up the house and take the whole family on any errand, journey, or excursion undertaken, and the neighbors, if there are any, often go too. Under these conditions it is impossible for them to keep domestic animals that require regular care.
>
> That this care-free, camp life existence has its distinctly attractive features must of course be admitted, and anyone who proposes to change it is open to the charge of trying to make the Indians over into white men. The fact is, however, that the economic basis upon which this type of existence was

predicated has largely gone and that the Indians must either be adjusted to a new economic basis or go through the slow, painful process of vanishing.[38]

Meyer found a similar problem on the Santee Reservation.

> The agents also objected to the tendency of some Santee to go on periodic visits to other agencies. Usually these visits had no purpose other than pure sociability, but at times they took on a religious coloration, as when an Episcopal convocation was held at Rosebud in 1880. Lightner, who had no quarrel with the Episcopalians, objected to the Indians' absence for three weeks just at a time when they should have been breaking new land and taking care of their wheat. Experience had shown, he said, that their cattle often got into the grain when the people were away from home.[39]

The agent on the Yankton Reservation related another problem. As Otis told the story:

> The Yankton agent in Dakota in 1887 found the traditional Indian neighborliness very disturbing so far as agricultural progress was concerned. "They want to be together," he said. He [the agent] told of seeing eight Indian teams in a less than eight-acre lot cultivating—between convivial rounds of sitting and smoking. He noted that all eight teams accomplished less in a day than a white man could. He had seen forty neighbors gathered around a threshing machine on which not more than ten men could work at a time. At the noon meal all were on hand, and at the end of the day everyone expected a sack or two of meal for lending his "gracious presence to the occasion." Under this system the owner of the field reaped for himself but a small fraction of what he had sown. . . .[40]

Yet another practice that disturbed the agents on the reservations of Plains tribes was that of keeping large herds of Indian horses. To the agent, these horses were an uneconomic burden. Indeed, they were a traditional form of wealth that may not have been well suited to the changed economic environment. Nonetheless, they were also the key means of transportation on the spread-out reservations of the plains. From an economic perspective, we can again see that the Plains Indians were making a painful reevaluation of the best way to hold one's wealth, as well as the best way to organize one's life.

Agents were also critical of the tradition of sharing that was common to many Indian peoples. Agent J. A. Smith in his report on the Yankton Reservation in 1897 complained that, "The Indians' hospitality, so far as means will permit, is boundless. He will divide his last morsel with his neighbor, however thriftless and improvident he may be."[41] Objections were voiced about two types of Indian generosity. The first objection was to the ritual exchange of gifts that accompanied dances or visits. At a time when the agents were endeavoring to encourage thrift, this behavior was seen as intolerable. On most reservations, it seems that the agents attempted to eliminate such practices as a part of the general campaign against "heathen" customs. In this, the results seem to have met with some "success." At least fewer references are made to such practices in the twentieth century.

The second complaint was that Indians were too generous to friends and relatives in difficult situations. To the agent, an Indian farmer who welcomed some member of his extended family and shared his possessions was squandering much needed capital. It is sometimes amusing to read complaints that Indians were both insufficiently Christian and too generous with their worldly possessions. The practice of sharing has proven to be persistent, and such behavior may have made sense in the context of Indian life in addition to its cultural significance among Indians.[42] Sharing is a common phenomenon among the poor, and such sharing provides a kind of insurance against fluctuations in income.[43] Obviously, it requires a detailed knowledge of a particular culture to understand fully the meaning of such behavior. As with other aspects of Indian culture discussed in this section, it is not clear that the behavior commented on by outside observers was "irrational," and it is not clear how the allotment of land was to bring about changes in this behavior.

Similarly, complaints that Indians did, and in fact do, waste the large cash payments received as settlements from the federal government also had merit. Indians had little experience in handling large cash settlements, and local merchants were certainly ready to suggest purchases and otherwise to engage in what were known as "sharp" practices. A new Indian farmer had to learn how to handle money and how to allocate it over time. As a guardian, the Office of Indian Affairs was strongly criticized by the Meriam Commission for doing little to prepare Indians to manage their finances. Often an Indian either had all of his money restricted or all controls lifted. Among the Santee, Meyer reported that in the mid 1890s:

> The money [which came from the sale of former reservation lands and unused appropriations] came at a good time, in the middle of the drought years, but unfortunately, it was not all spent as wisely as it might have been. Furthermore, the expectation of more such windfalls did irreparable damage to such habits of prudence, thrift, and industry as the Santees had acquired since 1866. The Episcopal missionary wrote in 1896: "Most if not all of what they expect is disposed of by credit at stores before it is received, and much is spent in rioting and drunkenness when it is obtained." The agents agreed that farming had fallen off, and habits of indolence had become prevalent. . . .[44]

Again, allotment appears to have been an uncertain vehicle for aiding Indians. Giving Indians a restricted property right did not allow them experience at making market transactions. Giving unprepared Indians an unrestricted property right, however, was all too often followed by a quick loss of their property. Indeed, some Indians expressed a preference for remaining under the supervision of the agent. Of course, the removal of restrictions was also followed by a loss of their tax-exempt status.

The agents' criticism of Indian customs should not necessarily be taken at face value, as the agents were hardly unbiased observers. The overwhelming goal was to make Indians over into hardworking Protestant farmers, and anything that interefered with that was condemned. As Meyer noted for the Santee Reservation, the urge to condemn all that was Indian could be carried too far. He wrote that:

> Some of the agents found sinister overtones in perfectly innocent Indian customs—customs which in some cases existed among white frontiersmen as well as among Indians. For example, Helms reported in 1891 that the Santee farmers had a tendency to form "bees" to do jobs most expeditiously managed by several people. He was encouraged however to think that the practice was on the wane. In other respects, too, when the Santees behaved much like the typically wasteful frontier farmer, their actions were denounced as characteristically Indian. One agent complained that they bought farm machinery on credit, then left it outdoors to be ruined by rain and snow. Sometimes a stock that had been issued to them was sold or neglected, and during the worst of the drought years they ate their hogs as soon as they were issued. When stallions were brought, the Indians sold the colts to white men or traded them for ponies. The limited amount of timber on the reservation had been used so prodigally that by 1892 there was little fuel left.[45]

Although allotment did not seem to directly help Indians adjust to the new demands of farming, it was perhaps an indirect "aid" in the eyes of the reformers in that it worked to undermine all aspects of traditional culture. But undermining Indian culture may have had perverse results. Also, the tendency of outside observers to label some Indian customs as "irrational" must be examined carefully. It is likely that some Indian customs that appeared strange to outsiders were sensible in terms of the available alternatives.

Allotment and Indian Welfare

The discussion to this point has examined allotment as it was presented by the reformers. The views of the Indian allottees themselves have not been considered. In part this omission reflects the conceptual difficulty of dealing with opposing systems of values. Confronted with evidence that most Indians did not want to be allotted, it would be totally consistent for the reformers to reject that fact as irrelevant. But it is conceivable that to at least some Indians, anything that hastened the end of a more traditional life-style was undesirable. Thus even if allotment had been as successful in promoting Indian farming as the reformers hoped it would be, it is not clear that an extreme traditionalist would agree that it was desirable. Economic analysis can say little about the welfare efficiency of alternative courses of actions involving redistributions of "benefits" among parties with conflicting tastes.

The absence of evidence of how Indians viewed allotment further limits this inquiry. Since allotment was not a permissive act, votes were not necessarily taken. Nor do we have the opinions of individuals and groups from different reservations. Of course, some objections to allotment were recorded. For example, the Yankton agent noted that:

> The most intelligent among the Indians have some dread of the day when the unallotted parts of the reserve shall be opened to white settlers. The Yanktons have always regarded their tribe as the primal stem of the Dakota Indians and they look upon the proposition to part with their reserve as a move toward the extinction of the race, which alarms them.[46]

On the other hand, J. P. Kinney concluded that either by desire or by resignation, most tribes were cooperating with allotment by the first decade of the twentieth century.[47]

Despite their difficulties, it is possible to consider a number of issues relating to allotment and Indian welfare. The model developed above clearly suggests that since Indians gained the ability to sell land after allotment, their welfare as measured with standard indifference curves increased. This is a straightforward result that can be seen in figure 4.4. Three aspects of this conclusion need to be examined. Even if one does accept the proposition that Indian welfare was potentially increased by allotment, a positive analysis can still be conducted. The clearly stated goal of federal policy was to promote farming regardless of the preferences of the Indians. Allotment can thus meaningfully be evaluated strictly in terms of its success in promoting farming. In the following chapters, we examine allotment as a policy that was designed to promote Indian farming but, for the reasons just discussed, may actually have discouraged Indian farmers. However, we also need to consider how allotment may have harmed Indian welfare.

First, allotment not only gave Indians the opportunity to sell or lease land to whites. As Trosper and others have emphasized, allotment also involved the unilateral termination of some rights of Indians on the closed reservations.[48] What were the losses and benefits to Indians of having their rights abridged in this manner? This is not a complete description of the costs and benefits of allotment but rather a starting point. More complex factors are considered later.

Starting from the cost side of the calculation, we need to ask what Indians lost when the closed reservation system was replaced by the allotted open reservation. At least five things were lost:

The inefficiency of the property right held by Indians. The unworkable inheritance system made land an uncertain means of transferring wealth to one's heirs. Additionally, the need to get approval for formal transfers of property added to the transactions costs associated with having an allotment. This would have been especially damaging where allotments were too infertile or too small to be efficient farms. In the long run, it is likely that these restrictions greatly hindered the progress of Indian farmers.

Surplus lands. If the amount that the government paid a tribe for the surplus lands was less than a fair market price, Indians clearly experienced a loss. More importantly, Indians no longer had the choice of retaining the surplus for future use. Certainly, contemporary development plans are hampered on many reservations by too small a land base due to the sale of allotted and surplus lands.

The loss of previously held rights, such as exemption from local taxation. The uncompensated cancellation of this right was a loss to Indians equal to the capitalized value of additional taxes and payments. Although land in trust was not immediately subject to local taxation, it was when the trust status was removed.

Incompetent guardianship. An Indian allottee was treated like a ward of the federal government. If an Indian did not need a trusteeship, his actions were needlessly restricted. If an Indian family did need a guardianship and the agent was corrupt or otherwise inefficient, a cost was imposed on an Indian allottee.

Loss of the right to add additional land to one's farm. After allotment, lands were surveyed and owned individually. A family that wanted to expand the amount of land that it was using no longer had access to undeveloped land beyond that which it already had. This might be especially true of cattle ranching, where one has an economic use for large tracts of undeveloped land for grazing.

The above is a list of some of the static disadvantages of allotment as seen by Indians. To calculate fully the economic costs, it would be necessary to specify a counterfactual situation.

Benefits to Indians arose largely because they now possessed different ownership rights to the land. The individual's right to sell or lease land was increased. Basically, allotment made it easier to exchange land for some other asset. In the world in which Indians lived, this usually meant that they could sell land and buy consumer goods. To the extent that Indians sold the land and moved to cities, allotment allowed Indians to make substantial adjustments in their lives. How often this option was actually exercised is examined later.

It may not be correct to conclude that allotment improved Indian welfare simply because it became easier to sell land. In the simplest case, if an Indian family was not informed enough to exercise its choices wisely, for example, a family that was either illiterate or so trusting that it could be cheated out of its land, allotment would not improve its welfare. A more difficult case arises from what might be called externalities in consumption. For example, suppose an Indian placed a high value on the functioning of tribal society, and the allotment of the reservation was accompanied by a scattering of the tribe and the disruption of tribal society. Such an individual is made worse off by allotment, although once allotted, he was presumably better off if he could sell the land if he wanted to. Allotment may also have created a type of "free-rider" problem. As mentioned above, many Indian tribes had strong traditions of sharing. Allowing some individuals the opportunity to sell land may have encouraged them to sell land and to depend upon friends and relatives, placing an added burden on the thrifty.

Still another exception could arise from externalities in production. Suppose that Indians were more productive farmers or learned farming more easily when other Indians were farming. Such an externality could have arisen if an Indian was able to learn farming more easily from another Indian than from a white farmer. Alternatively, economies of scale could have been realized in providing special services for Indians. If allotment did encourage Indians to reduce their farming, these spillover effects would also lead to too little Indian farming.

Allotment occurred in a world in which numerous other imperfections in the markets also faced Indian farmers. These imperfections raise second-best problems in considering allotment. It seems likely that these market distortions were most important in discouraging capital formation by Indians. If allotment further encouraged Indians to reduce the rate at which they farmed and hence acquired skills, allotment might lead them to improve their welfare but move farther away from their optimum level of capital formation in favor of current consumption. In the long run, this would help encourage Indian dissaving.

These issues are raised here as theoretical points to qualify the tendency of the economist to assume that allotment necessarily made Indians better off since it was easier to sell land after allotment.

It might be questioned whether a rational Indian family would pursue farming as a very low-return occupation to acquire skills for the future. This would be an unlikely course for a people with little knowledge of future events and no tradition in making long-term investments. The reformers themselves proved to be poor prophets about the development of farming. In light of low income levels, an uncertain future, and the vagaries of federal policy and local politics, discounting the future heavily had elements of a rational procedure.

Conclusions

Allotment emerges as a strikingly perverse policy. The reformers were willing to ignore the preference of Indians and accept the suffering of those Indians who lost their land following allotment to encourage Indians to become self-sufficient farmers. Yet if the model is correct, allotment encouraged Indian families to reduce the amount of labor and resources they employed in independent small farming.

The predictions made about the impact of allotment are obviously simplistic. If this study were an attempt to catalogue the success or failure of Indian farming and ranching on a particular reservation, certainly a large number of factors would enter into the picture. We would need to consider climate, the endowment of resources on the reservation, shifts in federal policy, changes in agricultural prices, the personality of the agent, the cohesiveness of the Indian community, and a myriad of other factors relating to changes in the culture of the people being studied.

This of course is not what is being attempted here. The concern in this study is the impact of allotment, by itself, on the economic position of American Indians. This concern will not seem odd to economists who are involved with evaluating the probable effect of a change in the economic environment holding all factors constant. Here the question is what allotment did to Indian farming. Was it a help or a hindrance? The task is aided by the fact that allotment was applied to a wide range of reservations in different parts of the country, each of which was at a different level of development before allotment. The basic technique in testing the model is to compare the aggregate and individual experiences of a number of Indian reservations before and after allotment and see if the predictions developed in this chapter are useful in explaining the observed behavior.

Notes

1. See Francis P. Prucha, ed., *Americanizing the American Indian*, passim.
2. Delos Sacket Otis, *The Dawes Act and the Allotment of Indian Lands*, pp. 10–11.
3. For a discussion of Social Darwinism, see Richard Hofstadter, *Social Darwinism in American Thought* (Philadelphia: University of Pennsylvania Press, 1944, revised ed., paperback, Boston: Beacon Press, 1955), passim.
4. See Lewis Meriam and Associates, *The Problem of Indian Administration*,

chap. 9; Otis, *The Dawes Act*, chap. 6; and Francis P. Prucha, *American Indian Policy in Crisis*, chap. 9.

5. See Meriam and Associates, *The Problem of Indian Administration*, pp. 540–41.

6. Cited in Donald Berthrong, "Legacies of the Dawes Act: Bureaucrats and Land Thieves on the Cheyenne-Arapaho Agencies of Oklahoma," *Arizona and the West* (Winter 1979): 341.

7. See Wilcomb E. Washburn, *The American Indian and the U.S.*, for other examples of official attitudes.

8. Berthrong, "Legacies of the Dawes Act," p. 354.

9. See, for example, Harold E. Fey and D'Arcy McNickle, *Indians and Other Americans*.

10. John C. Ewers, *The Blackfeet*, p. 321.

11. See below for a discussion of models of discrimination.

12. Otis, *The Dawes Act*, p. 11.

13. U.S. Department of the Interior, Bureau of the Census, "Agriculture on Indian Reservations," in *Twelfth Census of the United States, 1900, Vol. V: Agriculture*, pp. 717–40, passim.

14. Ewers, *The Blackfeet*, p. 318.

15. James B. Fitch, "Economic Development in a Minority Enclave: The Case of the Yakima Indian Nation, Washington" (Ph.D. diss., Stanford University, 1974), p. 87.

16. Ronald L. Trosper, "The Economic Impact of the Allotment Policy on the Flathead Indian Reservation" (Ph.D. diss., Harvard University, 1974), pp. 180–81.

17. Roy W. Meyer, *A History of the Santee Sioux*, p. 208.

18. Incidently, apparently at least one case occurred where the agent engaged in fraud in connection with the breaking of the land by conspiring with the outside contractors. See the Yankton agent's report in the *Annual Report of the Commissioner of Indian Affairs, 1885*, p. 58.

19. *Annual Report of the Commissioner of Indian Affairs, 1874*, p. 258.

20. Ibid., 1878, p. 47.

21. Ibid., 1883, p. 53.

22. Ibid., 1888, p. 70.

23. Trosper, "The Economic Impact of the Allotment Policy on the Flathead Indian Reservation."

24. See, for example, Wilcomb E. Washburn, *The Indian in America*, pp. 23–24.

25. Meyer, *The Santee Sioux*, p. 191.

26. Berthrong, "Legacies of the Dawes Act," pp. 352–53.

27. See Gary Becker, *The Economics of Discrimination*, 2nd ed. (Chicago: University of Chicago Press, 1971); Andrew Michael Spence, *Market Signaling* (Cambridge: Harvard University Press, 1974); Trosper, "The Economic Impact of the Allotment Policy on the Flathead Reservation," pp. 193–40.

28. The model developed here is similar to the one used by Fitch, "Economic Development in a Minority Enclave." Fitch, however, used the tribe, not the household, as the center of analysis. Fitch's model draws on work done by Steven Hymer and Steven Resnick. A reader interested in a further and more formal treatment of some of the points raised here is referred to Fitch, chap. 2. See also Hymer

and Resnick, "A Model of an Agrarian Economy with Nonagricultural Activities." *American Economic Review* 59 (September 1969): 493–506.

29. See Fitch, "Economic Development in a Minority Enclave," p. 20.

30. Figures 4.1a and 4.2 are drawn on the assumption that the production of traditional goods is a first degree linear homogeneous (constant returns to scale). If, for example, the production of traditional goods displayed decreasing returns to scale, the trade expanded production possibilities curve would be concave to the origin. This would not alter the conclusions.

31. See equations 5 and 6a above.

32. Economists have shown that predictions of a model of individual maximization hold under more general assumptions that do not require utility maximization but only assumptions about household behavior subject to budget constraints. See Warren C. Sanderson, "Does the Theory of Demand Need the Maximum Principle?" in *Nations and Households in Economic Growth: Essays in Honor of Moses Abramovitz*, ed. Paul A. David and Melvin W. Reder (New York: The Academic Press, 1974), and "Economic Theories of Fertility: What Do They Explain?" Working Paper No. 36, mimeographed (New York: National Bureau for Economic Research, March 1974).

33. See, for example, Meyer, *The Santee Sioux*, pp. 204–5, and Yankton agent in *Annual Report of the Commissioner of Indian Affairs, 1893*, p. 311.

34. Ewers, *The Blackfeet*, p. 321.

35. Meyer, *The Santee Sioux*, p. 191.

36. Ewers, *The Blackfeet*, p. 321.

37. Meyer, *The Santee Sioux*, p. 191.

38. See Meriam and Associates, *The Problem of Indian Administration*, p. 491.

39. Meyer, *The Santee Sioux*, pp. 192–93.

40. Otis, *The Dawes Act*, p. 55.

41. *Annual Report of the Commissioner of Indian Affairs, 1891*, p. 252.

42. Eicher voices similar complaints about the Rosebud Sioux in his 1960 study. Carl K. Eicher, "Constraints on Economic Progress on the Rosebud Sioux Indian Reservation" (Ph.D. diss., Harvard University, 1960). p. 197.

43. See, for example, Alexander Keyssar, "Men Out of Work: A Social History of Unemployment in Massachusetts 1870-1919" (Ph.D. diss., Harvard University, 1977), chap. 6, passim.

44. Meyer, *The Santee Sioux*, p. 195.

45. Ibid., p. 193.

46. *Annual Report of the Commissioner of Indian Affairs, 1892*, p. 473.

47. J. P. Kinney, *A Continent Lost—A Civilization Won*, p. 247.

48. Trosper, "The Economic Impact of the Allotment on the Flathead Indian Reservation," pp. 99–115.

5

INDIAN FARMING BEFORE ALLOTMENT

What effect did the allotment of Indian reservations have on Indian farming and ranching? Chapters 5 and 6 examine this straightforward, but far from simple, question. Although many factors are important in explaining year-to-year variations in Indian farming and differences between reservations, insofar as possible, we attempt to control for other factors and look at the effects of allotment by itself.

In practice, we examine the evidence that has bearing on two questions that relate to the primary question, but do not directly answer it: how successful was Indian farming and ranching before allotment and how did Indian agriculture fare after allotment? The first question is dealt with here and the second in the following chapter. The data allow for both cross-section comparisons of allotted and closed reservations and comparisons of Indian farming on a single reservation before and after allotment. The study is aided by the catholic way in which Indian reservations were allotted. Allotment was applied to peoples in scattered regions of the country and at different levels of economic development. Thus to some extent, the nonallotment factors can be expected to be random across the sample. The discussion in chapter 4 covered the analytical background for this examination of Indian agriculture.

Agriculture on the Closed Reservation

Reformers pictured the closed reservation period as one of economic stagnation in which Indians made relatively little progress in learning new ways of earning a living. Contrary to this view, the conclusion of this chapter is that substantial progress in Indian farming was made before allotment. In chapter 4, it was argued that the land-tenure system that existed before allotment was not a hindrance to Indians who wanted to become farmers. This can be treated as an empirical question: was Indian agriculture able to develop on the closed reservation system? Instances where Indian farming developed before allotment are consistent with this hypothesis and thus support the arguments made in chapter 4.

Reformers and others who discussed Indian policy in the 1880s and 1890s were confident that little of note had occurred or would occur on the closed reservations. This view was contradicted by a report in the 1900 *Census of Agriculture*, "Agriculture on Indian Reservations," which surveyed the progress of Indian farming on selected reservations and included many that were unallotted or had only recently been allotted.[1] The essay summarized the reports of the agents of the Office of Indian Affairs who supervised each reservation. The census report generally endorsed federal policy and praised the actions of the Indian agents, but it cited enough cases of unsuccessful federal policy to give it a ring of creditability. The report was encouraged by the progress of Indian farmers and expressed optimism about the future of Indians as farmers. The introductory section concluded that:

> Notwithstanding the numerous difficulties, there has been steady progress toward civilization in the past decade on most reservations. A number of tribes are now peaceable, self-supporting agriculturists, wearing citizens' clothing, and able to speak the English language with sufficient facility to carry on ordinary conversation. It is necessary, however, to issue rations to the aged and feeble, even on reservations where the Indians are self-supporting, for it is a significant fact that among all tribes, no matter how prosperous they may be, the aged are often neglected even by members of their own families.[2]

The report acknowledged that Indians faced a difficult time in any attempt to become farmers, one of the most important of which was the ". . . poor and unfavorably located land of many reservations."[3] The authors also noted that the administration of federal policy was a potent force for good or ill.

> Two prominent factors in the advancement of the Indian are the Indian agent and the Government schools. The position of the Indian agent is one of great responsibility and opportunity, and, if the confidence of the Indians be once gained, his influence over them is very great. Under a wise, judicious, and energetic administration, progress may be rapid; but, on the other hand, a tribe will quickly retrograde if intrusted to the care of an indifferent agent.[4]

The report, in the style of the period, passed an optimistic veridict on the capabilities of "the Indian."

Those who know the Indian best unite in recognizing his capacity for work and education. He had strength and endurance, and is reasonably industrious, but if he cannot see an immediate return for his labor, is easily discouraged. Once convinced, however, that his efforts in tilling the soil will repay him, he is usually willing to work.

Indians, as a rule, live from hand to mouth and accumulate but little. The most difficult agricultural lessons for them to learn are to cultivate their crops, to feed and care for their stock properly, and to save enough seed for the next season's planting. They depend too much upon the Government to furnish the seed, and upon nature to do the work after the seed is once put into the ground. The agricultural machinery furnished by the Government is usually left to the elements, but that purchased with their own money is protected.[5]

The 1900 census is quoted extensively, because it expressed a mood of optimism among contemporary observers that is too often ignored in modern discussions of the period. It should be remembered that the census was largely concerned with unallotted or only recently allotted reservations.

Pre-Allotment Agriculture: Reservation Histories

The optimistic assessment of Indian farming given by the 1900 census raises two important questions: does the history of farming on Indian reservations support this positive view, and, if so, were successful efforts to farm restricted to a few favored reservations or were they widespread?

Indians on different reservations had different backgrounds, and the reservations they lived on afforded a wide variety of opportunities. Some tribes had some experience with settled farming, and others had virtually none. Some tribes had a relatively long period of contact with whites before allotment, including, in some cases, many intermarriages between Indians and whites, and others were isolated from contact with whites and remained relatively unacculturated. Some were settled in regions plainly suited to farming without irrigation, and others lived in areas suited only to ranching, dry farming, or irrigated farming.

These factors were not independent of one another. Most tribes with a long history of contact with whites lived in areas that were suitable for general farming, and Plains tribes who resisted being placed on a reservation until late were often living on reservations best suited to dry farming or ranching.

Surprisingly, perhaps, many of the tribes with well-established traditions as farmers, such as the Pueblos in New Mexico and the Five Civilized Tribes in Oklahoma, or herders, such as the Navajos, were not allotted under the

Dawes Act. An exception were the Oneida Indians of Wisconsin. The Wisconsin Oneida had chosen to leave the other tribes of the Iroquois Nation in New York and settle in Wisconsin. In 1900 it was reported that, "They have long been a self-supporting, agricultural people, and all of them engaged in farming. . . ."[6] The Oneida farmers typically cultivated from three to sixty acres of grain, and most families had gardens as well. Some farmers had dairy cattle and swine in addition to farm horses. With a long tradition of settled farming, the Oneida had achieved the type of general farming on a small scale that the reformers advocated on a closed reservation before allotment. The pattern of farming after the Oneida lands were allotted in 1891 was simply a continuation of their previously successful methods.

A more common case was that of a tribe that had no tradition of settled farming, at least by males, but that had become acculturated to some degree into white society. One such tribe, actually a subtribe, was the Santee Sioux, one of the eastern three subtribes of the larger Sioux Nation. In 1862 the Santee in Minnesota, driven by hunger, white encroachment on their lands, and broken promises of aid, rebelled in a brief but bloody war on the white settlers. At the conclusion of that war, most of the Santee bands were settled on three scattered reservations: The Santee Reservation in Nebraska, the Sisseton Reservation in South Dakota (with parts in North Dakota and Minnesota), and the Devil's Lake Reservation in North Dakota. At the time of their expulsion, most of the Santee farming had been done by women, but as Roy Meyer noted, ". . . they had traveled much further on the road toward acculturation than had the western Sioux."[7]

Following their flight from Minnesota, the Santee living on the reservation of the same name in Nebraska made steady progress toward self-sufficiency.[8] The reservation was not allotted until 1885, and the output of Santee farmers grew throughout the closed reservation period. Meyer reported a steady improvement in the economic position of the Santees in the years before allotment. Expansion of agriculture slowed but continued despite a series of droughts beginning in 1887. Meyer reported that by 1884 the Santee had 184 wagons, 134 cross plows, 75 breaking machines, 28 mowing machines, 22 horse rakes, 10 reaping machines, and 3 threshing machines on the reservation. The agents gradually discontinued the practice of issuing rations to support the Indians as they approached self-sufficiency.[9]

To the north, the bands that settled on the Sisseton Reservation also made great strides in becoming self-sufficient farmers. In 1882 Agent Crissey optimistically announced that the "self-support of these Indians is forever settled."[10] The number of Indians supported by government rations had declined, and Meyer concluded that the Sissetons had made substantial progress towards the goal of self-support before the allotment of the reservation in 1888. As at Santee, each Indian farmed for himself. The changes among the Sisseton Indians did not come without conflict: a bitter split occurred between the traditionalists and the progressives, or church party. But as mentioned in chapter 4, some of the most active farmers on the reservation were members of the traditional group.[11]

The Devil's Lake Indians were among the least acculturated of the Santee bands, but at Devil's Lake, too, substantial progress in farming was made before its allotment in 1892. Acres cultivated by Indians grew from 1,500 acres in 1882 to 5,500 in 1889. The farming was done by the Indians themselves, supervised by the agent and his employees. Farm machinery was provided by the government or purchased by the Indians. In 1883 Agent Cramsie contributed $192 to help ten Indians at Devil's Lake buy a McCormick self-binder. In all Meyer concluded that, "Under [agent] Cramsie's direction, the Indians [at Devil's Lake] made some long strides towards the goal of complete self-support through agriculture."[12]

Nothing in the history of these three reservations suggests that the Santee Sioux were unwilling to farm or that individual Indians lacked private property rights to the land they cultivated. Aided by the agents, many Santee in the closed reservation era became farmers and gradually expanded the number of acres they cultivated.

The Fort Berthold Reservation is populated by three tribes: the Mandan, Arakara, and Gros Ventre. In the closed reservation period, the Fort Berthold Indians were less successful in becoming self-sufficient than the Santee, but they made a serious effort to farm and to raise cattle on the reservation. The Indians at Fort Berthold had traditionally lived in settled villages, and it was reported in the 1900 census that they had ". . . always been peaceable and agriculture has been carried on ʟy them to some extent for many years."[13] The report also praised their eagerness to improve their condition. Government policy had been to promote farming, which proved to be a mistake because of the uncertain amount of rainfall. By 1900 three straight droughts had led to a decline in the number of acres cultivated. Cattle raising, however, was a more promising activity and expanded rapidly in the years from 1890 to 1904. The number of Indian cattle on the reservation increased from 160 head in 1890 to 5,000 in 1904. Despite this progress, the Forth Berthold Indians relied on government rations for an estimated 60 percent of their subsistence. Although the reservation was allotted in 1891, by 1900 no evidence could be seen of substantial white entry on the reservation.[14]

Not all tribes showed the same degree of progress as farmers or the same willingness to try new ways of making a living as the Santee and Fort Berthold Indians. An interesting exception was the Indians in Kansas: the Sac and Fox, Potowatomies, and Kickapoos. Like the other tribes discussed so far, the Indians in Kansas were relatively acculturated, but they were notably unsuccessful as farmers. In the words of the census report:

> With excellent land and plenty of horses, wagons and agricultural implements, they [the Indians in Kansas] have every inducement to become good farmers, but in this respect they are making little advancement as a class. The system of allowing Indians to lease their land is accountable for their lack of industry, as their incomes from annuity payments and land rentals allow many to live in idleness.[15]

The disappointing performance of the Indians living in Kansas supports the proposition that allotment, accompanied by the right to lease or sell land, retarded the progress of Indian farmers.

Many tribes had not been as acculturated into white society as the Santee or the Indians in Kansas. Some of these tribes, however, were left in peaceful possession of a reservation for two or more decades before allotment and were aided by government agents and missionaries. Of course, not all agents were qualified or even honest, but some were a powerful force for change among the peoples they supervised.

One tribe with little contact with whites before signing a treaty in 1858 was another subtribe of the Sioux, the Yankton Sioux. The Yankton began to show an interest in farming after the buffalo disappeared. The evolution of property rights and the development of farming among the Yankton, from a small agency farm to more extensive cultivation by individuals on their own plots, was examined in chapter 4. Although the Yankton Reservation was allotted in 1890, the surplus was not opened for settlement until 1896. In 1895 Agent J. A. Smith reported that, "Quite a number of the more progressive farmers will harvest sufficient grain for their own subsistence."[16] Like their fellow tribesmen, the Santee, the Yankton had established small farms and developed a successful general agriculture on a closed reservation.

The Yakima in central Washington were primarily hunters and fishermen before signing a treaty and being settled on their reservation in the 1850s. The Yakima, like the Yankton, remained in peaceful possession of their reservation until its allotment in 1897. Fitch concluded that with the help of their agent, the Yakima had a workable system of individual property before the opening of the reservation. With the exception of the decade of the 1880s, when a number of Indians left the reservation to pick hops, the Yakima made steady progress as farmers and ranchers. In addition, members of the tribe constructed irrigation canals and worked in a tribal sawmill. It is incorrect, however, to picture the Yakima as making a complete shift from traditional to modern activities. Fitch found that many Yakima mixed their activities, combining farming and ranching with fishing and other traditional pursuits, and off-reservation labor.[17]

To the east of the Yakima, the Coeur d'Alene Indians of Idaho were perhaps the most successful Indian farmers in the closed reservation era.

Roman Catholic missionaries gained a wide following among Indians on the reservation and may have aided the Coeur d'Alene in becoming farmers.[18] Before 1906 the agent on Colville Reservation was in charge of the reservation, and day-to-day supervision was in the hands of the agency farmer. Left relatively to themselves, the number of acres farmed by the Coeur d'Alene grew from modest beginnings, until in 1900 it was reported that:

> . . . agriculture is their [the Coeur d'Alene] principle occupation, and, with few exceptions, their farms are well supplied with buildings and implements.
>
> Material progress is being made from year to year in the improvements on their farms. The acreage sown to crops in the census year was the largest ever cultivated and new land is being broken each year. Many of the Indian farms at Coeur d'Alene would compare favorably with those of the neighboring white men in the number of acres under cultivation.[19]

The Coeur d'Alene Indians were able to develop individual farms, some of which were quite prosperous, with relatively little direct supervision by the distant agent and without formal allotment.

Like the Yakima and the Coeur d'Alene, the Flathead Indians of western Montana made substantial progress as farmers and ranchers. Among the Flathead, much of the farming and ranching was done by persons of mixed Indian and white ancestry. The agent commented on the contrast between the mixed bloods, some of whom were well educated and nearly self-supporting, and the full bloods, who were often illiterate and poor. Trosper concluded that the Flathead had a recognized and workable system of private property on the closed reservation. Both the numbers of acres cultivated and the number of Indian cattle increased in the years before allotment of the Flathead Reservation in 1908.[20]

Most Indian bands on the Spokane and Colville reservations in central Washington were described in 1900 as making "commendable" progress, with the notable exception of Chief Joseph's band of Nez Perce.[21] These Nez Perce were separated from the rest of their tribe, despite earlier promises that they would be allowed to return to Idaho. According to the agent's account, Joseph and his followers defiantly resisted efforts to make them into farmers. The other tribes on the two reservations had been at peace for decades and were far more willing to experiment with farming. On the Spokane Reservation, the agent estimated that government rations accounted for only 5 percent of their support. Both reservations were allotted in 1909.

The Warm Springs Reservation in Oregon was peopled by the survivors of a number of tribes. Although some Indians still relied on hunting, others had become farmers. The Warm Springs Indians were described as "industrious," and it was reported that, "The majority of Indian farmers each had from 20 to 80 acres under cultivation, and a number owned range cattle."[22]

The outlook on the Nez Perce Reservation in Idaho was less promising.[23] In 1894, two years after allotment, the agent for the Nez Perce stated that, "I see no reason why the Nez Perce should not become a thriving and thrifty people."[24] By 1900 the agent was still optimistic about the prospects of the Nez Perce, but the evidence is that farming and ranching among the Nez Perce declined following allotment. It was estimated that in 1900 63 percent of the Nez Perce income came from leases or cash annuities. The number of Indian cattle declined from 7,000 in 1890 to 3,763 in 1900, confirming the fears of Indian cattlemen about the impact of allotment.[25] The promising development of farming among the Nez Perce occurred before allotment, not after.

The least self-supporting reservation Indians in the Northwest were tribes on the Umatilla Reservation, allotted in 1893. By 1900, "Only 20 of the 65 farms on the reserve are operated by Indians, the others being leased to white men, or alloted [sic] to families of squaw men."[26] The unwillingness of the Umatilla Indians to farm does not, of course, prove that if no allotment had occurred they would have eagerly seized the opportunity to till the soil, but it is consistent with the view that the opportunity to lease and sell land that accompanied allotment discouraged Indian farming.

Pre-Allotment Agriculture: Ranching

The tribes considered so far typically lived in regions suited to general farming without irrigation. The cultural backgrounds of the peoples considered so far differed widely, but they had remained settled on a reservation for a long time. Other tribes had less contact with whites before being confined to a reservation. The last peoples to come to terms with the federal government in the Northern Plains were those tribes who had hunted the buffalo. Were such tribes, settled on relatively arid reservations and isolated from contacts with whites, as successful as other tribes considered so far?

Without irrigation, land on reservations in the western Dakotas or eastern Montana was best suited to dry farming or ranching. A priori, it might be expected that these reservations were more suited to development through ranching than dry farming, since dry farming requires substantial acreage and capital to be successful. The government was trying to induce Indians to enter agriculture in gradual steps, and it was easier to promote small-scale cattle ranching than to leap into large-scale farming. Ranching also entailed a way of life that was familiar and attractive to Indians accustomed to a nomadic life in pursuit of the buffalo.

Some Indians on reservations in the western Dakotas (Standing Rock, Pine Ridge, Lower Brule, Crow Creek, Rosebud, and Fort Berthold) had considerable success as ranchers. The Fort Berthold Reservation was discussed above. All except Crow Creek were allotted in the first decade of the twentieth century, and all showed a similar pattern of economic growth. The data show relatively little change in the number of acres cultivated in the period from 1890 to 1900, but they show an increase in the number of cattle on the six unallotted reservations and a decrease in Indian herds only on the allotted Crow Reservation. The figures for the unallotted reservations in 1900 ranged from 3.2 to 8.0 cattle per capita.[27] Using an estimate of five persons per family, the average number of head per family ranged from 16 to nearly 40. These figures do not indicate that Indian cattlemen were self-sufficient, but they do indicate a healthy beginning.

The reports of the agents cited in the 1900 census confirm this picture of substantial progress, especially on the largest and most populous reservations: the Standing Rock, Cheyenne River, Pine Ridge, and Rosebud reservations. It was reported that on the Standing Rock Reservation, "They [the Indians] have begun to realize that their support must come from their cattle, and they give them great care, stock raising being even now their principal pursuit, although most of them grow a few small crops in addition to cutting large quantities of wild grass."[28]

A similar story was told for the Pine Ridge and Rosebud reservations. At Pine Ridge, it was reported that:

> Stock raising is their principle occupation, and the interest manifested in this industry is rapidly increasing, many having already become competent cattlemen. Recently an association was formed to protect their brands, to exterminate wolves and for other mutual benefits. At several districts on the reservation the Indians receive 50.0 percent of their subsistence from Government rations, while, at others, practically their entire support is provided.[29]

On the Rosebud Reservation, the report stated that, "They are making considerable progress in stock raising, with the exception of the older Indians, who did not take much interest in the industry."[30] In addition to stock raising, some Indians cut hay and planted gardens.

The Cheyenne River agent was more critical of Indian ranching practices, but the story was similar to that on other reservations:

> Stock raising is their principal occupation and there is scarcely an Indian on the reserve who does not own some ponies or cattle. The Indians need instruction in the care of their stock, as they usually allow their animals to range throughout the year without feed or attention, although many now put up enough wide hay to feed their stock during severe weather.[31]

Stock raising was less advanced on the Lower Brule Reservation in South Dakota, in part because a greater effort was made to promote farming. As at Fort Berthold, dry spells at Lower Brule made farming uncertain. Nonetheless, the agents were optimistic about the future of the Indian cattle industry. Across the Missouri River from Lower Brule was the Crow Creek Reservation. There, after a decline in Indian cattle between 1890 and 1900, by 1904 the number of Indian cattle had increased to 3,000 head or 2.9 per capita.[32]

Gordon Macgreggor's book *Warriors Without Weapons* examines the economic development of one reservation, Pine Ridge, in more detail. This respected study provides insight into the economic history of the reservation, especially the cattle industry.[33] The industry began in the 1880s when live cattle were issued by the army to the Indians along with their rations. These issues of live cattle led to the creation of small Indian herds. According to Macgreggor, this was hardly a modern cattle industry since, "They ran their cattle much as they ran their herds of ponies. However, an interest in cattle had been stimulated among those Indians who had accepted reservation life and wished to remain at peace with the white man."[34]

In the 1890s, the development of the cattle industry was slowed by efforts to promote farming as opposed to ranching. The Pine Ridge Indians were further hindered by what Macgreggor described as political scheming and fraud. In 1900 a new agent was appointed who was favorably disposed to the development of Indian ranching, and he remained for seventeen years. Under his direction, Indian cattle herds increased. Macgreggor reported that:

> *The livestock practice of this era was that of the open ranges . . . with little supervision.* Each spring and fall great roundups were held, which were important events to all the Indians. During these years the Pine Ridge Dakota became steeped in the life of the cowboy, his existence in the open, his dress, his skill with horses all of which would be extremely attractive to people who had been great horsemen and lived the life of the Plains Indians.[35] (Emphasis added)

The experience of the Pine Ridge Indians suggests some of the possibilities open to Indian cattlemen. Allotment, which divided the range and encouraged leasing, was at best of no consequence to Indian development and at worst a positive hindrance. Cattle ranching on the Pine Ridge Reservation combined open ranges with private ownership of cattle.

The growth of ranching among the Pine Ridge Indians stopped with the beginning of World War I. Indian cattlemen were encouraged to sell their cattle at the high war-time prices, and white ranchers pressed to lease Indian lands. A new agent, appointed in 1917, endorsed this practice, and from 1918 to 1921, most of the reservation was in the hands of white cattlemen. The leasing of Indian lands encouraged by the agent was described by

Macgreggor as ". . . the greatest disaster to befall the Pine Ridge Indians since the vanishing of the buffalo."[36] In the 1920s, Indian ranching failed to recover from the wartime decline.

The Sioux were not the only Indians to make progress as cattlemen in the pre-allotment period. The census found that stock raising on the open range was the major activity among the Blackfeet Indians in Montana. John C. Ewers concluded in his study that, "Between the years 1887 and 1900, the Blackfeet Indians of Montana made greater progress towards civilization than at any other period of equal duration in their history."[37] Like the Sioux, the Blackfeet found that their reservation was suited to grazing and that ranching was an appealing way of life. The development of the cattle industry among the Blackfeet before and after the allotment of their reservation is examined further in the next chapter. In the 1890s, other Indians in Montana also made progress as ranchers.[38]

Indians on the Fort Hall Reservation in southern Idaho developed a promising cattle industry before their allotment in 1914. The two tribes on the reservation were the Bannock and the Shoshoni. The Bannock, although numerically inferior and less acculturated than the Shoshoni, were described as the dominant tribe on the reservation. The census reported that, "They [the Fort Hall Indians] take much interest in stock raising, employ herders, and give as much attention to their cattle as white men."[39] Although the Indians demonstrated a willingness to become ranchers, the agent still played an important role. According to the census, "The stock of the reservation is of a good grade and well cared for, but government supervision and aid are necessary to prevent continual inbreeding and deterioration."[40] Some of the Fort Hall Indians were farmers, and a number of the more progressive members of the tribe had gardens. By 1900 the Fort Hall Indians had not reached a point of self-sufficiency nor the point at which they could compete with white ranchers without government aid. Nonetheless, before allotment they had made great strides in becoming independent of government rations.

The cases cited thus far present a picture of success by Indians as farmers and ranchers on a wide variety of reservations. Not all Indian reservations were this successful, of course. Some tribes in the Southwest and elsewhere were placed on reservations where opportunities in farming and ranching were extremely limited, such as the San Carlos Reservation in Arizona. Fishing was an important industry for some tribes in the Pacific Northwest, and hunting, gathering wild rice, and lumbering were important to some bands of Chippewa and other tribes in Minnesota, Michigan, and Wisconsin. Nonetheless, the cases support the view that with opportunities and sufficient incentive, Indians on a wide range of reservations could, and did, learn to farm or to ranch.

Pre-Allotment Indian Farming: Quantitative Evidence

The sample of reports from reservations of different types and locations cited above indicates that Indian farming and ranching were a success before allotment and were not, as the reformers argued, stagnating because of lack of private property or the unwillingness of Indians to be farmers. The question this raises is whether these cases of successful Indian farming were representative of Indian reservations before allotment. Since the central question of this chapter is whether Indians were able to become farmers without the "aid" of allotment, we are concerned with the question of whether, on reservations where Indians *could* succeed as farmers, they did in fact succeed *before* allotment.

To investigate Indian farming further, a sample of allotted reservations was selected using two criteria. The first criterion was whether Indians on the reservation were cultivating at least two acres per capita in 1904, the last year for which the Office of Indian Affairs published figures. This level could have been achieved before or after allotment. It is possible, however, that allotment, or the lack of allotment, led to a decline on some reservations, so that a second criterion is employed as well. This criterion is whether the Indians on a reservation cultivated one acre per capita in 1886, the year before the passage of the Dawes Act.

Thirty-three reservations and agencies satisfying either the first or second criterion are included in the sample. Reservations that were allotted before 1884 were omitted, to observe rates of change in Indian farming for at least a decade. Table 5.1 reports the compounded rate of change for each reservation of acres per capita cultivated by Indians and the output per capita measured in corn equivalent bushels.[41]

The sample includes the most successful reservations, in terms of agricultural output, of all allotted reservations. One might think that the reservations included in table 5.1 were small or unimportant reservations or that little of note occurred on reservations not included in the table. Neither assumption is correct. In 1904 the reservations included in table 5.1 had a combined population of 43,266. This was 16.5 percent of the entire Indian population of the United States and, of course, a far larger proportion of the allotted Indian population who were candidates for inclusion in the table.[42] Reservations where cattle ranching was the primary activity would not be included unless they also had substantial farming. The Five Tribes and unallotted reservations were automatically excluded.

The data in table 5.1 show that Indian farming before allotment was growing at a substantial rate. Looking first at the acres cultivated per capita by Indians, eighteen of the thirty-three reservations had compounded rates of growth in excess of 10 percent per year, including four that had growth rates in excess of 20 percent per year. Nine had rates of growth between 5

TABLE 5.1
The Growth of Indian Farming
Before Allotment: Selected Reservations

Reservations	Date of 10% Allotment	Period	Compounded Yearly Growth of Output	Compounded Yearly Growth of Acres Cult./Cap.
Southern Ute, Colo.	1896	1876-95	17.3%	27.8%
Coeur d' Alene, Ida.	1909	1886-1904	3.4	6.5
Fort Hall, Ida.	1914	1875-1904	11.3	14.8
Nez Perce, Ida.	1895	1875-92	7.0	9.4
Iowa, Kans.	1893	1877-92	21,6	14.6
White Earth, Minn.	1901	1875-99	8.1	11.5
Crow, Mont.	1907	1875-1904	13.6	14.6
Flathead, Mont.	1908	1875-1904	10.1	9.5
Omaha, Neb.	1884	1875-83	2.0	16.9
Ponca, Neb.	1890	1882-89	5.0	8.0
Santee, Neb.	1885	1875-84	10.2	21.4
Devil's Lake, N.D.	1892	1875-97	7.0	15.7
Fort Berthad, N.D.	1900	1875-99	7.9	8.2
Turtle Mountain, N.D.	1907	1875-1904	9.0	10.8
Sac and Fox Agency, Okla.	1890-94	1875-89	9.3	6.5
Quapaw Agency, Okla.	1890-94	1875-89	0.8	13.3
Pawnee, Okla.	1893	1876-92	22.6	24.4
Kaw, Okla.	1903	1875-1902	5.7	−2.9
Ponca, Okla.	1895	1879-94	50.2	12.0
Otoe and Missouri, Okla.	1899	1875-98	26.0	10.0
Osage, Okla.	1908	1875-1904	9.3	9.2
Kiowa, Okla.	1901	1875-1900	12.7	10.9
Grande Ronde, Oreg.	1891	1875-90	10.0	−5.6
Siletz, Oreg.	1894	1875-93	5.1	4.2
Umatilla, Oreg.	1893	1875-95	6.6	3.6
Warm Springs, Oreg.	1896	1875-95	−3.0	6.4
Sisseton, S.D	1888	1875-87	1.7	20.4
Yankton, S.D.	1890	1875-89	15.4	10.1
Unitah and Ouray, Utah	1905	1875-1903	2.8	7.2
Colville, Wash.	1900	1887-99	18.9	13.2
Spokane, Wash.	1909	1877-1904	0.2	0.8
Yakima, Wash.	1897	1875-96	6.6	14.0
Oneida, Wis.	1891	1875-89	2.9	−4.6

SOURCE: See appendix A, table A.6. Selection procedure discussed in text.

and 10 percent per annum, three grew at less than 5 percent, and three declined.

Output per capita also grew at impressive rates. Output on thirteen reservations grew in excess of 10 percent per year, including four that grew at a rate greater than 20 percent. On twelve reservations, output grew at rates between 5 and 10 percent per year. Seven had rates that were positive, but less than 5 percent, and one declined.

The measured rates of growth in Indian farming reported in table 5.1 are, in some cases, extremely high. Of course, Indian farming often started from an extremely small beginning, and this makes the measured rates of growth all the higher. This, however, does not make the success of Indian farmers less impressive.

At the time of allotment, the per capita acres cultivated by Indians ranged from a low of 0.26 acres to a high of 40.24 acres per capita. Using a figure of five persons per family as a rough estimate of the averge extended family, the per capita figures can be converted into per family averages. Thus at the time of allotment, the number of cultivated acres per family ranged from just over 1 to over 200 acres. More typically, twenty-four of the thirty-three reservations averaged between 10 and 30 acres per family. For most reservations, the average number of acres per family was undoubtedly far smaller than an equivalent figure for white farmers in similar circumstances, but it was a solid beginning.

These data on average acres per family, combined with the substantial rates of growth in the number of acres cultivated, support the proposition that Indians had made steady progress toward the goal of self-support through subsistence farming before allotment.

The data used in this section were taken from the reports submitted by agents to the commissioner of Indian affairs. Along with the statistical information, the agents submitted a written report describing the activities on the reservations. A comparison of the agents' written reports with the figures reported in table 5.1 and the appendix allows for the examination of two questions: were the agents' narrative reports consistent with the reported figures on output and acres cultivated, and what was the size distribution of Indian farms?[43] The figures in table 5.1 are per capita averages and do not give any information about the size of Indian farms or the number of Indians participating in agriculture.

On some reservations, the data and the agents' reports tell a story of widespread Indian participation in farming. In 1900 the agents for the Devil's Lake reservations reported that the Indians had cultivated 5,835 acres, or 5.61 acres per person.[44] This translates into an average of 28 acres per family. The census report described the majority of Indians as cultivating between 20 and 80 acres each.[45] Since the typical Indian farm was close to the average per family as calculated from the agents' figures, it is probable that most of the farming at Devil's Lake was done by individuals with relatively modest farms, and that many Indians were participating in farming.

The Oneida in Wisconsin also had extensive participation in farming. In 1891 the Oneida were reported as cultivating 1.71 acres per capita, or 8.5 acres per family. The 1900 census reported that most of the Oneida had their own farms, and that the majority of farms had between 3 and 60 acres of cultivated land.[46]

Again, the description is consistent with the idea that most of the farming on the Oneida Reservation was done by numerous individuals cultivating modest farms and not by a few individuals with massive farms.

As explained above, the census reported that the farms of the Coeur d'Alene Indians were comparable to those of whites. The Coeur d'Alene cultivated 40.26 acres per person, a figure that implies both that many Coeur d'Alene did indeed have farms as large as those of whites and that farming was widespread.[47]

We should not, however, conclude that all Indians were farmers. It appears that while some Indians farmed, others devoted their efforts to more traditional activities. As reported above, the typical farm on the Warm Springs reservations in Oregon was from 20 to 80 acres, and the average acres cultivated was 4.2 per capita or 20.1 per family. This is consistent with the agent's report that some Indians in Oregon were primarily farmers and others depended on hunting and fishing.[48] Similarly, on the Fort Berthold reservations in North Dakota, the agent said the majority of farms were between 5 and 40 acres, and the average number of acres cultivated was 1.50 per capita, or roughly 7.5 acres per family. Again, it is likely that some families did little or no farming.[49]

The output figures reported for the Osage Reservation, however, lead to a far different interpretation. In 1904 it was reported that Indians cultivated 35,000 acres or 18.47 acres per capita. Much of this, however, apparently was accounted for by a few mixed bloods or whites married to Indians. The census reported that most Osage leased land to whites and that this widespread leasing encouraged idleness.[50] Much of the farm output reported for the Osage was apparently accounted for by a large farm operated by the white husband of an Indian woman.

In general, agents' descriptions of Indian farming are consistent with the quantitative evidence and show that Indian participation in farming was widespread. Of course, it is likely that a number of Indian families did little beyond planting a garden. Most Indian farming, however, was accounted for by numerous individuals with relatively modest farms, not by a few mixed bloods or whites married to Indians. Since farming was relatively widespread, many Indian families were acquiring skills and habits needed for future gains in productivity and the future growth of Indian farming. Such widespread participation in farming supports the optimism expressed by contemporary observers.

The data and accounts in this chapter have drawn heavily upon the commentaries and reports of the agents of the Office of Indian Affairs stationed on each reservation. Although some agents filed inaccurate or biased reports, it appears that many of these biases were offsetting (e.g., as likely to be positive as negative) and hence should not affect the overall conclusions.[51]

Conclusions

The story of Indian farming on the closed reservations was more hopeful than one might have expected, reading the accounts of reformers. It was argued in chapter 4 that a workable system of private property right existed on the closed reservations. The evidence presented here shows no evidence that Indians were hindered by a lack of title to their land; their rights to property were recognized, and many, although certainly not all, had displayed enough interest in becoming independent of government rations to begin modest farms or small herds of cattle. Thus any evaluation of the impact of allotment on Indian farmers needs to acknowledge the promising beginnings made by Indians on the closed reservations.

Notes

1. U.S. Department of the Interior, Bureau of the Census, "Agriculture on Indian Reservations," in *Twelfth Census of the United States, 1900, Vol. V.: Agriculture*, pp. 717–40.

2. Ibid., p. 717.

3. Ibid.

4. Ibid.

5. Ibid.

6. Ibid., pp. 719–20.

7. Roy W. Meyer, *A History of the Santee Sioux*, p. viii.

8. In addition to the Santee on the reservation, a small band left the reservation in the 1870s to take up homesteads near Flandereau, South Dakota, determined to become farmers. Despite a lack of government aid, the colony persevered. See Meyer, *The Santee Sioux*, chap. 16.

9. Ibid., pp. 183–84.

10. Quoted in ibid., p. 213.

11. Ibid., pp. 212–13.

12. Ibid., p. 235.

13. "Agriculture on Indian Reservations," pp. 721, 722.

14. Ibid., p. 721.

15. Ibid., p. 723.

16. *Annual Report of the Commissioner of Indian Affairs, 1895*, pp. 304–5.

17. James B. Fitch, "Economic Development in a Minority Enclave: The Case of the Yakima Indian Nation, Washington" (Ph.D. diss., Stanford University, 1974).

18. "Agriculture on Indian Reservations," p. 735.

19. Ibid.

20. Ronald L. Trosper, "The Economic Impact of the Allotment Policy on the Flathead Indian Reservation" (Ph. D. diss., Harvard University, 1974).

21. Chief Joseph had attracted national attention in 1878 when he and other Nez Perce chiefs led their band in a nearly successful attempt to evade the army and enter Canada. See chapter 1. For a popularized account, see Dee Brown, *Bury My Heart at Wounded Knee*.

22. "Agriculture on Indian Reservations," p. 738.

23. The Nez Perce Reservation, Idaho, was the home of that part of the tribe that came to terms with the federal government in the 1850s plus that part of Chief Joseph's band that was allowed to settle there.

24. *Annual Report of the Commissioner for Indian Affairs, 1894*, p. 134.

25. "Agriculture on Indian Reservations," p. 783; and *Annual Report of the Commissioner of Indian Affairs, 1890*, p. 468, and *1900*, p. 660.

26. "Agriculture on Indian Reservations," p. 738.

27. See tables 3.1 and 3.2 in chapter 3.

28. "Agriculture on Indian Reservations," p. 722.

29. Ibid., p. 723.

30. Ibid.

31. Ibid., p. 722.

32. Ibid., p. 723.

33. The Pine Ridge Reservation was the sight of the Wounded Knee Massacre in 1891, cited in chapter 2.

34. Gordon Macgreggor, *Warriors Without Weapons*, pp. 38–39.

35. Ibid., p. 39.

36. Ibid.

37. John C. Ewers, *The Blackfeet: Raiders on the Northwestern Plains*, pp. 314–15.

38. See "Agriculture on Indian Reservations," pp. 728–29.

39. Ibid., p. 735.

40. Ibid.

41. The growth rates in table 5.1 are taken from table A.6 in the Appendix A. The procedure for calculating the output index is included in the notes to that table.

42. *Annual Report of the Commissioner of Indian Affairs, 1904*, pp. 594–614. Population figures reported by the Office of Indian Affairs do not equal those reported by the census due to different methods for determining who is an Indian. Total Indian population in 1904 was reported as 274,706.

43. In general, the agents' reports were rough estimates and undoubtedly contained measurement errors. For the purpose the data are used here, however, measurement errors should not bias the conclusions.

44. *Annual Report of the Commissioner of Indian Affairs, 1900*, p. 624.

45. "Agriculture on Indian Reservations," p. 721.

46. Ibid., p. 719.

47. Ibid., p. 735.

48. Ibid., pp. 737–38.

49. Ibid., p. 722. Also some were cattlemen. See above.

50. Ibid., p. 725.

51. Professor Mary Young, in private correspondence, suggested a noticeable tendency for an agent to exaggerate the problems among the Indians at the agency when he took office and then overstate the progress of Indian farmers during his term of office. Such a strategy would make it appear to his superiors that the agent had done a good job of teaching farming to the Indians on the reservation. Since agents on the reservation were changed frequently, it is reasonable to assume that such errors would cancel out each other and hence the estimates of the long-run trends discussed here would be unbiased in the statistical sense of the term. Individual reports or measurements of year-to-year fluctuations need to be viewed carefully, however.

6

INDIAN AGRICULTURE IN THE ERA OF ALLOTMENT, 1900-1930

On a number of reservations, as discussed in chapter 5, Indians had made and were making progress in self-sufficient agriculture before allotment. It was not an easy process. Some individuals fared better than others, and Indians on some reservations were clearly more successful than Indians on other reservations. But the evidence supports the proposition that Indians had a workable system of land tenure and that allotment was not needed to establish individual rights to the land.

We must evaluate the impact of allotment against this background of substantial progress in subsistence agriculture. Of course, such an evaluation need not naively extrapolate past trends into the future. The conclusion drawn from theoretical considerations in chapter 4 was that the impact of allotment on an already functioning system of property rights would have been to discourage self-sufficient agriculture. In the long run, it also would have retarded the rate at which Indians learned farming and reduced the level of investment in farm capital. These predictions about the impact of allotment must be examined in light of the available evidence.

Indian Farming After Three Decades of Allotment: Contemporary Accounts

The 1900 census was encouraged by the progress of Indian farmers and was optimistic about their prospects for the future. By the late 1920s, however, responsible observers were deeply concerned about the economic and social problems of American Indians. The sorry state of Indian agriculture attracted particular attention. The Meriam report is one of the most highly regarded and thorough studies ever done on the social and economic conditions in the United States. Not surprisingly, the bleak picture of the economic position of Indians painted by the Meriam report has strongly influenced historical accounts of the entire allotment era. It is not the purpose of this study to challenge these findings; indeed, the descriptions of the sorry state of Indian farming in the late 1920s is consistent with the arguments and evidence given here.

The Meriam report was not a historical work. The commission surveyed the social and economic position of American Indians in 1927 to recommend programs to alleviate their social, economic, and health problems.

The Meriam report began by describing the overall poverty of Indians:

> An overwhelming majority of the Indians are poor, even extremely poor, and they are not adjusted to the economic and social system of the dominant white civilization.
>
> The poverty of the Indians and their lack of adjustment to the dominant economic and social systems produce the vicious cycle ordinarily found among people under such circumstances. Because of the interrelationships, causes cannot be differentiated from effects.[1]

The report's assessment of the economic activities of Indian men was also bleak:

> The main occupations of the men are some outdoor work, mostly of an agricultural nature, but the number of real farmers is comparatively small. A considerable proportion engage more or less casually in unskilled labor. By many Indians several different kinds of activity were followed spasmodically, a little agriculture, a little farming, hunting, trapping, wood cutting, or gathering of native products, occasional labor and hauling and a great deal of just idling. . . .[2]

Indian farms presented an additional cause for concern. It was found that:

> . . . although a few Indians were visited who could really be called farmers in the ordinary sense of the word, they were distinctly exceptional. The agricultural activities of a great majority of them were very limited, and are considerably below any satisfactory standard for subsistence farming. Frequently, as has been said, their crops did not greatly exceed those raised by suburban white gardeners who give the operations only their spare time. Cows, poultry, and hogs are the exception rather than the rule. . . .[3]

Not surprisingly, the commission was sharply critical of the government programs that were supposed to have assisted Indians in becoming farmers. Agricultural instruction in Indian schools was poor, and the "farmers" hired to assist Indians on the reservation were in reality little more than low-paid clerks with few real skills and many other tasks to perform. Although the commission did not reject allotment *qua* allotment, it placed a large share of the blame for the low level of Indian farming on errors in the administration of the policy of allowing or even encouraging Indians to lease or sell their lands and live off the proceeds.[4]

The Meriam Commission lacked the expertise to investigate irrigation projects. This void was filled by a congressional study on irrigation projects and irrigated farming on Indian reservations prepared by Preston J. Porter and Charles A. Engle (the Preston-Engle report). Many of the largest irrigation projects were supposed to serve both Indians and white farmers who purchased surplus land or bought or leased land from Indians. The report found that in 1927, 32 percent of the irrigated lands on Indian reservations, or 117,189 acres, was farmed by Indians, with 68 percent or 244,829 acres, farmed by white owners (37 percent) or white lessors (31 percent).[5] On some reservations, Indians farmed almost no irrigated lands, choosing instead to lease or sell the irrigated land to white farmers. Indeed, almost 40 percent of the reported total of Indian irrigated farming was conducted by Indians on the Pima Reservation in Arizona and the Unitah Reservation in Utah. In addition to the low use of irrigated lands by Indians, it was found that "on many projects the acreage utilized by Indians is continuously decreasing, while the acreage utilized by whites is increasing."[6] On irrigated land, the average Indian farmer produced crops worth $21 per acre, and the average white farmer produced crops worth $40 per acre.

The Preston-Engle report found that many Indian families on irrigated lands were scraping by on very low earned incomes. In the words of the report:

> Many Indians, particularly those on the northern projects, are securing only trifling returns from their irrigable lands. This can be explained principally due to the fact that most of the land is not farmed but used only for growing wild hay. On a few of these projects the climatic conditions are such as to make farming any crops other than hay extremely hazardous, and hence discouraging particularly for an Indian.
>
> On a few of the projects the income or annual crop return is so low as to make it a matter of speculation as to how an Indian exists. It can be explained only by the fact that some members of the family occasionally find outside employment, sell a few cattle, or some may receive rations. On some projects the farm income for those families actually engaged in farming is as low as $60 to $80 each or only $15 to $20 for each individual. In view of this it seems probable that undernourishment may be a principle cause of unsatisfactory health conditions among Indians.
>
> On the Colorado River Reservation, Ariz., the Unitah Reservation of Utah, and the Ahtanum Project of Washington, the farm income per individuals of the Indian families actually engaged in farming ranges from $200 to $300 each.[7]

Thus the two most thorough studies of Indian agriculture in the 1920s painted a dismal picture of the status and prospects for the future of Indian farmers. It does not follow, however, that the far more optimistic assessment of Indian farming made by observers at the turn of the century was inconsistent with these reports. If allotment was followed by a period of stagnation or decline in Indian farming, the pessimistic appraisal of Indian farming of the Meriam report can be reconciled with the encouraging appraisal of Indian farming presented in chapter 5. The question addressed below is whether such a decline in Indian farming occurred after allotment.

Indian Farming After Allotment: Reservation Histories

A model was presented in chapter 4 that predicted how allotment would affect Indian farming. The argument rested on the proposition that Indian farmers had a workable system of individual property before allotment and that Indians were able and willing to be farmers. The success of Indian farmers who cultivated land before allotment, described in chapter 5, supports that proposition. The conclusions of the model are straightforward. The allotment of Indian land is expected to have led to the following results: an increase in the amount of Indian land leased and sold to whites, a decrease in the rate of capital accumulation by Indian farmers, a decrease in the rate at which Indians learned farming, and a reduction in group cooperation in economic matters that would further retard Indian agriculture. In short, allotment by itself would discourage Indian farmers, not stimulate their efforts. The model is not formally tested in this chapter; rather, it is used as a guide to interpret the history of Indian farming from 1900 to 1930.

One of the clearest predictions developed in chapter 5 was that the introduction of leasing would discourage Indian farming. Indeed, we can observe a close tie between the leasing of Indian land and a decline in Indian farming. For example, according to the 1900 census, Indian farming in Oklahoma was retarded by the spread of leasing. In the words of the census report:

> Much of the Indian land is suitable for either agriculture or grazing, and many Indians have made slow but steady progress in the development of their allotments: but the influx of settlers has had a retarding influence. Annuity payments and the returns from leased lands have allowed many to live in idleness and general regression has been the result.[8]

Similarly, the stagnation of farming among the Omaha Indians in the 1890s, as well as a generally demoralized attitude on the part of the members of the tribe, was attributed to the increased leasing of allotted land.[9]

Following allotment, Indian farming declined on many of the reservations studied in chapter 5. On both the Santee Reservation in Nebraska and the Sisseton Reservation in South Dakota, allotment led to increased poverty and a sharp decline in the amount of farming done by Indians. Roy Meyer concluded that:

> . . . the history of the Sisseton Reservation in the late nineteenth century followed much the same pattern as Santee: a brave beginning, with considerable enthusiasm among both Indians and agents, followed by gradual progress toward self-sufficiency, *culminating in allotment, which proved to be not the crowning achievement of the process as intended, but actually a disaster for the Indians, succeeded by deterioration and a return to poverty*. . . .[10] (Emphasis added)

Along with the decline in Indian participation in farming at Santee and Sisseton came a decrease in school attendance, an increase in drunkenness, and an overall decline in group cooperation. The Indians at Santee and Sisseton became more, rather than less, dependent on government support and assistance. Although allotment was not the only cause of the problems of the Santee and Sisseton Indians, Meyer assigned it a major part of the blame.[11]

The Devil's Lake Indians were the least acculturated Santee band before allotment, but as explained in chapter 5, they too had progressed as farmers before allotment. According to Meyer, "Allotment in severalty proved to be the same tragic failure at Devil's Lake as elsewhere."[12] In 1922 a member of the Board of Indian Commissioners toured the Devil's Lake Reservation and was appalled by the poor condition of Indian farms and ranches. Only 5,120 acres were cultivated by Indians, about as much as in 1891, and one-third of that total was accounted for by five individuals. In general, Commissioner McDowell reported that "there was too much tuberculosis and trachoma; too much dirt; too many filthy homes; too many children out of school; too much sickness and too much backwardness on this reservation. . . . "[13] Allotment and leasing again played a prominent role in the decline of Indian farming at Devil's Lake. In 1922, 425 allotments were leased for $45,000, and Indian farmers grew crops worth only $104,000.[14] Three decades after allotment, the Devil's Lake Indians were, if anything, farther from being self-sufficient than they had been before they were allotted. The constrast between Commissioner McDowell's pessimistic appraisal and the optimism expressed three decades earlier is clear and understandable. In 1900 the agent saw the prospects of the Devil's Lake Indians in light of their successes in the relatively recent past. In 1922 Commissioner McDowell viewed the Devil's Lake Reservation after two decades of stagnation. It is not surprising that he found little cause for optimism.

After allotment, the Coeur d'Alene Indians, perhaps the most successful

Indian farmers of any on the closed reservations, granted extensive leases to white farmers and contracted the number of acres they farmed for themselves. By 1933 the Coeur d'Alene, who had been allotted 104,072 acres in 1909, owned only 62,400 acres on the reservation and leased 45,120 acres of that total to white tenants. After the reservation was opened to white settlement, tribal leaders lost much of their influence among members of the tribe, and drunkenness, gambling, and general lawlessness increased. Those who sold their lands moved in with friends and relatives, and those who leased the land managed to scrape by without having to work.[15] The success of the Coeur d'Alene farmers before allotment stands in sharp contrast to their decline after allotment.

Of course, not all reservations fared as badly as those discussed so far. In 1922 Commissioner McDowell commented on the substantial progress made by the Fort Berthold Indians. Crops were planted on over 10,000 acres, and the cattle on the reservation were healthy and improved breeds. Much of the credit for the progress on the reservation was given to Superintendent Jermark, who worked closely with Indian leaders and helped create a mood of industry and optimism.[16] In some ways, however, the success of the Fort Berthold Indians is an exception that is consistent with the view that allotment discouraged Indian farmers. The reservation was relatively isolated from contact with white settlers, and the superintendent was able to devote time and energy to promote Indian farming. In general, this was not the case. Allotment was typically followed by an increase in paper work, a decline in the authority of the agent, and, too often, a belief that Indians should be given minimal assistance.

An important part of the growth of Indian agriculture after the turn of the century was the expansion of the cattle industry. As described in chapter 5, on some reservations Indian cattle were grazed on unfenced range. Allotments were often too small to be efficient ranches, and allotment only encouraged the lease or sale of Indian land. On a number of important reservations, Indian ranching had declined by the 1920s—a decline in which the lease and sale of allotted lands played an important role.

The agents in charge of the Blackfeet Reservation had viewed the allotment of small, irrigated farms as the vehicle for Indian economic development. Yet, according to John C. Ewers, virtually no irrigated farming was done by the Blackfeet:

> By the middle-teens it was becoming clear to the planners as it had been to their predecessors two decades earlier, that the Blackfeet Reservation was better adapted to the raising of livestock than for farming. A considerable number of progressive mixed-bloods and some of the full bloods were prospering as cattlemen. . . . But the unprogressive and the shiftless, as well as the aged and physically handicapped, leased their allotted lands to white stockmen and tried to live on their meager returns in lease money.[17]

Cattle raising offered the Blackfeet an attractive way of life, and for a time, the industry prospered. According to Ewers:

> For a brief period during World War I, when cattle prices were high, the reservation cattlemen prospered. . . . Then disaster struck. Two years of summer drought withered crops in the fields. No hay could be cut for winter feed. The reservation range became over stocked. When the dry summer of 1919 was followed by one of the severest winters on record, thousands of weak, underfed cattle and horses froze to death. White settlers on lands in northern Montana suffered along with the Indians. Many of them abandoned their homes and sought employment elsewhere. But the Indians had no other place to go. They were wiped out.[18]

While drought was wiping out cattle, federal agents were granting patents in fee to the recently allotted Blackfeet. A Senate investigator a decade later concluded that, "In nearly every case the issuance of the patent meant that the Indian was defrauded of his land."[19] By 1921 many Blackfeet were dependent on government rations for support.

Other Indians in the 1920s were in much the same position as the Pine Ridge and Blackfeet Indians. The growing Indian cattle industry of the first decade of the twentieth century had stagnated or declined, and much of the range was leased to whites. Some Indian ranchers appear to have been prosperous, but many were not. On the Cheyenne River Reservation in 1922, Commissioner Vaux found that much of the range was leased to whites. He reported that, "As respects [sic] the Indians themselves the most serious problem here, as [it is] so frequently, is their lack of industry."[20] Of course, by the 1920s, all ranchers, Indian and white, faced low prices and hard times. Nonetheless, the commissioner's pessimistic view of the willingness of the Cheyenne River Indians to become cattlemen was a marked change from earlier reports.

Indian ranchers in Oklahoma experienced much the same fate as Indians in the Northern Plains. The experience of the Commanche Indians in Oklahoma provides another illuminating example of how allotment disrupted Indian ranching. The Kiowa and Commanche Reservation was allotted by special legislation and opened in 1901. According to William Hagan, the years before allotment saw the Commanche at their most prosperous. The Indians received both federal aid and "grass payments" from white cattlemen who grazed their herds on reservation land. "In addition, some of the Commanches had opened farms and most of them owned cattle, a few holding herds that ran into the hundreds."[21]

The opening of the reservation brought the promising growth in cattle ranching by the Indians to an abrupt end. According to Hagan, this decline was the result of the encroachment of white squatters and cattle thieves, the application of the territorial herd law (which made Indians liable for the damage their animals inflicted upon the claims of white farmers), and the reduction in support provided by the federal government that led the Indians to consume their breeding stock to provide meat for family and friends. The net result of the opening of the reservation was that:

> By 1910 few Indians held any cattle, although most retained a horse or two. The Commanches received from the interest on tribal funds held in the United States Treasury annual per capita payments that seldom exceeded $100. Some Indians also worked part-time as farmhands, chopping and picking cotton or working in the grain harvest. From these varied sources the Commanche family would receive an income of $400 or $500 a year. Living in their own houses and cultivating small gardens on tax-free land, attending government schools and using government medical facilities, the Indians were able to eke out an existence . . . secure in the knowledge that if emergencies occurred he could turn to the government or to friends and relatives who would not deny a fellow Commanche help.[22]

The Commanche chiefs had predicted dire results if their reservation was allotted and opposed the legislation that allotted the reservation. Despite their best efforts, however, the reservation was opened.[23]

Irrigated farming by allotted Indians was, as the Preston-Engle report emphasized, one of the most *unsuccessful* of Indian economic activities. On the Yakima Reservation in Washington, James Fitch reported that little growth occurred in the number of irrigated acres farmed by Indians, and the value of crops per acre grown by Indians declined steadily relative to that of whites. Profitable irrigated farming in the West was a high-technology, resource-intensive form of agriculture, and the Yakima shifted their efforts to cattle ranching, nonirrigated farming, or fishing.[24]

The Flathead experienced a similar decline in irrigated farming after 1910. Ronald Trosper found that the number of irrigated acres farmed by Indians on the Flathead Reservation fell. Trosper concluded that the attempt by irrigation project managers to serve both Indians and whites worked to the disadvantage of the Indians. Primarily interested in large yields on project lands, the managers discriminated against Indians in favor of white farmers who had greater access to capital inputs.[25]

As noted above, Ewers found that virtually no Blackfeet were willing to farm irrigated lands. This he attributed to "the persistent prejudice of many Indians against farming. . . ."[26] The evidence cited by Ewers can be given an alternative interpretation, however. Prior to 1920, Indians elected to avoid irrigated farming, an input-intensive activity, in favor of cattle ranching, a flourishing industry and one that allowed them to pursue a way of life similar to that they had known. A decade later, following the collapse of the cattle industry, a number of Blackfeet, including many full bloods, enthusiastically responded to a program that encouraged subsistence farming.

The rejection of irrigated farming by the Blackfeet does not imply that they rejected all farming. Some members of the tribe refused to farm, but when farming became an attractive alternative, a number of Blackfeet responded and did try to become farmers.[27]

In general, the failure of the Indians to succeed on irrigated lands is hardly surprising. Faced with the choice of dealing with a difficult, input-intensive form of agriculture and possible discrimination by project managers, or leasing or selling their land, many Indians chose not to farm irrigated lands for themselves.[28]

These scattered case studies from the teens and twenties tell a far different story of Indian farming from that of only two or three decades earlier. On some reservations, the situation was dismal: little increase or even a fall in the number of acres farmed by Indians, a decline in government support, and often an increase in social problems such as excessive drinking or the avoidance of school. On other reservations, the situation was better: houses were in good repair, and the Indians were making some progress as farmers. On balance, the story is consistent with that told by the Meriam report: occasional bright spots amid what otherwise was a tale with little cause for optimism. The new dimension added by this study is that the sorry state of Indian farming in the 1920s can be seen as the result of two or three decades of stagnation or decline following allotment.

The story is consistent with the model developed in chapter 4. Allotment, accompanied by the opportunity to lease and sell land, encouraged a decline in Indian farming. Of course, it is not claimed here that allotment was the only factor that mattered in shaping economic changes among Indians. Some Indians with the right mix of skills, luck, motivation, and desire succeeded as farmers or at other occupations. Some reservations in more favorable circumstances were more prosperous than others. On the whole, however, allotment does seem to have played a key role in the decline in Indian farming of the reservations discussed above. The question that remains is whether this story is representative of what happened to American Indians after allotment. Thus we need to consider a broader, more quantitative picture of Indian farming after allotment.

The Scale of Indian Farming

An important question left unanswered by the reservation histories examined above is how Indian farmers fared relative to their white neighbors. The reformers hoped that allotment would free Indian farmers to compete successfully with white farmers. The reformers wanted Indians gradually to close the gap separating them from white farmers. The reservation histories suggest that, in fact, Indian farming after allotment, in its structural characteristics and level of prosperity, diverged further from the rest of American agriculture. Was this indeed the case?

The question of the success of allotment in promoting Indian farming and ranching is approached here by comparing how Indian farmers fared relative to white farmers in the same state. In both cases, the unit of analysis is the family farm. Farms operated by individual families remained the dominant form of organization in United States agriculture until 1940. William Parker concluded that, "If the family was indeed the minimal unit of social life, there were few technological or economic reasons for making the minimal production unit any larger in terms of labor requirements."[29] One of the reasons cited by Parker for the success of the family farm was that a family could ride out bad times by reducing its level of consumption, something corporate farms could not do.[30]

In comparing Indian and white farms, it is assumed that agriculture was a competitive industry in which the typical farm was operating with minimum, long-run average costs. The typical firm in a competitive industry earns a "normal" return to all inputs but no economic profits in equilibrium. If the average Indian farm were substantially smaller than the average white farm in the same state, it is reasonable to infer that the Indian farm was operating at less than the profit-maximizing scale. This assumes that the average Indian and the average white farm have the same amount of labor available and that Indians were not using more of other inputs; for example, farming in a more capital intensive manner. This latter assumption is shown below to be justified by the facts. Of course, if a family were operating their farm to maximize utility rather than income, it might choose to work fewer hours and take more time as leisure. It is unlikely, however, that this explanation can account for all differences between Indian and white farmers observed in the data.

The argument developed here rests on the assumption that Indian farmers employed less of all nonlabor inputs, not merely that they cultivated fewer acres of land. If Indians cultivated their farms more intensively than whites, we would expect contemporary observers to have commented on this, secondary studies to have uncovered evidence that this occurred, and the measured value of land and improvements and equipment per farm to reflect this more intensive cultivation. As described earlier, Indian farmers were the least successful on irrigated land, the most input-intensive form of agriculture. I have found no evidence to suggest that Indians used more nonlabor inputs, and indeed, accounts of Indian farming picture Indians as using fewer of all inputs. As explained below, the measured value of land and other inputs as well were also far lower on Indian farms than white farms.

Even without economies of scale, a smaller farm and fewer capital inputs meant that the return to a family's labor would be lower than it was for a white family. In the presence of economies of scale, the competitive disadvantages of Indian farmers would be increased. Economies of scale could arise from indivisibilities associated with purchasing and using farm equipment or from fixed costs involved in marketing crops. If labor's return is treated as a residual to the operation of the family farm, we can then explain why Indians sometimes believed they could get a larger return from leasing their land than working it themselves.[31]

Learning-By-Doing and Indian Agriculture

Indian farmers operated on a much smaller scale than white farmers. The small size of Indian farms suggests that constraints prevented farmers from adopting the same scale and technology as white farmers. For simplicity, these constraints can be categorized as human capital (the skills and habits needed to be a farmer), physical capital, and land.

All three operated to limit the expansion of Indian farming and ranching. Capital was a constraint, since Indians lacked funds to improve the land or to buy machinery. Access to loanable funds depended on sporadic government programs, since white lenders could not be relied upon.[32] Tribal funds distributed to members of the tribe were an unreliable source of capital. Many Indians lacked enough good land, especially those who received poor land as an allotment. The inheritance scheme formulated by the General Allotment Act left other Indians with fragmented, scattered holdings.

The last and perhaps greatest obstacle facing Indian farmers was a lack of skills, work habits, and good health needed to succeed. Indeed, that was the view taken by the Meriam Commission. Thus the problem in helping Indians to become farmers was simultaneously to ease all of these constraints, clearly a formidable task.

Surprisingly, the pro-allotment reformers and the Meriam report four decades later arrived at the same basic conclusion about how to promote Indian farming. The reformers pictured Indians as becoming hardy, independent yeoman farmers by gradually building their allotments into prosperous farms. Without indulging in the poetic nostalgia of the reformers, the Meriam report reached similar conclusions:

> The obvious course is to place the emphasis on subsistence farming for the support of the Indian families. The advancement of the Indians in farming should be along the natural lines indicated by the general history of agriculture. They cannot be expected to succeed at first in the highly specialized forms of commercial farming or, broadly speaking, even in the ordinary forms of commercial farming. Commercial farming, especially one crop farming, implies an ability to buy and sell and transact business that most Indians do not at present possess. Their need is aid, advice, and encouragement in the

production of an abundance of grains and feeds, garden vegetables, fruit, milk, butter, poultry and eggs, and hogs for domestic use, with some small surplus of these and other farm products to sell. As they develop they may be brought to specialize in certain crops for which their lands are particularly adapted, but for a considerable time emphasis will have to be placed on subsistence farming.[33]

The reformers believed the transition to subsistence farming would occur as a natural result of allotment, but the writers of the Meriam report prepared hundreds of pages of suggestions for improving programs to assist Indians, including health, education, and economic aid. Nonetheless, both the Meriam report and the reformers saw subsistence farming as the primary vehicle for assisting Indians to become self-supporting.

By farming their own land, Indians were to learn the skills necessary to increase their productivity and become successful farmers. William Parker found that a similar process was a necessary part of any successful farming endeavor in the nineteenth and early twentieth centuries. According to Parker:

> . . . still, in the absence of technical knowledge of wide applicability—of reliable "book farming"—the acquisition of the particular knowledge required to farm a modest farm was the task of a generation living on the soil, surviving through risk and frequent failure, and transmitting this knowledge to its successor. Farms were amateur research laboratories, and technical schools as well as production organizations, and these functions have been shed only slowly as scientific agriculture has grown reliable and dominant.[34]

Subsistence agriculture and small-scale ranching were the best, and sometimes the only, way for Indians to enter self-managed agriculture. Thus the criterion used in this study for judging the success or failure of the Dawes act is the extent to which it encouraged Indians first to become subsistence farmers on small ranches and then gradually to attempt more market-oriented forms of agriculture.

Agriculture, 1900-1930

Most Indian farmers received their allotments in the years from 1890 to 1910. The market conditions faced by these newly allotted Indian farmers were favorable. According to Mary Hargreaves:

> Beginnng in 1897, farm prices mounted steadily until 1920. Wheat, though climbing much less spectacularly than the general level, rose from an index of 56.2 (1910-1914 = 100) in 1894 to 106.4 in 1904, maintained a high level much

of the interval through 1915, and soared to 248.6 under the war time demand from 1916 to 1919. Moreover, this growth far outstripped the growth in farm costs. . . .[35]

The long period of prosperity led farmers to expect continually high prices after 1919, and farmers made an enormous investment in farm land on the assumption that demand for agricultural products and appreciation in land values would be growing. The optimistic expectations of the late teens ended abruptly in 1920 as farm prices fell with onset of the postwar depression. Farm prices remained low throughout the 1920s, and farm incomes remained substantially below the wartime level.[36]

According to Parker, the boom of the 1915-18 period resulted in overexpanded production of wheat, cotton, and beef throughout the 1920s.[37] This was echoed by the Meriam report, which found that income earned by cattle ranches in the 1920s was typically very low. After two decades of prosperity, the 1920s were hard years for American farmers and ranchers.

In the twentieth century, two relatively novel types of agriculture became important in the western states where many allotted Indians lived: irrigated farming and dry farming. Many of the large irrigation projects constructed between 1890 and 1930 were built on Indian reservations. Using reservation land made it easier to develop large areas while avoiding conflicts with existing property rights. As described above, irrigated farming was a high technology, input-intensive form of agriculture.

Dry farming is a land-intensive agriculture in which the low yields per acre are compensated for by large acreages under cultivation. Although little evidence exists to suggest that Indians were engaged in dry farming, it did create an additional outside demand for Indian lands on relatively arid reservations. The dry farming movement had two phases. The first phase lasted from the turn of the century until the drought of 1917-19 and the low prices after 1919. According to Hargreaves:

> By the mid-twenties a second phase of the dry farming movement was under way. With relatively favorable weather conditions from 1920 to 1928, grain growers in the semi-arid region adjusted their operations to overcome the problem of demand . . . with such innovations [as improved credit facilities and mechanized equipment suitable to the family farm] in the early twenties, dry farmers undertook to maximize low acreage income by a vast expansion in the area under cultivation.[38]

The second phase of the dry farming movement led to a massive increase in cultivated lands in eastern Montana and the western Dakotas.

With the exception of dry farming and irrigated agriculture, the technology of general farming did not change markedly. William Parker

characterized the years from 1910 to 1940 as a time in which there was
". . . minor technological improvement, [and] replacement of animal by
mechanical power."[39] By the twenties, the tractor was beginning to become
prominent in American agriculture. The amount of farm machinery used
per farm increased, but it should not be concluded that the decades covered
in the previous chapters were not mechanized. Plains farmers, in particular,
used a variety of horse-drawn implements. According to Parker, "the small
grains had moved into the mid-west so completely by 1910 because
machinery had been invented which was ideally suited to the terrain."[40] According to the census, the value of implements and machinery per farm increased from $186 per farm in 1900 to $981 in 1930 for the West-North Central
region.[41]

The History of Indian Farming, 1900-1930: Aggregate Evidence

The central question is whether the decline in Indian farming discussed
above for selected reservations was representative of what occurred among
all allotted farmers. The analytic framework and propositions being tested
are unchanged. We are examining the question of whether allotment,
accompanied by the lease and sale of Indian lands, retarded the development of Indian farming. In practice, this means that we are concerned with
the changes in the number of Indians in agriculture, the changes in the
amount of Indian farming, and the position of Indian farmers relative to
white farmers, that is, whether they were catching up with white farmers.
Data for this section comes from the *Census of Agriculture,* 1900-1930. Of
course these data must be interpreted with care; in particular it must be kept
in mind that there were variations from census to census as to who was
counted as an Indian.[42]

Identifying the impact of allotment on Indian agriculture necessitates
distinguishing between allotted and unallotted farmers. The method
employed here is to analyze Indian farming in states where the majority of
Indian land was allotted. Table 6.1 gives the official total for tribal lands
and reservations allotted as of June 1929.[43] The third column gives the ratio
of allotted land to tribal land. The analysis centers on those states where the
ratio of allotted land to tribal land is greater than one, that is, a majority of
Indian land was allotted. It is assumed that most Indian farming in such
states was done by Indians on allotted land. As explained in chapter 2, most
reservation land left in tribal hands was not of high quality, since neither
whites nor Indian allottees wanted it. It is likely that the most economically
valuable tribal lands were those used for grazing or forestry.

In eleven states, a majority of Indian land was allotted to individuals
rather than owned by the tribes. These allotted states are Idaho, Kansas,

TABLE 6.1
Total Allotted Land, Total Tribal Land, 1929, by State

State	Total Land Allotted	Tribal Land June 1929	Allotted Tribal Land
North Dakota	2,192,903	1,107	1,980
Michigan	273,574	155	1,768
Oklahoma	19,145,906	38,957	491
Kansas	271,478	1,183	229
Nebraska	352,652	7,405	48
South Dakota	6,408,755	263,111	24
Idaho	619,847	57,359	10.8
Montana	5,759,301	770,135	7.4
Minnesota	935,299	555,726	1.6
Washington	1,136,917	854,901	1.3
Wisconsin	330,874	273,585	1.2
Oregon	619,063	1,123,875	0.55
Utah	111,947	340,680	0.33
Colorado	82,011	396,143	0.21
California	99,840	495,331	0.20
Wyoming	246,822	1,997,000	0.12
New Mexico	353,971	3,534,850	0.10
Nevada	15,227	832,182	0.02
Arizona	172,868	20,290,152	0.01
Florida	0	26,741	0
Iowa	0	3,480	0
New York	0	87,677	0
North Carolina	0	63,211	0

SOURCES: U.S. Department of the Interior, Office of Indian Affairs, *General Data Concerning Indian Reservations (Revised to June 30, 1929)* (Washington, D.C.: U.S. Government Printing Office, October 15, 1929), p. 21.

NOTE: Totals do not include public domain allotments.

Oklahoma, Michigan, Montana, Nebraska, North Dakota, South Dakota, Washington, and Wisconsin. The eleven states had a combined Indian population of 188,049 in 1930, over half of all Indians living in the United States.[44] In terms of total allotted acres, these states had 37,425,258 acres of the total of 39,192,258 acres of reservation land allotted by June 1929. Thus we are considering states that included the majority of allotted Indian land and states where most Indian farmers were allottees and not farming on tribal land.

In the tables and analysis that follow, Oklahoma is considered separately from the other allotted states (referred to as the ten allotted states). Oklahoma had roughly half of the Indian population in the eleven-state sample and a number of unique characteristics. The lands of the Five Civilized Tribes were divided among members of the tribe under agreements that differed from the Dawes Act. Members of the Five Tribes received a share of the tribal land, and they were permitted to dispose of part of it as they saw fit, but reservations in the western half of the state were allotted under the Dawes Act and had more restrictions placed on the lease and sale of land. It should also be recalled that the Five Tribes had a long agricultural tradition and extensive experience as farmers before the opening of their lands.

Using the census, the development of Indian agriculture in each state is followed from 1900 to 1930, and we can observe the effects of allotment on Indian farming over the course of three decades. It is reasonable to conclude that the level of Indian farming in 1900 was achieved before allotment. This is clearly true for the two most important states in the sample: Oklahoma and South Dakota. Most allotments were issued between 1890 and 1910, and allotment activity declined sharply after 1910. Thus in comparing the level of Indian farming achieved in 1900 and 1910 with the levels in 1920 and 1930, we are comparing what Indians achieved either before allotment or in the immediate post-allotment period with what they achieved after two or more decades of allotted farming. It is not a perfect comparision, and it is understood that other factors also changed. The interest here is in the broad trends in the development of Indian farming after allotment.

This is not to suggest that, had Indians not been allotted, their farming and ranching would have continued to grow at the same rate it had before allotment. However, Indians might have made some progress as farmers and ranchers if the reservations had remained closed. Important changes were occurring that radically altered the economic environment. A number of these changes, like increased use of machinery in farming, might be expected to create difficulties for Indian family farmers. But not all changes would have had a negative impact. For example, literacy and the ability to speak English were far more common by 1930 than they were in 1900.[45]

The first topic to be considered is how Indian participation in farming changed after allotment. The reformers had hoped that, by giving each family its own farm, Indians would have been encouraged to become farmers. As it turned out, this was not the case. No evidence exists to show that Indian participation in farming increased after allotment. If anything, the number of Indian farmers following allotment declined. Table 6.2 reports the number of farms run by Indians for the years from 1900 to 1930. For the ten allotted states, the number of Indian farms increased by 316 between 1900 and 1930. Comparing 1910 and 1930, years that included large numbers of mixed bloods in the totals, a decline of 517 farms is evident. No state shows more than a nominal increase in the number of farms from 1910 to 1930. Oklahoma follows the same pattern, with an increase of 988 farms between 1900 and 1930 but a decline when 1910 and 1930 are compared.[46]

Table 6.3 gives the number of Indians per farm in each state. The rise in Indians per farm from 1900 to 1930 indicates that relatively *fewer* Indians were independent farmers at the later date. The full meaning of this decline,

TABLE 6.2
Number of Indian Farms

	1900	1910	1920	1930
Total U.S.	19,910	24,251	16,680	26,817
Idaho	563	334	336	511
Kansas	83	157	103	95
Michigan	347	306	182	131
Minnesota	341	264	174	217
Montana	281	1,146	987	1,135
Nebraska	249	347	260	176
North Dakota	1,316	721	517	791
South Dakota	1,788	2,740	1,563	2,698
Washington	960	673	460	700
Wisconsin	462	541	615	258
Total Ten State	6,396	7,229	5,197	6,712
Oklahoma	6,872	7,459	5,315	7,760
California	658	591	578	758
Colorado	15	405	83	126
Oregon	443	452	300	368
Utah	199	200	209	343
Arizona	1,770	3,159	537	3,735
Nevada	155	148	208	289
New Mexico	1,401	2,087	1,833	3,245
Wyoming	167	44	134	217

SOURCE: U.S. Department of the Interior, Bureau of the Census, *Fifteenth Census of the United States, 1930: The Indian Population of the United States and Alaska,* p. 227.

of course, depends upon the alternative occupations of Indians in 1930, a question examined below.

Even though allotment was not followed by an increase in the number of Indian farmers, we need to consider whether those Indians who were farmers prospered after allotment. The first step in examining how Indian farmers fared after allotment is to consider the amount of land in farms operated by Indians. These data are reported in table 6.4. The data in this table must be interpreted with care. The figures for 1910 are interpolated from figures for all nonwhite farmers, not just Indians.[47] Since Indians constituted over 70 percent of the total nonwhite farmers in many important states, the possibility of error is limited.

The total acres farmed by Indians in the ten allotted states peaked in 1910 at an estimated 2,131,477 acres. After 1910 Indian farming declined in every state except Montana. The relative slightness of the decline in total acres farmed between 1910 and 1920 is due largely to a sharp increase in acreages farmed in Montana, but the other nine states recorded a decline of 667,000 acres or 35.7 percent. Even allowing for undercounting in 1920, post-allotment Indian agriculture was stagnating at best. By 1930 the decline was

TABLE 6.3
Indian Population per Farm

State	1900	1910	1920	1930
Idaho	7.5	10.4	9.2	7.1
Kansas	25.7	15.6	22.1	25.8
Michigan	18.3	24.5	30.8	54.0
Minnesota	26.9	34.3	50.4	51.0
Montana	40.3	9.4	11.1	13.0
Nebraska	13.3	10.1	11.1	18.5
North Dakota	5.3	8.9	12.1	10.6
South Dakota	11.3	7.0	10.5	8.1
Washington	10.5	16.3	19.7	16.1
Wisconsin	18.1	18.7	15.6	44.8
Wt. Average	12.8	11.6	14.4	14.2
Oklahoma	9.4	10.0	10.8	11.9

SOURCES: Table 6.2; Appendix A, Table A.5.

universal. This trend was widespread, with many states showing a sharp decline in Indian farming in the 1920s. Apparently the bad harvests, droughts, and low prices of the 1920s led many Indian farmers to cultivate fewer acres.

Among the ten allotted states, four reported the peak number of acreages farmed by Indians in 1900 and five in 1910. Only Montana peaked as late as 1920. Much of the increase in Indian acres farmed after 1900 was due to increases in Montana and South Dakota, states in which many reservations were allotted relatively late.

A similar story was true for Oklahoma. The number of acres farmed by Indians was highest in 1900 was then declined. By 1930 Indians were farming fewer acres than in either 1900 or 1910. The totals show an increase in the decade of the twenties, which may be a spurious result since many mixed-blood individuals were not reported as Indians in 1920. The tribal governments in the Indian Territory were gradually eliminated after 1897. Thus the decline in Indian farming was coincidental with increased opportunities to lease and sell land and a loss of political control by Indians in Oklahoma.

The number of acres in Indian farms measure only one input, raw land. An additional measure of the inputs employed by Indian farmers is the amount of improved land on Indian farms. Unfortunately, data on the amount of improved acres in Indian farms are available only for 1900 and 1920 and are reported in the appendix.[48] The data do not show any substantial increase in the number of acres of improved land used by Indians. The total number of improved acres in the ten allotted states increased between 1900 and 1920, as a result of sharp rises in South Dakota and Montana. Since the total number of improved acres in Oklahoma showed a steep decline, virtually no change occurred in the total number of improved areas in Indian farms in all eleven states. The total number of acres in Indian farms fell between 1900 and 1920, and, therefore, improved land as a percentage of the total rose. For the ten allotted states, the percentage of improved land rose from 15.0 percent in 1900 to 22.5 percent in 1920, and in Oklahoma the percentage rose from 37.3 percent in 1900 to 47.5 percent in 1920.[49] Although these figures show some improvement, they do not suggest that Indian farms were becoming substantially more capital intensive.

The most comprehensive indicator of the amount of land and fixed capital improvements employed by Indian farmers is the value of the land and buildings per farm. It was hoped that, after allotment, Indian farmers would close the gap and be more competitive with white farmers. The ratio of the average value of land and buildings in each Indian farm relative to

TABLE 6.4
Land in Indian Farms, in Acres

State	1900	1910	1920	1930
Idaho	101,869	47,918[a]	33,468	41,760
Kansas	13,016	22,252	12,398	10,381
Michigan	15,144	13,711	7,494	6,921
Minnesota	61,378	21,917[a]	17,922	18,392
Montana	36,554	285,746[b]	634,956	385,382
Nebraska	31,691	49,005[b]	29,959	12,598
North Dakota	144,716	181,676[a]	175,376	147,203
South Dakota	1,103,854	1,410,390[a]	829,954	776,058
Washington	111,180	85,665	67,465	105,392
Wisconsin	52,138	35,084[a]	30,019	15,281
Total Ten States	1,671,538	2,131,447	1,836,191	1,519,368
Oklahoma	1,231,738	1,087,424	667,903	904,053
California	55,326	61,101	75,434	83,457
Colorado	2,320	69,247	12,822	16,151
Oregon	201,826	194,083	61,122	87,209
Utah	18,968	19,753	31,242	28,563
Arizona	43,502	93,521	52,825	94,731
Nevada	5,635	6,636	10,883	17,861
New Mexico	62,472	151,321	57,133	223,108
Wyoming	22,380	na	13,670	27,540

SOURCES: U.S. Department of the Interior, Bureau of the Census, *Fifteenth Census of the United States, 1930: The Indian Population of the United States and Alaska*, p. 228; *Twelfth Census of the United States, 1900, Vol. V: Agriculture*, pp. cxii–cxiii; *Thirteenth Census of the United States, 1910, Vol. V: Agriculture*, pp. 209–15; *Fourteenth Census of the United States, 1920, Vol. V: Agriculture*, pp. 203, 207–13.

NOTE: Data for 1910 interpolated from data on all nonwhite farms, number of Indian farms. See Appendix A, table A.2. and Appendix B.
[a]Greater than 80 percent of all nonwhite farmers were Indians.
[b]Greater than 70 percent of all nonwhite farmers were Indians.

the average for white farmers in the same state is reported in table 6.5. For the ten allotted states, a weighted average of Indian farms relative to white farms has been computed as well.[50]

The story told by the data is of a marked deterioration in the position of Indian farmers. In the ten allotted states, the weighted average of the value of land and buildings in Indian farms reached a peak in 1910, when it was 44 percent of that of the average white farm. This had declined to only 31 percent in 1930. In Oklahoma, the highest year was 1900, when the value of land and buildings on Indian farms, was 88 percent of that of white farms, and the low was 1930, when the average was only 59 percent. Only Montana and Michigan had their high points after 1910. That peak occurred in 1920 in Montana, which is consistent with other evidence showing an increase in Indian farming in Montana through 1920. The high for Michigan was 71 percent in 1930, but this occurred only after a sharp drop in the number of Indian farms and acres farmed. The data again show that the hard times of the 1920s hit Indian farmers especially hard. The overall picture shows Indian farmers in a significantly less competitive position by 1930 than in 1900 or 1910.

The data in table 6.6 on the relative size of Indian and white farms tells much the same story of decline. The data are harder to interpret, since land per farm includes both valuable improved land and less important, unimproved land. For example, Indian farms in South Dakota were much larger than white farms and much less valuable, suggesting that they were largely unimproved pasture land. Again, the ratio of Indian to white acres per farm shows a clear pattern of decline.[51]

TABLE 6.5
Indian-White Value of Land and Building per Farm

State	1900	1910	1920	1930
Idaho	0.56	0.59	0.53	0.48
Kansas	1.08	0.85	0.60	0.43
Michigan	0.25	0.32	0.32	0.71
Minesota	0.45	0.29	0.23	0.21
Montana	0.30	0.34	0.65	0.34
Nebraska	0.49	0.48	0.44	0.25
North Dakota	0.78	0.35	0.33	0.21
South Dakota	0.46	0.48	0.32	0.22
Washington	0.34	0.51	0.32	0.50
Wisconsin	0.43	0.39	0.26	0.34
Wt. Averages	0.36	0.44	0.40	0.31
Oklahoma	0.82	0.72	0.74	0.59

SOURCE: Table A.8 in Appendix A.

TABLE 6.6
Indian-White Land per Farm

State	1900	1910	1920	1930
Idaho	0.98	0.83	0.49	0.36
Kansas	0.64	0.58	0.47	0.39
Michigan	0.50	0.49	0.42	0.52
Minnesota	1.06	0.47	0.61	0.51
Montana	0.14	0.47	1.06	0.36
Nebraska	0.52	0.47	0.31	0.21
North Dakota	0.31	0.66	0.72	0.37
South Dakota	2.89	3.10	1.15	0.65
Washington	0.44	0.60	0.73	0.78
Wisconsin	0.96	0.54	0.42	0.49
Wt. Average	1.21	1.52	0.82	0.53
Oklahoma	0.82	0.93	0.74	0.59

SOURCE: Table A.9 in Appendix A.

TABLE 6.7
Value of Indian Implements and Machinery per Farm
and Indian-White per Farm

State	1900 ($)	1900 Ind/White	1930 ($)	1930 Ind / White
Idaho	217	1.16	453	0.47
Kansas	127	0.74	328	0.32
Michigan	45	0.32	173	0.28
Minnesota	119	0.61	283	0.29
Montana	262	0.95	476	0.34
Nebraska	103	0.50	307	0.15
North Dakota	78	0.25	307	0.20
South Dakota	139	0.59	298	0.22
Washington	123	0.64	355	0.49
Wisconsin	81	0.47	268	0.29
Wt. Average		0.57		0.29
Oklahoma	97	0.97	229	0.46
California	52	0.18	211	0.21
Colorado	83	0.43	172	0.20
Oregon	97	0.54	441	0.57
Utah	80	0.53	134	0.27
Arizona	38	0.22	138	0.15
Nevada	50	0.11	199	0.15
New Mexico	38	0.38	121	0.27
Wyoming	6	0.26	205	0.18

SOURCES: U.S. Department of the Interior, Bureau of the Census, *Twelfth Census of the United States, 1900, Vol. V: Agriculture*, pp. cxiv-cxv, cii-ciii; *Fifteenth Census of the United States, 1930, Vol. IV: Agriculture*, pp. 301, 240-46.

Another important input in farming was the machinery and implements on each farm. Table 6.7 reports the dollar value of implements and machinery per farm of Indians and the ratio of the value of machinery on Indian farms relative to white farms for 1900 and 1930, the only years for which data are available. Between 1900 and 1930, the value of Indian farm machinery increased but fell sharply relative to the average of white farms. In 1900 the weighted average of Indian farms in the ten-state sample had machinery that was 57 percent as valuable as that of the average white farmer. By 1930 this had fallen to only 29 percent. In Oklahoma the value of machinery per farm fell from 97 percent of that of the average white farm in 1900 to 46 percent in 1930.

As shown above, Indian livestock raising, especially cattle raising, was also an important part of the story of the development of Indian agriculture. In table 6.8, the value of Indian livestock in 1900 is reported, as well as the value of all nonwhite livestock from 1900 to 1920. These are the only data available from the census returns. In 1900 Indians in six states owned more than $500,000 in livestock. Of these six states, Montana, North Dakota, and South Dakota were the states in which more than 90 percent of all nonwhite farmers were Indians in 1910 and 1920, making it possible to follow Indian livestock ownership after 1900 by analyzing the data for all nonwhite farmers.

A marked increase occurred in the value of livestock owned by nonwhites in Montana and South Dakota from 1900 to 1910, but North Dakota stayed

TABLE 6.8
Value of Livestock

	All Non-White			Indian
	1900	**1910**	**1920**	**1900**
Idaho	$ 601,189	$ 417,294	$ 403,942	$ 593,199
Kansas	649,286	1,052,069	1,136,100	86,115
Michigan	211,612	395,574	474,428	42,796
Minnesota	91,474	136,096	256,781	82,643
Montana	558,362	2,020,697	2,732,182	540,778
Nebraska	121,160	332,294	550,604	52,159
North Dakota	783,229	737,519	753,055	769,215
South Dakota	1,433,393	4,032,814	3,236,043	1,417,938
Washington	583,661	703,066	1,372,426	558,447
Wisconsin	100,215	180,739	376,074	81,890
Oklahoma	$9,934,090	$9,998,510	$12,012,922	$7,769,497

SOURCES: U.S. Department of the Interior, Bureau of the Census, *Twelfth Census of the United States, 1900, Vol. V: Agriculture, Part I*, p. cxiv, cxv; *Thirteenth Census of the United States, 1910, Vol. V: Agriculture*, pp. 216-23; *Fourteenth Census of the United States, 1920, Vol. V: Agriculture*, pp. 226-33.

roughly the same. This supports the idea that much of the growth in Indian farming in South Dakota and Montana was due to growth in the Indian cattle industry. Montana showed continued substantial increases in the value of livestock through 1920, with no change in North Dakota and a decline in South Dakota. Figures are reported in current dollars. The average value of cattle, except milk cows, reported by the census and the U.S. Department of Agriculture was $24.97 in 1900, $19.07 in 1910, and $43.22 in 1920.[52] If cattle constituted most of Indian livestock, this confirms a picture of growth in the number of cattle owned through at least 1910.

Taken as a whole, the data used in this section are remarkably uniform in suggesting that in the years from 1900 to 1930 a clear and widespread pattern of stagnation and decline was evident among the newly allotted Indian farmers. No single piece of data presented above is meant to be conclusive, but the overall consistency of the data is impressive. This broad phenomenon was undoubtedly caused by a wide range of economic and social factors. But the story of Indian agriculture that emerges from both the individual reservation histories and the aggregate evidence supports the model developed in chatper 4. As predicted, allotment was followed by a dramatic decline in Indian farming. The story is, of course, still incomplete. The interpretation of the decline in Indian farming depends in part upon the alternatives pursued by those Indians who were not farmers.

Occupational Changes Among American Indians, 1900-1930

A possible explanation of the decline of Indian farming could have been that a type of adverse selection process operated to leave the least capable Indians in agriculture. If allotment allowed the most industrious Indians to leave farming, this might explain the relatively poor performance of Indian farmers after allotment. However, as explained below, this was not the case. Most Indians remained in agriculture and did not leave rural areas.

In general, allotment was not followed by a massive exodus of Indians off the reservation or into new occupations. Some important developments had taken place, but they were still in their formative stages and had not yet touched most Indians. For example, one possible result of allotment could have been that Indians were freed to move to cities, joining the black migration from the rural South. This did not occur. In 1910, 4.5 percent of the Indian population of the United States lived in urban areas, and by 1930 this had increased to only 9.9 percent of the Indian population. Over the same period, the percentage of blacks in urban areas rose from 27.4 percent to 43.7 percent.[53] The proportion of Indians in cities almost doubled in the twenty years from 1910 to 1930, but most Indians still lived in rural communities or on farms. Roughly nineteen out of twenty Indians lived in rural areas in 1900, and eighteen out of twenty still lived in rural areas in 1930. Although blacks were leaving rural poverty and moving to cities in large numbers, Indians were not to join the movement to cities in large numbers until a later date. Of course, these figures are for the entire population, but no evidence shows that allotted Indians moved to cities in much greater proportions than the national average.[54]

A surprising feature of the economic position of the Indians in the first decades of the twentieth century was the relatively low percentage of Indians who were gainfully employed. In 1930 only 65.0 percent of Indian males over ten were gainfully occupied, versus 73.4 percent of native whites, 88.4 percent of foreign-born whites, and 80.2 percent of blacks.[55] Foreign-born whites and blacks, the two groups we might expect to be most like Indians in that they were also poor and faced discrimination, responded to their circumstances by entering the labor market in relatively large numbers. It appears that, because of discouragement, ill health, or other reasons, many Indians were not gainfully employed or, as the Meriam report suggested, were employed only on an occasional odd job. Indian women also figure very little in the story of market-oriented employment. Only 15.4 percent of Indian women over ten were gainfully employed in 1930, the lowest percentage of any population group in the census.[56] The percentage of Indian men and women gainfully employed in most allotted states appears to have been even lower than the national average for all Indians.

Agricultural and other outdoor occupations remained the primary activity of those Indian males who were reported as gainfully employed in the census. The percentage of Indians in agriculture fell from 74.7 percent in 1910 to 64.5 percent in 1930. Thus despite the dismal picture of allotted Indian farming, most Indians who worked remained in agriculture. Some allotted states showed relatively low proportions of Indians in agriculture, but Oklahoma and South Dakota, the two most important allotted states, had percentages of males employed in agriculture of 63.7 and 82.8 percent respectively.[57]

As measured by the *Census of Occupations*, in 1930, slightly less than half of the Indian men employed in agriculture were employed as farm workers, 25,124 farm laborers versus 26,521 farmers. In 1910 the picture was much the same, with more Indians reported as farm laborers, 26,490, than farmers, 21,997.[58] As reported in table 6.2, the number of Indian farms in the *Census of Agriculture* in the eleven allotted states declined between 1910 and 1930, which suggests that the increased number of Indians who were reported as farmers were living on unallotted reservations. This conclusion is consistent with other data in the census. These figures must be viewed with some care, since the definition of an Indian farm does not correspond exactly to the number of Indians reported as farmers. The data are for the entire nation, but the evidence is that in 1930 nearly half of all Indians in agriculture in allotted states were farm laborers as well. It is likely that many of the Indians reported as farm laborers were sporadically employed in planting and harvesting and, undoubtedly, had low earned incomes.

Most Indian males were either farmers or unskilled laborers in 1930. In 1910, 54.3 percent of Indian males were classified as workers in unskilled jobs, including farm labor; in 1930, 51.1 percent. Excluding agriculture, the number of Indians in semiskilled, skilled, or professional jobs increased from 8.1 percent in 1910 to 13.4 percent in 1930,[59] an important increase. Nonetheless, most Indians remained tied to jobs in which they acquired few skills and had few prospects for the future. Again, these figures are national totals, but little is found to suggest that allotted Indians fared better than the national average.[60]

Some bright spots in this picture of the economic and social position of Indians were the marked declines in the percentage of Indians who were illiterate and the percentage of Indians who could not speak English. In 1900, 56.2 percent of Indians over ten were reported as illiterate, and in 1910, 27.7 percent of Indian males over ten were unable to speak English. By 1930 the percentage of illiterates had declined to 25.7 percent, and the percentage of Indian males unable to speak English had declined to 14.8 percent (17 percent of the total male and female population). Indians in allotted states typically had lower rates of illiteracy than the national average.[61] According to these important measures, Indians seemed in a far better position to compete in white society than they had two or three decades earlier. Despite some important changes, however, the picture of Indian economic life that emerges from the above statistics is of a people who were still tied to agriculture or to some form of rural employment. In 1930 Indians, either because of a desire to remain on the reservation or through the lack of any other alternative, remained in an environment where agriculture was the major industry. Thus the failure of government programs to aid Indians becoming farmers discussed above acquires added significance.

Changes in Indian Land Ownership in the Allotment Era

Since Indians remained a primarily rural people whose livelihood was tied to agriculture, the amount of land remaining in Indian control was very important. After 1930 programs to aid Indians and the economic and social changes that occurred among Indians were critically influenced by the amount of land available to Indian tribes.

As historians know, a vast amount of land passed out of Indian control in the era of land allotment. Indian lands under the supervision of the Office of Indian Affairs declined from 104.3 million acres in 1890 to 52.7 million acres in 1933.[62] The decline came about in numerous ways: through the sale of unallotted (surplus) lands, through agreements and orders reducing the size of a reservation, and through the passing of allotted land into fee-simple status, free of government regulations. Indians not only lost land; reservations were sometimes expanded by adding tracts of land from the public domain, and new reservations were established for tribes that did not previously have a reservation.[63] The most notable increase came on the Navajo Reservation in Arizona and New Mexico.

The ten allotted states considered above plus Oklahoma accounted for much of the decline in Indian land ownership. In the ten allotted states, the amount of land under the supervision of the Office of Indian Affairs fell from 37.47 million acres in 1890 to 27.95 million acres in 1900 to 16.82 million acres in 1933.[64] Reductions in Indian land holdings before the turn of the century were through the sale of unallotted, surplus lands or direct cession of the land to the federal government. After 1900 the loss in Indian land was more directly related to sales by individual Indians as allotments themselves were released from the control of the Office of Indian Affairs or sold directly to non-Indians. The removal of land from trust status was not uniform across reservations. On some reservations, almost all allotted land remained in trust status in 1934, and on other reservations, most allotted land had been removed from trust status.

In all, approximately 26.11 million acres were allotted under the Dawes Act or by special treaty. Another 15.79 million acres were divided among members of the Five Tribes. In 1940, 61.8 percent or 16.14 million acres of the land allotted under the Dawes Act or by special treaty were still under government supervision, and only 9 percent or 1.45 million acres were held in trust for members of the Five Tribes.[65] Excluding the Five Tribes, most of the allotted land removed from trust status was the result of direct federal action: either by the direct sale of land for Indian allottees or by issuing patents in fee in advance of the end of the twenty-five-year trust period. A total of 3.7 million acres were sold either as heirship lands or directly for noncompetent Indian allottees. In addition, an incomplete total of land removed from trust status by administrative action is 4.58 million acres.[66] The best available evidence suggests that up to 80 percent or more of Indians granted patents in fee sold it or had it sold for them on account of delinquent mortgage or tax payments within a few years of being declared competent.[67]

A much larger percentage of land was divided among members of the Five Tribes than was allotted to Indians under the Dawes Act. The restrictions on the lease and sale of land divided among members of the Five Tribes were initially far more liberal than those of lands granted under the

Dawes Act, and restrictions were quickly eased further once the land was in Indian hands. Authority over some aspects of Indian property was transferred to the the state government, sometimes with regrettable consequences. For example, the property of minor allottees in the Five Tribes was placed under the jurisdiction of the Oklahoma probate courts, an action that often led to the defrauding of Indian minors of their inheritances.[68]

The way in which Indian land passed out of government supervision after allotment raises important questions about how federal policies were carried out and what would have been the best policy from the point of view of Indian welfare. These questions go beyond the scope of this study, but some conclusions can be reached. The failure of Indian farming was caused, in part, by the way in which allotment discouraged Indian farmers and encouraged the lease and sale of lands to non-Indians. I consider possible alternatives to allotment in the concluding chapter.

Conclusions

The evidence on the development of Indian farming in the first three decades of the twentieth century is remarkably consistent. Allotted Indians did not farm in any greater numbers by 1930, and those Indians who were farmers were farther behind white farmers than they had been in 1900. Allotment as a means of promoting self-sufficient farming among Indians was a failure. The propositions developed in chapter 5 on the negative impact of allotment on Indian farming are consistent with what actually occurred.

The Meriam Commission found that Indians were often in the most isolated parts of the reservations because they chose to be near a water supply or a source of firewood or because, "Frequently the better sections of the land have fallen into the hands of the whites, and the Indians have retreated to the poorer lands remote from markets."[69] This pattern of withdrawal and perhaps isolation of allotted Indians is the opposite of the picture envisioned by the reformers. They saw allotment as promoting the mixing of whites and Indians and hence speeding the transfer of skills.

The picture of Indians having little contact with their white neighbors parallels William Parker's description of the origins of rural poverty in the United States. Parker concluded that:

> The rather sharp adjustment of regions to new markets, products and processes were not without cost. In each adjustment, some farmers were left behind; in regions less well favored by transport—in the hill country of New England, the Appalachians, and the Ozarks; in the cutover country of northern Minnesota; in areas of the Southeast with damaged soils; and in the southern

plains—the vicious circles characteristic of agriculture in underdeveloped countries appeared. People removed from progressive farming by isolation, poverty and ignorance on which it was built. . . .[70]

Allotment had been intended to increase the incentives for Indians to farm their own land and to make it easier for Indians to learn new skills. It had the opposite result in many cases. Indians often reduced the amount of land they farmed and remained relatively isolated from the white settlers, who sometimes became a majority of the people on the reservation.

Notes

1. Lewis Meriam and Associates, *The Problem of Indian Administration*, p. 3.
2. Ibid., p. 5.
3. Ibid., p. 491.
4. Ibid., p. 7.
5. U.S. Congress, Senate, "Report of Advisors on Irrigation in Indian Reservations," by Porter J. Preston and Charles A. Engle. *Review of Conditions of the Indians in the United States: Hearings Before the Commission on Indian Affairs*, 71st Cong., 2d sess., U.S. Senate Res. 78 and 308, 1930, pp. 2210–2661 (hereafter cited as *Preston-Engle Report*).
6. Ibid., p. 2218.
7. Ibid., p. 2248.
8. U.S. Department of the Interior, Bureau of the Census, "Agriculture on Indian Reservations," in *Twelfth Census of the United States, 1900, Vol. V: Agriculture*, pp. 724–25.
9. Delos Sacket Otis, *The Dawes Act and the Allotment of Indian Lands*, p. 130.
10. Roy W. Meyer, *A History of the Santee Sioux*, p. 219.
11. Ibid., p. 217.
12. Ibid., p. 238.
13. U.S. Department of the Interior, Board of Indian Commissioners, *Annual Report of the Board of Indian Commissioners to the Secretary of the Interior for Fiscal Year Ended June 30, 1922*, pp. 20–21.
14. Ibid., p. 21.
15. Jack Drozier, "The Coeur d'Alene Land Rush," *The Pacific Northwest Quarterly* 53 (October 1962): 149.
16. *Annual Report of the Board of Indian Commissioners, 1922*, p. 20.
17. John C. Ewers, *The Blackfeet: Raiders on the Northwestern Plains*, p. 318.
18. Ibid., p. 319.
19. Cited in ibid., p. 319.
20. *Annual Report of the Board of Indian Commissioners, 1922*, p. 27.
21. William T. Hagan, *United States-Commanche Relations*, p. 219.
22. Ibid., p. 271.

23. Ibid., p. 250.

24. James B. Fitch, "Economic Development in a Minority Enclave: The Case of the Yakima Indian Nation, Washington" (Ph.D. diss., Stanford University, 1974), chap. 3., passim.

25. Ronald L. Trosper, "The Economic Impact of the Allotment Policy on the Flathead Indian Reservation" (Ph.D. diss., Harvard University, 1974), pp. 188–96.

26. Ewers, *The Blackfeet*, p. 318.

27. Indeed, the skepticism of the Blackfeet about irrigated farming on the reservation may well have been warranted. The Blackfeet project was so unsuccessful that the *Preston-Engle Report* recommended it be abandoned, since operating costs outweighed the benefits. See the *Preston-Engle Report*, pp. 2219–20.

28. In addition, the *Preston-Engle Report* concluded that the efforts made to instruct Indians in irrigated farming techniques were grossly inadequate. See ibid., p. 212.

29. William Parker, "Agriculture," in *American Economic Growth: An Economist's History of the United States*, ed. Lance Davis, Richard Easterlin and William Parker, et al, p. 395.

30. Ibid., pp. 395, 404.

31. See for example, Fitch, "Economic Development in a Minority Enclave," chap. 3; and Otis, *The Dawes Act*, p. 125.

32. A white lender could not acquire a mortgage claim to trust-status allotted lands and hence would not have been willing to lend money. Even if an Indian had a patent in fee, he might have been considered a poor credit risk. This could easily result from a mix of prejudice with market signaling—Indians might have been seen as less creditworthy than a typical white, regardless of the merits of the individual applicant.

33. Meriam and Associates, *The Problem of Indian Administration*, pp. 490–91.

34. Parker, "Agriculture," p. 395–96.

35. Mary Wilma H. Hargreaves, *Dry Farming in the Northern Great Plains*, p. 17.

36. W. Eliot Brownlee, *The Dynamics of Ascent: A History of the American Economy* (New York: Alfred Knopf, 1974), p. 273.

37. Parker, "Agriculture," p. 406.

38. Hargreaves, *Dry Farming*, pp. 19–20.

39. Parker, "Agriculture," p. 372.

40. Ibid., p. 387.

41. U.S. Department of the Interior, Bureau of the Census, *Fifteenth Census of the United States, 1930, Vol. V: Agriculture*, pp. 72–73.

42. The census data require some care in interpretation. The census identified as an Indian anyone who said he was an Indian. In two of the four years studied here, 1910 and 1930, special questionnaires on Indians were included in the census. This led to more mixed-blood individuals being included as Indians than in 1900 or 1920. In general, Indians who passed as some other race in 1900 and 1920 were more like white Americans: they had higher literacy rates, faced less discrimination, and had larger farms and better jobs. This should be kept in mind in comparing the data for 1910 and 1930 with those of 1900 and 1920. See U.S. Department of the Interior, Bureau of the Census, *Fifteenth Census of the United States, 1930: The Indian Population of the United States and Alaska*, p. 2.

43. The totals include lands allotted to members of the Five Tribes but do not appear to include lands allotted from the public domain.

44. See table A.5 in appendix A.

45. See tables A.20 and A.21 in appendix A and the discussion below.

46. As mentioned above, data on the level of Indian farming and per farm averages are both biased upwards for 1910 and 1930 relative to 1900 and 1920 by the inclusion of more mixed-blood Indians. Since we are concernred with whether allotment led to a decline in Indian farming, the upward bias of the data for 1930 is *against* the hypothesis and strengthens any conclusion that allotment did lead to a decline in Indian farming.

47. See the explanation of the interpolation procedure in appendix B. Totals are constrained to add up to the total for all nonwhites.

48. See table A.7 in appendix A.

49. See table 6.4 and table A.7 in appendix A.

50. See table A.8 in appendix A. Again, data for 1910 have been interpolated from the totals for all nonwhite farms.

51. See table 7.6 and table A.9 in appendix A.

52. U.S. Department of Agriculture, *Yearbook of Agriculture, 1920*, p. 729.

53. See table A.12 in appendix A.

54. See Meriam and Associates, *The Problem of Indian Administration*, chap. XII, passim.

55. See table A.16 in appendix A.

56. See table A.16 in appendix A.

57. Source: Tables A.13, A.14, and A.15 in appendix A. Data on Indian participation rates by state were reported only for selected states in 1930. The number of Indians reported as farmers by the *Census of Occupations* differs from the number of Indian farms reported in the *Census of Agriculture*. See the *Fifteenth Census of the United States, 1930: The Indian Population of the U.S. and Alaska*, p. 227.

58. See table A.14 in appendix A.

59. See table A.15 in appendix A.

60. Many of the Indians in nonagricultural, off-reservation jobs mentioned in the Meriam report were from unallotted tribes such as the Pueblos or Navajos. See Meriam and Associates, *The Problem of Indian Administration*, chap. XII, passim.

61. See tables A.20 and A.21 in appendix A.

62. See table A.2 in appendix A.

63. One way that reservations were created was through an executive order from the president, transferring unclaimed land from the public domain to Indian control.

64. See table A.1 in appendix A.

65. See table A.1 in appendix A.

66. See tables A.3 and A.4 in appendix A.

67. See Meriam and Associates, *The Problem of Indian Administration*, pp. 471–72; Lawrence F. Schmeckebier, *The Office of Indian Affairs*, pp. 154–64; U.S. National Resources Board, Land Planning Committee, *Indian Land Tenure, Economic Status, and Population Trends*, 1935, p. 6.

68. See Schmeckebier, *The Office of Indian Affairs*, pp. 172–75.

69. Meriam and Associates, *The Problem of Indian Administration*, p. 5.

70. Parker, "Agriculture," p. 409.

PART FOUR
Implications

7 | PROPERTY RIGHTS, POLITICS, AND PROGRESS

The New Deal and the passage of the Indian Reorganization Act in 1934 brought to an end the nearly fifty-year history of the allotment policy. The Dawes Act had been part of a set of policies that had the stated intention of improving the material and economic position of Indians in the United States. By 1930 significant social changes had occurred among Indians, and some of these changes can be quantified and suggest that improvements had occurred. In the years from 1900 to 1930, the proportion of Indians who were illiterate declined from over one-half of the population to roughly one-fourth; the proportion of the population that was unable to speak English declined as well.[1] The percentages of Indians unable to read or unable to speak English were even lower in allotted states. Such changes could have been expected to improve the economic opportunities of Indians. Yet in 1930 Indians were little better off, if at all, than they had been in 1900. Indeed, the Meriam report of 1928 painted a picture of widespread poverty and related social problems among Indians.[2]

This study has looked at the role of the Dawes Act in promoting change among American Indians. Specifically, two major topics have been explored: how the Dawes Act was carried into effect and how the Dawes Act as a major land reform affected American Indians as farmers. Allotment began under special treaties in the late 1860s and continued under the Dawes Act until 1934. Models were developed to explore how reservations were chosen for allotment. The first model formalized the official position of the Office of Indian Affairs and was referred to as the "guardianship model." Legally, the Office of Indian Affairs was charged with protecting the interests of Indians by delaying allotment until members of the tribe were ready for allotment. The model concluded that the Office of Indian Affairs would have delayed allotment until members of a tribe had demonstrated their ability to support themselves and hence were ready to take advantage of owning private property. The guardianship model is similar to the "public-interest" view of regulation, which sees economic regulation by government as an effort to correct distortions or inequities in the market.

The second hypothesis was referred to as the "demand for allotment model" and concluded that the Office of Indian Affairs chose reservations for allotment as a direct response to the interests of whites who wanted to develop reservation lands. The allotment of an Indian reservation offered substantial benefits to non-Indians: surplus land was opened for settlement, and the allotments themselves could be leased or sold to whites, often on very favorable terms. Settlers and merchants were all well aware of these potential benefits and pressured the Office of Indian Affairs to allot desirable reservations both directly, by attempting to influence its employees, and indirectly, by working through Congress. The evidence clearly shows that congressmen worked to speed the allotment of desirable reservations. If the demand for allotment model is correct, the first reservations to be allotted were those that yielded the greatest benefits to non-Indians.

The guardianship and the demand for allotment models were both tested using aggregate data for the entire United States. One test of the demand for allotment model uses multiple regression. A regression of the date of a reservation's allotment on five independent variables reflecting attractiveness of the reservation for allotment (white population density in the state, percentage of all land that was improved farm land, rainfall, and two dummy variables) explains 65 percent of the variation in the dates of allotment. In addition, nonparametric statistical tests of the relationship between the order in which reservations were allotted and the attractiveness of a reservation to whites also yielded statistically significant results. The guardianship model was tested using measures of the self-support of reservation Indians and proved to be far less satisfactory.

The statistical tests and literary evidence provide support for the demand for allotment model. In some cases, however, the statistical evidence may be given more than one interpretation. Thus the demand for allotment and guardianship models were also tested using case histories of the allotment of reservations in the Northern Plains states of Nebraska and North and South Dakota. In general, the attractiveness of land for agriculture in these states declines as one moves from the eastern to the more arid western regions. The eastern regions were the first to be settled and are still the most densely populated. The eastern reservations in these states were the most attractive to settlers and, according to the demand for allotment model, should have been the first to be allotted. Indeed, a definite east to west movement was evident in allotment of reservations in the Northern Plains. Although most reservations in these states were allotted in the 1880s and 1890s, the large reservations in the western Dakotas were not allotted until after 1900, when interest increased in the development of those lands for dry farming. An illuminating example of how federal agents responded to white pressure for land is provided by the Rosebud Reservation, where fertile land in the eastern part of the reservation was opened to white settlers before allotment had been completed in the arid western portion.

If the guardianship model is correct, Indians on the reservations allotted relatively late should have demonstrated an increased readiness for allotment. As measured by increased self-sufficiency in farming, however, Indians on the last reservations allotted were no more ready to benefit from allotment than they had been a decade earlier. Thus the conclusion of this section was that the administration of the Dawes Act was determined by the economic interests of non-Indians. This does not necessarily imply, however, that Indian policy was a thinly veiled scheme to expropriate Indian land. Rather, it suggests that an open-ended federal policy was bent and shaped by outside economic interests.

The second major section of this study examined the consequences of allotment as an important land reform. The reformers saw allotment as a way to encourage the economic and cultural assimilation of American Indians. Discussions of allotment by the reformers and others implied that Indians, before allotment, held and worked their lands in common. In such a case, allotment would have created private property rights where none had existed before. A study of Indian reservations before allotment, however, shows that this was not the case. On most reservations, an Indian had a recognized right to land that he cultivated—a right that was respected both by the agents and the tribe. Thus formal allotment made it easier for an individual Indian to sell or lease land while making collective or coordinated actions by Indians more difficult and costly. A model was developed to explore how utility-maximizing Indian farmers would allocate time and resources before and after allotment. The conclusion was that, after allotment, a rational Indian farmer would devote *fewer* resources to his own farming, choosing instead to acquire market goods by leasing land to whites and working for a wage. In addition, a decline in Indian farming would have made it harder for an Indian to learn from another Indian and reduce the benefits from cooperation among Indians—which would have further retarded Indian farming. Since the primary way for an Indian to learn farming was to do it himself, encouraging a decline in Indian farming would have contravened the stated intentions of the reformers.

The analysis rests on the proposition that Indians had a workable system of private property before allotment, and they were willing and able to become farmers. Historians and others have often neglected the study of farming and ranching by Indians before allotment on the assumption that nothing of significance had occurred. A survey of case histories of Indian reservations, however, showed that many Indians were small-scale farmers and ranchers who had made substantial progress in the years before allotment. Individuals had recognized rights to the land they cultivated, and farming was carried out by families on their own land. Indeed, on a number of reservations, Indians made long strides toward becoming self-sufficient through farming in the years before allotment.

Some tribes whose members became successful farmers, such as the Santee Sioux, were relatively acculturated before being placed on a reservation. Other tribes that had little contact with whites before being placed on a reservation, including some important tribes in the Pacific Northwest, were also successful as farmers and ranchers before allotment. On some reservations, a good agent or missionary gave valuable aid to Indian farmers. Not all Indians, however, were settled in areas suited to conventional farming. Many of the Plains tribes were settled on reservations best suited to grazing, and some members of these tribes found ranching a colorful and attractive way of life and became successful cattlemen.

This picture of successful Indian farming, drawn from selected reservation histories, was confirmed by data on acres cultivated and output taken from thirty-three reservations and agencies where successful farming was possible. Looking at the years from 1875 until the date of allotment, most reservations in the sample had very high compound rates of growth in both acres cultivated and output. Over one-third had rates of growth in excess of 10 percent per year; only one reservation had a decline in acres cultivated, and only three had a decline in output before allotment. Of course, not all Indians were willing and able to become farmers, and not all Indian tribes were as successful as others in becoming farmers. Nonetheless, a substantial number of Indians were farmers or ranchers before allotment, and although their farms were typically small, they had improved at a rapid pace. No evidence is found to suggest that Indians needed allotment to stimulate their efforts.

The history of Indian farming after allotment was quite different. As predicted by the model developed in this study, allotment was often followed by a decline in Indian farming and an increase in the lease and sale of allotted lands to whites. Along with this decline in Indian farming came a continued dependency on the federal government—rather than a reduction in federal supervision—and a rise in alcoholism and other social problems. Ranching on the Plains reservations was less affected at first, but after a brief period of prosperity, much Indian ranch land ended up in white hands.

The story of stagnation and decline in Indian farming that emerges from individual reservation histories is consistent with the overall position of allotted Indian farmers, as shown by aggregate evidence. Between 1900 and

1930, Indian farming in the ten states in which a majority of Indian land was allotted, plus Oklahoma, showed a marked decline.[3] Fewer Indian farmers were farming fewer acres in 1930, after allotment, than in 1900, before allotment. In addition, the value of the average Indian farm as a percentage of the value of the average white farm fell after 1910. For ten allotted states in 1930, the average Indian farm was only 31 percent as valuable as the average white farm, down from 44 percent in 1910. In Oklahoma, the average Indian farm was worth only 59 percent as much as the average white farm in 1930, down from 82 percent in 1900. Indian farmers used less of inputs other than land as well. Rather than "catching up" with white farmers, Indian farmers slipped into an even more marginal position relative to white farmers. This evidence of a low level of Indian farming three decades after allotment was confirmed by the Meriam Commission in 1928. The commission found that most Indians mixed a variety of activities to earn a meager living and that relatively few Indians were prosperous farmers.

The decline in Indian farming cannot be explained by arguing that the most industrious Indians left agriculture and moved to new occupations. Although the proportion of Indians living in cities and the percentage of Indians who were in semiskilled trades rose in the first decades of the twentieth century, most Indians still remained in rural areas where they depended on agriculture or some form of unskilled labor for a livelihood. In 1930 only 9.9 percent of all Indians living in the United States lived in cities, and 64 percent of all Indian males over ten were reported as either farmers or farm laborers. The picture is similar when only allotted Indians are considered.

Certainly, many factors contributed to the economic and social problems of Indians in 1930, but the decline in Indian farming that followed allotment was an important contributor to those problems. This decline was substantial and is completely consistent with the theoretical expectations developed in this study concerning the impact of the Dawes Act. Those theoretical expectations, however, were derived from a model that recognized the existence of property rights among Indians before allotment and thus avoided the fallacy embraced by the reformers—that Indians lacked individual rights to property before allotment.

The Dawes Act and the Goals of the Reformers

In light of the conclusions of this study, what can be said about the success or failure of allotment? To evaluate the Dawes Act as federal policy, we need to consider what the reformers were trying to achieve. The goals of the reformers included the following: (1) to open unused Indian land to development by industrious white settlers, (2) to protect Indian title to at least a part of their lands, (3) to promote Indian farming and other "civilized" activities, (4) to promote the assimilation of individual Indians into white culture, and (5) to reduce the burden to taxpayers of the cost of aiding reservation Indians.

As discussed in chapter 6 and shown in appendix A, table A.1, allotment and related policies were spectacularly successful in achieving the goal of opening Indian land to white settlement. For example, in the ten allotted states, Indian land in trust status declined from 82 million acres in 1881 to 37.5 million acres in 1890 to 16.8 million acres in 1933. In Oklahoma Indian land in trust status fell from 41 million acres in 1881 to 39 million acres in 1890 to 2.9 million acres in 1933.[4] Most of the land that was removed from trust status passed out of Indian ownership altogether, and part of the land in trust status was leased to white farmers and ranchers. Since agriculture was a competitive occupation, it is likely that most land that passed from Indian hands ended up in its highest valued uses. We can be less sanguine that the way in which land was transferred was efficient or fair.

Looking at how efficiently land was transferred from Indians to whites, the story is mixed. Surplus lands were opened in a manner similar to the Homestead Act. Presumably, this transfer was as efficient as any other federal land-distribution program and hence no more costly than the most likely alternative distribution scheme. The record, however, with respect to allotted lands is poor. Allotments could only be leased or sold subject to administrative regulations and the approval of the agent. This increased the cost to whites of acquiring Indian lands and reduced the return to Indians from leasing or selling land. Heirship lands present an extreme case, since in some cases, the title to the land became so encumbered that it was not used at all. The administration of allotted and tribally held lands offered chances for favoritism and corruption in the worst of cases and increased the costs of information and negotiating transactions in cases where agents were conscientious.

Allotment was not only intended to transfer land from Indians to whites; the reformers also wanted to guarantee Indians sufficient land with which to become farmers. As discussed in chapter 6, 26.12 million acres were allotted under the Dawes Act or by special legislation. Another 15.79 million acres were divided among members of the Five Tribes. As of June 1940, 61.8 percent of the land allotted to Indians, other than members of the Five Tribes, was still under government supervision.[5] Accounts from the period state that much of the land removed from government supervision was sold to white farmers. Most land was removed from trust status either by issuing the allottee a patent in fee or by the sale of the land of an allottee by the federal government in its role as trustee. In general, reservations that were allotted early had a higher percentage of land removed from governmental supervision than reservations allotted at a later date.

The Dawes Act contained no provisions for the allotment of land to future generations. Population growth and the sale of allotted and surplus tribal lands have left many tribes with a relatively small land base; in some cases, modern efforts to develop a reservation have been hindered by insufficient land and the fragmented nature of Indian land holdings.[6] Thus the Dawes Act can be seen as leaving Indians in a relatively poor position for future development; again, the actual performance of the allotment policy fell short of what the reformers intended.

The main economic objective of the reformers was to encourage Indians to become farmers. Yet Indian farming did not prosper after allotment. Previous explanations of the poor showing of reservation Indians have focused on three things: the blindness of reformers, policymakers, and field workers to the true problems and unique cultural values of American Indians; the inadequate and ill-conceived programs to assist Indians; and the unwillingness of Indians to abandon traditional values and adapt to new occupations such as farming. Allotment, as part of a misguided attempt to force assimilation, is also assigned a role.

This study has not challenged the first two propositions. Federal programs to assist Indians were often ill-conceived, poorly implemented, and in conflict with the wishes of the Indians. The Meriam report gave a powerful account of the need to have better educational programs, to give assistance in acquiring capital, and to provide training and aid to Indian farmers and other Indians, as well as to provide better health care and training in health and hygiene. With a higher level of assistance, the story of the social and economic development of American Indians in the first decades of the twentieth century might have been happier.

Criticism of the reformers for not stressing programs to aid Indian farmers is also in order. This study has challenged the proposition that Indians were unwilling or unable to respond to incentives to become farmers or learn new occupations. The reformers pictured Indians as learning farming by a gradual process of accumulating skills and capital necessary for successful farming. Yet this is the type of gradual development that in fact took place before allotment. The Dawes Act discouraged Indians from continuing to develop as farmers.

The failure of allotment can be seen, in part, as a consequence of the inability of reformers to reconcile conflicting aims. On the one had, reformers wanted to eliminate differences between Indians and non-Indians. It was hoped that, by granting individual property rights, the Indians would be in a position to respond to the same economic incentives as non-Indians. Politically, Indians were encouraged to abandon the tribe and use the franchise to move local politicians to defend their interests.

On the other hand, reformers realized that Indians were not yet ready to either compete or to be allowed to compete on equal terms with white farmers.

Indians often needed special assistance and supervision. Thus Indian property rights were entangled in a complex set of rules and regulations that severely restricted the rights of the individual allottee, without really solving the problem of encouraging and assisting Indians in becoming farmers. Over time, these restrictions became more burdensome.

Existing legal forms assumed that an individual was ready to handle his or her own affairs and that the person would receive equal treatment in legal and market transactions. No wonder that modifying the legal institutions to serve a completely different situation led to the creation of a costly, complicated, and perverse set of institutions.

To the reformers, promoting Indian farming was part of the broader and more important goal of encouraging Indians to assimilate into white society. As revealed in chapter 4, little reason can be found to conclude that allotment *qua* allotment did much to discourage the customs and values that were pictured as hindering the development of Indian farming. It is difficult to assess how much allotment promoted the assimilation of Indians into white culture. In the end, however, Indian values and cultures proved to be far more enduring and were far more viable than the reformers ever conceived was possible.

The Dawes Act deliberately gave Indians little voice in devising Indian policy. They were especially opposed to political action by the tribe. The reformers saw the tribe as an archaic relic of an earlier stage of development, and they feared that conservative individuals in the tribe would thwart the efforts of those willing to advance economically, or that a tribal government would be unfair to some group or individual. The reformers were also fearful that, if Indians were given a significant role in the formulation of Indian policy, they would be able to oppose needed reforms and programs. Ward politics and political action by immigrant nationalities in big cities were an anathema to the reformers, and they were strongly opposed to letting Indians act in a similar manner.

In general, these efforts were successful. Tribes as units of government and political action were relatively ineffective during the allotment era. The results of this suppression of tribal activity, however, might have surprised many members of the reform movement. With collective action through the tribe blocked, Indians were placed at a severe disadvantage in pressing for funds or in acting to change federal policy or protecting their own interests.

Reformers wanted Indians to act through state and local government. Yet Indians did not rise to prominence in local politics, and little evidence exists that local white politicians courted the votes of Indians or reflected their interests. On many reservations, Indians quickly became a minority group with little or no direct political influence. Limiting Indian influence in shaping Indian policy appears to have had the opposite effect from that intended by the reformers. Rather than allow the federal government to devise programs that would best serve the long-run interests of Indians, the policies of the Office of Indian Affairs in the first decades of the twentieth century were carried out with great conviction but little success, and Indians could do little to correct the situation.

One of the long-run aims of the Dawes Act was to end the dependency of Indians on the federal government and to reduce federal expenditures to aid Indians. Indeed, shortly after the passage of the Dawes Act, Commissioner of Indian Affairs Thomas J. Morgan boasted that the Dawes Act would eventually lead to an end of the need for special programs to aid Indians and the disappearance of the Office of Indian Affairs.[7] Ironically, the passage of the Dawes Act saw instead a continued growth of federal appropriations to aid Indians. Allotment itself required considerable expenditures to survey allotments and to assign one to each individual on the reservation. Once an Indian was allotted, his or her property was administered separately, and the volume of paper work required grew with these new demands. As mentioned above, the number of employees of the Office of Indian Affairs in Washington increased by more than two and one-half times between 1900 and 1920. Congressional appropriations to run the Office of Indian Affairs grew from $9.6 million in 1903 to $15 million in 1928. In addition, the federal government used funds due to tribes and individuals as compensation for treaty or other settlements to administer some programs or to make direct per capita payments to individuals. In 1926 all federal expenditures on Indians, including per capita payments and disbursements from tribal funds held in trust for the various tribes, totaled $48.5 million.[8] Clearly, the Office of Indian Affairs had not withered away with the coming of allotment.

Indians also did not cease to rely on federal aid for survival. The poor showing of allotted Indian farmers and the generally depressed state of American agriculture in the 1920s meant that many Indians depended upon federal services or payments from the federal treasury or tribal funds for survival. These services and payments were uneven, with some individuals and/or tribes receiving generous payments and others for various reasons receiving very little.

On balance the Dawes Act failed to achieve most of the goals of its enthusiastic adherence. Indeed, the allotment of Indian lands led to what many of the reformers feared would happen even without allotment: the rapid transfer of Indian land to white settlers and little progress by Indian farmers. This is not to suggest that the reformers faced an easy task in designing policies to deal fairly and effectively with Indians. The allotment policy not only raised questions that the reformers were unable to solve, it also raised theoretical issues for economists interested in the economics of property rights. As an exercise to appreciate the dilemmas faced by the reformers, I consider below both the theoretical problems raised by allotment and propose a hypothetical alternative to allotment.

Reflections on the Economics of Property Rights

Allotment in severalty, judged either as a program to advance the welfare of American Indians or to promote economic development among reservation Indians, was a disaster. Rather than encourage Indian farmers, it led to a significant decline in Indian farming. No student of the property-rights literature or, indeed, economic theory will be surprised that the complicated and heavily supervised property right that emerged from allotment led to inefficiencies, corruption, and losses for both Indians and society. Issues related to allotment, however, do illustrate points that sometimes have been neglected in the property-rights literature. From the failure of allotment, one might conclude that a person is better off, *certeris paribus*, with a property right that is restricted with respect to lease or sale than one that is unrestricted. But in fact, that argument does not hold. Allotment introduced numerous changes into the economic environment faced by Indians, and the right to sell and lease property was only one of these changes. It is instructive, however, to consider the welfare implications of granting Indians restricted, as opposed to unrestricted, titles to their allotments.

Consider first the case of a family with a trust patent on a reservation that had been allotted, the surplus opened for sale to non-Indians, and other families already granted fee patents. Assume that the family was rational in an economic sense and in possession of sufficient information to make wise decisions. It seems clear that, *certeris paribus*, such a family would have its welfare improved if it had the right to petition to have restrictions on its right to lease or sell land removed. Even if the family became liable for property taxes upon receiving a fee patent, it would be better off if at its own option it could request fee-patent status. If the family were granted fee-patent status without its consent, the maximum value of loss would equal the capitalized value of the tax payments that would otherwise have been avoided.

If members of a family were not in possession of sufficient knowledge to act wisely in their own interests, they should have been protected. Such a guardianship is similar to that imposed on children and others in society judged not able to handle their own affairs. The problem is to design a program to supervise the property of noncompetent individuals and to assist them in acquiring the necessary skills and judgment to act in their own interests. The government and the Office of Indian Affairs have been strongly and correctly criticized for their handling of the property and education of Indians classified as incompetent. At least in theory, however, the problem is straightforward.

But it does not follow that the program of allotting all Indian land in severalty, as opposed to giving one family the right to sell land, automatically improved the welfare of allotted Indians, as a straightforward application of economic theory might conclude. Allotment was part of a broader program of assimilation, and its welfare implications cannot be considered apart from these other changes. Also, as discussed in chapter 4, interdependencies (externalities) may have existed among Indians that allotment made more difficult to take into account (increased transaction costs).

Indians were operating in an economic environment that contained important market imperfections. Indians could obtain capital and skills only at a significantly greater cost than non-Indians; their initial level of skills with respect to farming was below that of white farmers; discrimination was evident in market transactions and in the actions of government agencies and the courts; and group cooperation and coordination among Indians to capture economies of scale in operating farms were deliberately hampered. In technical terms, the removal of restrictions on Indian allottees occurred in a second-best situation.

The general theory of the second best holds that removing one market imperfection in such a situation may well move the equilibrium away from a global maximum for efficiency and welfare, not closer.[9] *A priori* reasoning suggests that Indians were acquiring too few skills, too little capital, and engaging in too little market-oriented labor, as judged by their own preferences and certainly as judged by the preferences of the reformers. Allotment made it easier to sell land and reduce participation in farming without encouraging other activities that plausibly would have been associated with improving the welfare of American Indians in the long run. Of course, after allotment some Indians could buy more land, if only from other Indians, but before allotment they could claim unused tribal land. The net gain to Indians seems to have been small at best. Another set of issues is raised by the fact that Indians possessed a different culture and values than the population at large, had a different endowment of skills and resources, lacked experience with white-dominated institutions and legal arrangements, and were discriminated against by non-Indians and may in turn have avoided or discriminated against non-Indians. It is in the spirit of the property-rights literature to conclude that the costs and benefits to Indians of receiving land in fee simple would be very different from those to non-Indians. Indians might have benefited from a different set of legal and property arrangements. For example, during the allotment era, the tribe was not recognized as a political or economic unit. Yet as discussed chapter 4, the tribe might have served as an aid to reservation development programs. Discussions in the property-rights literature often assume that populations are homogeneous in tastes and in the ability to benefit from a particular set of institutional arrangements. These assumptions should be reexamined in situations where groups differ in important economic characteristics.

Studies of the impact of alternative property-rights arrangements have often focused on the efficiency of these changes—whether the allocation of resources between competing uses was improved after allotment. The effect of different assignments of property rights on income and wealth distributions have often been assigned a secondary role. On theoretical and empirical grounds, the redistributive effects of allotment cannot be neglected. Important redistributions of wealth in property occurred between Indians and whites and, within the tribe, between Indians and Indians. The way in which redistributions occurred affected the nature and rate of economic change among Indians.

The long-run effect of allotment on Indian land ownership, the transfer of much of Indian land holdings to whites via lease or sale, provides support for a simple-minded version of the Coase Theorem. After allotment, land may have been employed in its highest valued use. Farming was a competitive industry, and it is likely that anyone using Indian land would employ it to earn a competitive return. It is possible that an alternative program that offered greater incentive to Indians to use their own land would have reduced production on reservation lands. It does not follow, however, that a program that made it easy to transfer land to whites was necessarily better than a policy that restricted such transfers or at least kept title to reservation lands in Indian hands.

This reasoning suggests that an evaluation of a policy such as allotment cannot be accomplished by examining changes in first-order conditions for efficiency. Allotment was a nonmarginal change that removed some barriers to Indian development and strengthened others. Alternative policies must be evaluated in terms of their net effect on Indian and non-Indian welfare. Even if the transfer of Indian lands under allotment did lead to a higher level of GNP, important questions of efficiency versus equity remain, as well as the question about whether it is better to maximize aggregate ouput now or to encourage Indians to become more productive in the future.

An Alternative to Allotment

As an exercise to gain appreciation for the difficulties and dilemmas faced by reformers, this section proposes a counterfactual alternative to allotment. Certainly, any alternative to allotment requires that conflicting goals and values be reconciled. As the primary policymaking body, Congress would have had to decide the level of assistance that would be provided for Indians and the extent to which Indians would be allowed to retain reservation lands. For Indians the problem of choosing a livelihood was closely tied with reconciling traditional values with new values adapted from white society and adjusting to new ways of earning a living.

The position taken in this study is that Indians should have been allowed to adapt or retain those features of traditional culture that they chose and to accept or reject ideas and values taken from white society with a relatively small amount of interference from federal agents. At the same time, economic development of reservation resources and the training of Indians in new occupations should have been encouraged. These two goals could have been in conflict. In essence, the Meriam Commission endorsed a similar set of values in 1928. These are not the only values that have received serious attention. The reformers were committed to a combination of economic development and cultural assimilation. Others, both Indian and white, have suggested that Indians should be encouraged to retain traditional cultures and values as much as possible and to reject economic change when it threatens this goal.

A number of issues need to be considered in contemplating alternatives to the allotment of Indian lands:

1. The amount of land that was to be transferred from Indian to white control and conditions under which land was to be transferred.
2. The nature of land tenure and other property rights that would exist on Indian lands.
3. The role of the federal government, the tribe, and individual initiative in shaping the development of a reservation and its resources.
4. The incentives created for Indians to learn farming or other occupations and the nature of programs to assist Indians.
5. The protections offered to individuals and groups within the reservation community.

The level of federal support for Indian programs must be considered in assessing the impact of alternative programs. One alternative would have been to accompany the allotment of Indian lands with large-scale federal programs to train, aid, and assist Indians in economic development. Such a ''Great Society'' approach to Indian policy might have succeeded in advancing Indian welfare within the framework of the allotment policy. It is inconceivable, however, that in the first three decades of the twentieth century, Congress would have authorized spending on a scale large enough to make such a program effective.

With respect to Indian holdings, little can be resolved. Congress made it clear that Indians were not to be allowed to retain the large reservations that were held by some tribes in the 1880s. It was an important question and, like the question of funding to aid Indians, the answer would depend upon how Congress reconciled competing claims for scarce resources between Indians and whites and recognized the legal and moral claims of Indians. As a simplification, it is assumed that Congress specified how much land was to be transferred from Indians to whites, the amount of compensation, and how and when the land was to be opened to non-Indians. After the initial cession of land, it is assumed that any further transfer is part of the overall question of federal supervision of Indian land.

The alternative considered further here would have been to replace the Dawes Act with a policy that would have treated the reservation as the central unit of economic development. Land on the reservations would have been transferred to the ownership of nonprofit tribal corporations supervised by the federal government. Individual Indian families wanting to farm or ranch could lease the land from the tribe under relatively long-term, renewable leases. Renewal could be made automatic if the family demonstrated that it was using the land productively. Such long-term leases should be designed to protect the rights of individuals to capital improvements made in the land, so as not to discourage investment in the land. Perhaps after a certain period, the family would be allowed to buy the land from the tribal corporation. Subleasing the land without permission or failure to use the land properly would lead to forfeiting the lease. Such a system of land tenure is in keeping with pre-allotment Indian land tenure and would be both flexible, in that tribal development programs would not be blocked by complicated ownership claims, and secure for the individual Indian farmer.

Maintaining the reservation as a land unit under a tribal corporation would have allowed for a wide range of development programs. For example, William Brophy and Sophie Aberle reported that range associations that combined individual ownership of livestock with a coordinated use of the range land were successful on some reservations in the 1930s, 1940s, and 1950s.[10] Such an organization could have been set up easily on a reservation where land was held by a corporate authority. Programs to encourage individual farmers through low rents, subsidies, or low-cost loans would be another alternative. Demonstration farms or credit facilities geared to the needs of Indians could have been developed by the tribal corporation. Land could have been leased to whites, if Indians were unwilling or not ready to use the land.

Nothing in the proposal guarantees that the administration of Indian lands would have been all-knowing or just or that all Indians would have been ready to farm and ranch. The agent might well have been corrupt or the Indians themselves discouraged and unwilling to farm or ranch. Land might have been leased to whites, which might have discouraged Indian farmers. The reformers feared that if Indians had had a steady outside income, such as that provided by leases to outsiders, they would not have chosen to work. It would not have been difficult, however, to insure that most of the land remained in Indian hands, even while it was being leased. Future generations of planners and farmers would not have been frustrated by an inadequate land base. Even in the worst situations, it is likely that Indians would have been left with better prospects for future development than they were under the Dawes Act.

Conflicts between tribal authority and the federal government might have arisen as they have under the Wheeler-Howard Act. On the one hand, the federal agents might have been unwilling to transfer authority to tribal governments or to listen to tribal officers when opinions differed from official policy. On the other hand, the tribal governments might have lacked all the necessary skills and continuity to act wisely in economic matters. Such problems are real, but it is unlikely that they would have been worse than under federal Indian policy as it actually operated under the Dawes Act or later under the Wheeler-Howard Act.

A more fundamental problem would have been to protect individual rights. The proposal being contemplated here would have left wide authority to the tribe and the tribal corporation. As has been emphasized, however, Indian tribes were not homogeneous populations. Programs that benefited one group may not have been in the interests of another group. Leaders might have granted the right to lease good land to political allies or in return for bribes. Clearly, the rights of minority groups within the tribe would have required the protection of legal procedures. However, it should be noted that the huge Navajo reservation has never been allotted, and the rights of individuals to pursue their own economic interests have been protected.

Another problem would have been created by the individual who decided to leave the reservation, perhaps to move to an urban job. How would such a person receive his share of the tribal assets? If no provision were made for separation, a severe burden would have been placed on individuals who wanted to migrate, and individuals suited to employments away from the reservation might have been prevented from leaving. If one's share of tribal assets were too easily claimed, however, the tribe might have been broken up by individuals rushing to claim their share. A possible solution might be to give individuals funds to set up housekeeping in cities and perhaps a share of tribal assets if they stayed away from the reservation for, say, three years. Alternatively, they might be given stock in the tribal corporation.

The above scheme is largely designed to suggest ways in which the weak points of the Dawes Act, criticized in this study, might have been overcome. It is also possible that keeping the tribe as a unit and limiting the benefits accruing to non-Indians from federal decisions would have encouraged the Office of Indian Affairs to act more in the interests of Indians, or at least Indians who wanted to work through the tribes, and less in response to the perceived benefits to non-Indians.

Notes

1. See tables A.20 and A.21 in appendix A.
2. See Lewis Meriam and Associates, *The Problem of Indian Administration*, chap. X, passim. Among the problems of Indians were severe public health problems. See chap. VIII, passim.

3. These states are Idaho, Kansas, Michigan, Minnesota, Montana, Nebraska, North Dakota, South Dakota, Washington, Wisconsin, and Oklahoma.

4. See table A.1 in appendix A.

5. See table A.2 in appendix A.

6. William A. Brophy and Sophie D. Aberle, *The Indian: America's Unfinished Business*, p. 67.

7. U.S. Department of the Interior, *Annual Report of the Commissioner of Indian Affairs, 1892*, pp. 6–7.

8. Laurence F. Schmeckebier, *The Office of Indian Affairs*, pp. 514, 515, 535, 536.

9. Richard Lipsey and Kevin Lancaster, "The General Theory of the Second Best," *Review of Economic Studies* 24 (1956–57): 193–210, passim.

10. Brophy and Aberle, *The Indian*, pp. 81–83.

STATISTICAL
APPENDICES

Appendix A

TABLE A.1
Supervised Indian Land Holdings by State, 1881-1933

	1881	1890	1900	1911[a]	1933
Idaho	2,748,981	2,273,421	1,364,500	770,706	803,239
Kansas	137,747	102,026	28,279	273,408	34,821
Michigan	66,332	27,319	8,317	153,910	20,233
Minnesota	5,026,447	2,254,781	1,566,707	1,480,647	549,320
Montana	29,356,800	10,591,360	9,500,700	6,263,151	6,055,009
Nebraska	436,252	136,947	74,592	344,375	69,280
North Dakota		5,861,120	3,701,724	2,786,162	1,034,123
South Dakota	36,616,448	11.661,360	8,991,791	7,221,939	5,544,424
Washington	7,779,348	4,045,248	2,333,574	2,948,708	2,712,915
Wisconsin	526,026	512,129	381,061	590,094	395,919
Total	32,050,381	37,465,711	27,951,245	22,833,100[a]	16,823,364
Oklahoma	41,100,915	39,156,040	26,397,237	22,736,473[a]	2,919,886
Arizona	3,092,720	6,603,191	15,150,757	17,358,741	18,657,984
California	415,841	494,045	406,396	437,629	625,354
Colorado	12,467,200	1,094,400	483,750	556,621	443,751
Nevada	885,015	959,135	954,135	696,749	866,176
New Mexico	7,228,731	10,002,525	1,667,485	4,520,652	6,188,964
Oregon	3,853,800	2,075,240	1,300,225	1,719,561	1,718,510
Utah	2,039,040	3,972,480	2,039,040	219,101	1,571,020
Wyoming	2,342,400	2,342,400	1,810,000	318,543	2,249,576
Total U.S.	155,632,312	104,314,349	78,372,185	71,464,393[a]	52,651,393

SOURCE: "Statistical Supplement to the Annual Report of the Commissioner of Indian Affairs, for the Fiscal Year ended June 30, 1940," p. 37.

[a]Totals include all allotted land.

TABLE A.2
Total Indian Land Allotted and Percentage in Trust Status, 1940

All Land Allotted as of June 30, 1920:
Reservation land:[a]	35,897,069
Public domain:	1,261,586

All Land Allotted as of June 30, 1920, to 1934:
Reservation land:	4,442,980
Public domain:	313,389

Totals
Reservation lands:	40,340,249
Public domain:	1,574,475
	41,915,224

Land Allotted to the Five Tribes:
Cherokee:	4,346,233
Choctaw:	3,800,190
Chickasaw:	4,291,036
Creek:	2,997,114
Seminole:	359,535
	15,794,108

Residual:
Land allotted under the Dawes Act and individual allotment bills: 26,121,116

Land held in trust, Jan. 1, 1940:
Five Tribes:	1,430,723
All others:	16,143,213
	17,573,936

Percent in Trust Status:
General:	61.8 %
Five tribes:	9.06%

SOURCES: Annual Reports of the Commissioner of Indian Affairs, 1920-1934; Statistical Supplement to the Annual Report of the Commissioners of Indian Affairs, 1940, pp. 30-37.

[a]Includes Five Civilized Tribes.

NOTE: See Table A.26 for amount of allotted acres, surplus by state.

TABLE A.3
Patents in Fee Issued, 1907-34

Applications Approved	Acres
38,122	4,579,225

SOURCE: Annual Reports of the Commissioner of Indian Affairs, 1920-34; Laurence F. Schmeckebier, The Office of Indian Affairs, p. 154.

NOTE: Total number of applications approved is not reported for 1929 and 1934. Total acres are not reported for 1921, 1925, 1926, 1927, 1934. Canceled patents in fee are not removed from the totals.

TABLE A.4
Annual Sales of Indian Allotted Lands, 1903-34 Inclusive

Year	Sales of original allotments			Sales of inherited lands			Total sales of land		
	NUMBER OF TRACTS	ACREAGE	PROCEEDS	NUMBER OF TRACTS	ACREAGE	PROCEEDS	NUMBER OF TRACTS	ACREAGE	PROCEEDS
Total	11,325	1,280,526	$23,203,877	20,129	2,499,739	$44,612,555	31,454	3,752,923	67,816,430
1903	—	—	—	—	44,494	757,173	—	44,494	757,173
1904	—	—	—	1,236	122,222	2,057,464	1,236	122,222	2,057,464
1905	—	—	—	978	90,215	1,393,131	978	90,215	1,393,131
1906	—	—	—	643	64,448	981,430	643	64,448	981,430
1907	—	—	—	820	106,359	1,248,793	820	106,359	1,248,793
1908	92	7,991	159,318	768	91,303	1,302,508	860	99,294	1,461,827
1909	235	34,060	442,762	753	102,708	1,321,258	988	136,768	1,764,021
1910	520	82,656	1,245,639	873	129,360	1,956,315	1,425	216,191	3,268,415
1911	494	56,198	978,588	638	79,666	1,503,960	1,294	154,347	2,542,028
1912	324	34,391	568,880	392	43,652	889,285	716	78,043	1,458,165
1913	208	20,779	407,315	109	10,798	285,097	317	31,577	692,413
1914	529	45,526	779,526	418	45,242	773,309	947	90,768	1,552,835
1915	422	34,429	584,724	393	68,245	715,568	815	102,674	1,800,293
1916	583	54,959	969,611	324	35,762	694,241	907	90,721	1,663,852
1917	588	69,849	1,040,202	655	75,892	1,546,965	1,243	145,741	2,587,167
1918	662	74,126	1,541,178	438	49,216	1,174,855	1,100	123,342	2,716,033
1919	463	57,947	1,224,823	507	57,450	1,580,309	970	115,397	2,805,132
1920	1,206	147,047	3,566,816	1,000	155,794	4,007,558	2,206	302,841	7,574,374
1921	667	69,193	1,651,832	1,268	135,893	4,061,906	1,935	205,086	5,713,738
1922	416	40,817	917,614	590	63,997	1,315,219	1,006	104,814	2,232,833
1923	419	48,447	938,393	767	76,652	1,965,944	1,186	125,099	2,904,337
1924	409	45,911	913,875	746	94,452	1,752,233	1,155	140,363	2,666,108
1925	397	39,548	735,717	764	99,916	1,759,698	1,161	139,464	2,495,415

(continued)

TABLE A.4 (continued)
Annual Sales of Indian Allotted Lands, 1903-34 Inclusive

Year	Sales of original allotments			Sales of inherited lands			Total sales of land		
	NUMBER OF TRACTS	ACREAGE	PROCEEDS	NUMBER OF TRACTS	ACREAGE	PROCEEDS	NUMBER OF TRACTS	ACRES	PROCEEDS
Total	11,325	1,280,526	$23,203,877	20,129	2,49,739	$44,612,555	31,454	3,752,923	67,816,430
1926	433	44,217	855,544	770	81,834	1,858,257	1,203	126,051	2,713,801
1927	430	45,299	806,803	854	96,123	1,758,730	1,284	141,422	2,565,533
1928	417	49,731	804,020	851	101,682	1,534,754	1,268	151,413	2,338,774
1929	421	66,718	735,603	909	114,695	1,570,905	1,330	181,413	2,306,508
1930	290	35,773	505,799	596	72,742	1,101,996	886	108,515	1,607,795
1931	206	19,132	282,452	438	50,663	726,086	644	69,795	1,008,538
1932	265	26,316	230,145	300	45,368	436,368	565	71,684	666,524
1933	139	16,416	163,398	189	22,501	260,170	328	38,917	423,569
1934	90	13,050	153,293	142	20,395	321,052	232	33,445	474,345

SOURCE: United States National Resources Board Land Planning Committee, 1935. *Indian Land Tenure, Economic Status, and Population Trends*. The table has been checked against the *Annual Reports of the Commissioner of Indian Affairs* for the appropriate years, and some errors were found and corrected. Totals to 1926 are consistent with figures in Schmeckebier, *The Office of Indian Affairs*, p. 177.

NOTE: Does not include Five Civilized Tribes; does include Osage and Kaw.

TABLE A.5
Indian Population by State
Census Figures

	1890	1900	1910	1920	1930
Total U.S.	248,253	237,196	265,683	244,437	332,397
Idaho	4,223	4,226	3,488	3,098	3,638
Kansas	1,682	2,530	2,444	2,276	2,454
Michigan	5,625	6,354	7,519	5,614	7,080
Minnesota	10,096	9,182	9,053	8,761	11,077
Montana	11,206	11,345	10,745	10,956	14,798
Nebraska	6,431	3,322	3,502	2,888	3,256
North Dakota	8,174	6,968	6,486	6,254	8,387
South Dakota	19,854	20,225	19,137	16,384	21,833
Washington	11,181	10,039	10,997	9,061	11,253
Wisconsin	9,930	18,372	10,142	9,611	11,548
Total	88,402	82,163	83,513	74,903	95,324
Oklahoma	64,456	64,445	74,825	57,337	92,725
California	16,624	15,377	16,371	17,360	19,212
Colorado	1,092	1,437	1,482	1,383	1,395
Oregon	4,971	4,951	5,090	4,590	4,776
Utah	3,456	2,623	3,123	2,711	2,869
Total	26,143	24,388	26,066	26,044	28,252
Arizona	29,981	26,480	29,201	32,989	43,726
Nevada	5,156	5,216	5,240	4,907	4,871
New Mexico	15,044	13,144	20,573	19,512	28,941
Wyoming	1,844	1,686	1,486	1,343	1,845
Total	52,025	46,526	56,500	58,751	79,583

SOURCES: U.S. Department of Commerce; U.S. Department of the Interior, Bureau of the Census, *Fifteenth Census of the United States, 1930: The Indian Population of the United States and Alaska*, pp. 10-32.

TABLE A.6
Pre-allotment Indian Agriculture: Selected Reservations

Reservation (Date of 10% Allotment)	DATE	POPULATION	Acres Cultivated			Output (Corn Equivalent BU.)		
			TOTAL	PER CAPITA	YEARLY CHANGE [COMP]	TOTAL	PER CAPITA	YEARLY CHANGE [COMP]
So. Ute, Colo. (1896)	1876	900	3	0.003		2,377	0.26	
	1895	1,142	296	0.26	7.8%	4,737	4.15	7.3%
Coeur d'Alene, Ida[a] (1909)	1886	487	6,100	12.5		80,536	165.4	
	1904	497	20,000	40.24	6.5	151,601	305.0	3.4
Fort Hall, Ida (1914)	1875	1,500	42	0.03		3,695	0.25	
	1904	1,351	3,000	2.22	4.8	7,319	5.42	1.3
Nez Perce, Ida[b] (1895)	1875	2,800	2,100	0.75		22,375	7.99	
	1892[b]	1,828	6,775	3.71	9.4	48,355	26.45	7.0
Iowa, Kan. (1893)	1877	213	750	3.52		5,061	23.8	
	1892	159	5,000	31.45	4.6	91,131	604.6	1.6
White Earth, Minn. (1901)	1875	2,732	530	0.19		11,890	4.35	
	1899	1,990	6,000	3.02	1.5	60,525	30.41	8.1
Crow, Mont. (1907)	1875	4,200	106	0.03		1,030	0.25	
	1904	1,826	3,815	2.09	4.6	23,708	12.98	3.6
Flathead, Mont. (1908)	1875	1,566	1,500	0.96		5,311	3.39	
	1904	1,834	28,000	16.26	9.5	117,253	63.90	0.1
Omaha Neb. (1884)	1875	1,005	1,500	1.49		28,968	28.82	
	1883	1,192	6,000	5.74	6.9	40,073	33.62	2.0
Ponca, Neb. (1890)	1882	168	189	1.13		6,642	39.5	
	1889	224	511	2.28	8.0	12,579	56.2	5.0
Santee, Neb. (1885)	1875	800	481	0.60		15,141	18.93	
	1884	1,056	4,357	4.13	1.4	50,135	47.48	0.2
Devil's Lake, N.D. (1892)	1875	800	265	0.29		6,599	8.25	
	1891	1,030	3,693	3.59	5.7	44,480	26.12	7.0

Location (Year)	Year							
Fort Berthold, N.D. (1900)	1875	1,920	400	0.21		3,660	1.91	
	1899	1,118	1,673	1.50	8.2	14,195	12.70	7.9
Turtle Mountain, N.D. (1907)	1885	914	311	0.34		3,746	6.03	
	1904	2,714	1,500	2.64	0.8	91,339	33.65	9.0
Sac and Fox Agency, Okla.[c] (1890-94)	1875	1,419	1,551	1.09		444,389	31.3	
	1889	2,180	5,960	2.73	6.5	251,976	115.6	9.3
Quapaw Agency, Okla.[d] (1890-94)	1875	1,301	4,695	3.61		128,435	98.72	
	1889	1,150	26,640	23.17	3.3	126,926	110.37	0.8
Pawnee, Okla. (1893)	1876	2,026	100	0.05		2,737	1.4	
	1892	798	1,986	2.49	4.4	41,487	2.0	2.6
Kaw, Okla. (1903)	1875	273	404	1.48		11,632	42.6	
	1902	222	146	0.66	-2.9	5,121	23.1	5.7
Ponca, Okla. (1895)	1879	620	200	0.37		12	0.02	
	1894	588	1,320	2.24	2.0	21,566	36.68	0.2
Otoe and Missouria, Okla. (1899)	1882	274	250	0.91		507	1.85	
	1898	360	1,614	4.48	0.0	42,692	118.6	6.0
Osage, Okla. (1908)	1875	3,001	3,876	1.29		22,677	7.54	
	1904[e]	1,895	35,000[e]	18.47[e]	9.2	213,125[e]	112.47[e]	9.3
Kiowa, Okla. (1901)	1875	3,180	450	0.14		9,917	3.12	
	1900	3,834	8,065	2.16	0.9	276,431[g]	74.05[g]	2.7
Grande Ronde, Oreg. (1891)	1875	743	3,900	5.25		7,861	10.58	
	1890	379	862	2.27	-5.6	18,501[e]	48.85	10.1
Siletz, Oreg. (1894)	1875	1,000	610	0.61		8,231	8.23	
	1893	530	668	1.26	4.2	10,903	20.68	5.1
Umatilla, Oreg. (1893)	1875	682	1,500[f]	2.20		14,766	6.99	
	1895[f]	1,113	5,000[f]	4.49[f]	3.6	28,854[f]	25.92	6.6
Warm Springs, Oreg. (1896)	1875	680	800	1.18		5,053	7.43	
	1895	945	3,090	4.24	6.4	3,861	4.09	-3.0
Sisseton, S.D. (1888)	1875	1,807	795	0.44		15,091	8.35	
	1887	1,519	7,740	5.10	0.4	41,144	10.26	1.7
Yankton, S.D. (1890)	1876	2,000	1,200	0.60		10,330	5.16	
	1889	1,760	4,332	2.46	0.1	78,188	44.42	5.4

(continued)

TABLE A.6 (continued)
Pre-allotment of Indian Agriculture: Selected Reservations

Reservation (Date of 10% Allotment)	DATE	POPULATION	Acres Cultivated			Output (Corn Equivalent BU.)		
		TOTAL	TOTAL	PER CAPITA	YEARLY CHANGE [COMP]	TOTAL	PER CAPITA	YEARLY CHANGE [COMP]
Unitah-Ouray, Utah (1905)	1875	650	325	0.50		1,833	2.82	
	1903	1,512	5,202	3.53	7.2	9,066	6.16	2.8
Colville, Wash. (1900)	1887	2,268	5,200	2.29		8,981	3.96	
	1899	1,625	18,125	11.19	3.2	62,279	38.3	8.9
Spokane, Wash. (1909)	1887[h]	323	1,500	4.64		16,197	50.15	
(Wash.)	1904[h]	242	800	3.31		2,448	10.12	
(Idaho)	1904[h]	77	500	6.49	0.8	14,028	182.2	0.2
Yakima, Wash. (1897)	1875	3,650	5,280	1.45		27,007	7.40	
	1896	1,821	16,500	27.65	14.0	54,215	29.77	6.6
Oneida, Wash. (1891)	1876	1,387	4,322	3.12		19,737	14.23	
	1889	1,716	2,926	1.71	-4.6	33,445	20.60	2.9

SOURCE: All data are taken from the *Annual Reports of the Commissioner of Indian Affairs* for the appropriate years.

NOTE: The table includes all reservations for which data are available, allotted in or after 1884, that satisfy either of two criteria: acres cultivated by Indians in 1904 exceeded 2.0 per capita or the total number of acres cultivated by Indians in 1886 exceeded 1.0 per capita.

The output index is in corn equivalent Bu. Weights are nutritional units taken from W. A. Henry and F. B. Morrison, *Feeds and Feeding*, 17th ed. (Madison, Wis.: Henry Morrison Co., 1940). The procedure is taken from Roger Ransom and Richard Sutch, "Debt Peonage in the Cotton South after the Civil War," *Journal of Economic History* (September 1972): 660. Weights: wheat = 1.104, oats = 0.433, Irish potatoes = 0.220. It was assumed that all of oats and barley (0.966) were oats, and that all vegetables were Irish potatoes. This gives a slight downward bias.

[a] First time listed separately.

[b] Data for 1893, 4 includes white lessors.

[c] Includes the Sac and Fox, Shawnee, Mexican Kickapoo reservations, 1875.

[d] Includes a number of reservations in Eastern Shawnee, Miami, Modoc, Ottawa, Peoria, Quapaw, Seneca, Wyandotte.

[e] Suspected that totals include whites leasing Indian lands. See U.S. Department of the Interior, Bureau of the Census, "Agriculture on Indian Reservations," in *Twelfth Census of the United States, 1900, Vol. V: Agriculture*, p. 725.

[f] Data for 1895 were used, since the totals for 1892 are very large and appear to include white lessors.

[g] Output figures for 1900 are much larger than years before or after. Using 1898 gives an output of 64,744. Data are incomplete or missing for years around allotment.

[h] The Spokane are listed as a tribe under the Colville Agency in 1887. By 1904 part of the tribe had a separate reservation, and part were on the Coeur d'Alene Reservation (totals omitted from the Coeur d'Alene totals) all under the Colville Agency.

TABLE A.7
Improved Land in Indian Farms

	1900	1920
Idaho	26,782	14,015
Kansas	7,841	9,369
Michigan	7,056	4,040
Minnesota	15,148	6,201
Montana	18,539	140,678
Nebraska	9,976	17,636
North Dakota	40,208	40,608
South Dakota	77,876	143,263
Washington	29,896	20,589
Wisconsin	10,607	13,057
Total (ten states)	251,510	317,672
Oklahoma	460,947	317,406
California	11,624	17,147
Colorado	257	3,315
Oregon	40,926	21,180
Utah	5,808	8,712
Arizona	26,782	14,015
Nevada	2,552	7,278
New Mexico	23,544	17,588
Wyoming	1,885	5,581

SOURCES: *Twelfth Census of the United States, 1900, Vol. V: Agriculture*, pp. cxiv-cxv; *Fourteenth Census of the United States, 1920, Vol. V: Agriculture*, pp. 313.

TABLE A.8

Average Value Land and Buildings per Farm: Indian and White

	Indian Farms				White Farms			
	(1) 1900	(2) 1910	(3) 1920	(4) 1930	(5) 1900	(6) 1910	(7) 1920	(8) 1930
Idaho	$1,377	$4,673[a]	$ 7,373	$4,859	$2,457	$ 7,988	$13,858	$10,074
Kansas	4,042	8,342	10,317	5,892	3,739	9,817	17,187	13,784
Michigan	720	1,881	2,362	4,859	2,872	4,362	7,325	6,863
Minnesota	1,955	3,359[a]	4,203	2,388	4,335	8,096	18,513	11,482
Montana	1,409	3,359[a]	8,875	3,883	4,718	9,892	13,556	11,291
Nebraska	2,338	6,718[b]	13,002	4,803	4,760	14,012	29,876	19,299
North Dakota	353	3,848[a]	6,273	2,603	4,506	11,133	19,249	12,298
South Dakota	1,960	6,311[a]	10,728	3,439	4,261	13,186	33,625	15,862
Washington	1,212	5,247	4,511	5,527	3,554	10,227	13,961	10,991
Wisconsin	1,729	2,640[a]	2,993	3,284	4,049	6,798	11,587	9,536
Oklahoma	1,356	2,947	5,472	3,834	1,653	4,079	7,423	6,494

SOURCES: *The Indian Population of the United States and Alaska, 1930, 1930,* p. 229; *Twelfth Census of the United States, 1900, Vol. V: Agriculture,* pp. cxiv-cxv, cii-ciii; *Fifteenth Census of the United States, 1930, Vol. IV: Agriculture,* pp. 267-80; *Thirteenth Census of the United States, 1910, Vol. V: Agriculture,* pp. 208-23.

NOTE: Data for 1910 interpolated. See appendix B.
[a]Greater than 90 percent of nonwhite farmers were Indians.
[b]Greater than 80 percent of nonwhite farmers were Indians.

TABLE A.9
Average Acres per Farm: Indian and White

| | Indian Farms | | | | White Farms | | | |
	(1) 1900	(2) 1910	(3) 1920	(4) 1930	(5) 1900	(6) 1910	(7) 1920	(8) 1930
Idaho	180.9	143.4[a]	99.6	81.7	183.8	171.9	200.2	226.7
Kansas	156.8	141.7	120.4	109.3	242.2	245.1	275.7	283.7
Michigan	43.6	44.8	41.2	52.8	86.6	91.6	97.0	101.2
Minnesota	180.0	83.0[a]	103.0	84.8	169.7	177.4	169.4	167.0
Montana	130.1	249.3[a]	643.3	339.5	904.9	529.7	608.0	345.8
Nebraska	127.3	141.2[b]	103.7	71.5	246.4	298.3	339.9	345.8
North Dakota	110.0	251.9[a]	339.2	186.1	349.7	383.5	467.0	499.0
South Dakota	617.4	489.0[a]	531.0	287.6	214.0	157.7	462.7	445.7
Washington	115.8	127.3	147.1	150.6	260.9	216.9	202.1	192.7
Wisconsin	112.9	64.9[a]	48.8	59.2	117.0	119.1	117.2	120.4
Oklahoma	179.2	145.4	125.7	116.5	222.9	156.8	165.1	175.9

SOURCE: Tables 7.2 and 7.4.

NOTE: Data for 1910 interpolated. See appendix B.
[a]Greater than 90 percent of nonwhite farmers were Indians.
[b]Greater than 80 percent of nonwhite farmers were Indians.

TABLE A.10
Total Nonwhite Farms

State	1900	1910	1920	1930
Idaho	595	405	508	698
Kansas	1,866	1,691	1,238	1,036
Michigan	973	946	733	561
Minnesota	372	293	207	245
Montana	328	1,196	1,063	1,184
Nebraska	329	462	384	270
North Dakota	1,334	743	543	801
South Dakota	1,806	2,808	1,612	2,740
Washington	1,090	1,125	1,266	1,349
Wisconsin	520	591	663	316
Oklahoma	13,225	20,671	18,725	22,937
California	1,607	3,078	6,486	5,472
Colorado	73	574	553	601
Oregon	551	627	573	683
Utah	243	276	414	568
Arizona	1,803	3,203	646	3,953
Nevada	173	161	219	311
New Mexico	1,418	2,148	1,875	3,345
Wyoming	173	65	169	263

SOURCES: *Thirteenth Census of the United States, 1910, Vol. V: Agriculture*, p. 176; *Fifteenth Census of the United States, 1930, Vol. IV: Agriculture*, pp. 170-6.

TABLE A.11
Proportion Indian in All Nonwhite Farms

State	1900	1910	1920	1930
Idaho	0.95	0.82	0.66	0.73
Kansas	0.047	0.093	0.083	0.092
Michigan	0.36	0.32	0.25	0.23
Minnesota	0.92	0.90	0.84	0.89
Montana	0.86	0.96	0.93	0.96
Nebraska	0.76	0.75	0.88	0.65
North Dakota	0.99	0.97	0.95	0.99
South Dakota	0.99	0.98	0.97	0.98
Washington	0.88	0.60	0.36	0.52
Wisconsin	0.89	0.92	0.93	0.82
Oklahoma	0.52	0.36	0.28	0.34
California	0.41	0.19	0.09	0.14
Colorado	0.21	0.71	0.15	0.21
Oregon	0.80	0.72	0.52	0.54
Utah	0.82	0.99	0.50	0.60
Arizona	0.98	0.99	0.83	0.94
Nevada	0.80	0.92	0.95	0.93
New Mexico	0.99	0.97	0.98	0.97
Wyoming	0.97	0.68	0.79	0.83

SOURCE: Table 7.2 and Table A.12.

TABLE A.12
Percentage of the Population in Urban Areas

	1900	1910	1920	1930
Total population	40.0	45.8	51.4	56.2
Negro	22.7[a]	27.4[a]	34.0	43.7
Indians		4.5	6.2	9.9

SOURCES: The Indian Population of the United States and Alaska, 1930, p. 5; Fifteenth Census of the United States, 1930, Vol. II: Population, p. 14; Thirteenth Census of the United States, 1910, Vol. I: Population, p. 190.

[a]Taken from the thirteenth census, 1910. Definition of urban areas changed by the 1930 census. In 1900, 40.5 percent of the total population was in urban areas; 46.3 percent in 1910, by the 1910 census definition.

TABLE A.13
Gainful Workers Over Ten Year Old in Agriculture: Farmers (Owners and Tenants), Managers, and Agricultural Laborers

	1910	1920	1930
Males: Total population	35.2%	29.0%	25.1%
Native white	38.4	31.1	26.0
Foreign-born white	14.9	12.5	10.3
Negro	56.1	46.8	40.7
Indian	74.7	69.5	64.5
Females: Total population	22.4	12.7	8.5
Native white	14.4	7.3	4.8
Foreign-born white	4.7	3.5	2.3
Negro	52.2	38.9	26.9
Indian	29.7	30.3	26.0
All persons: Total	32.5	25.6	21.4
Native white	33.8	26.3	21.9
Foreign-born white	13.3	11.2	9.1
Negro	54.6	44.2	36.1
Indian	66.9	63.4	57.5

SOURCES: The Indian Population of the United States and Alaska, 1930, pp. 203-5; Fifteenth Census of the United States, 1930, Vol. II: Occupations, pp. 74-75.

TABLE A.14
Indians Gainfully Employed in Agriculture by State

State	Males Over Ten				Females Over Ten			
	TOTAL	GAINFULLY EMPLOYED	NUMBER IN AGRI.	% EMPLOYED IN AGRI.	TOTAL	GAINFULLY EMPLOYED	NUMBER IN AGRI.	% EMPLOYED IN AGRI.
Kansas	1,052	674	304	45.1%	818	89	6	6.7%
Michigan	2,917	2,087	514	24.6	2,348	336	11	3.3
South Dakota	8,242	4,952	4,102	82.8	7,627	345	114	33.0
Washington	4,307	2,761	1,098	39.8	4,022	293	160	54.6
Oklahoma	32,890	19,997	12,735	63.7	32,502	2,866	693	24.2
Arizona	16,083	11,153	8,658	77.6	14,877	4,467	731	16.4
California	7,811	5,357	2,966	55.4	7,013	967	137	14.2
Colorado	582	374	228	60.9	466	67	24	35.8
New Mexico	10,568	7,501	5,775	76.9	9,840	3,493	691	19.8
New York	2,736	2,004	652	32.5	2,520	510	39	7.6
North Carolina	5,680	4,416	4,114	93.1	5,522	1,656	1,540	92.9
Total U.S.	123,469	80,306	51,771	64.5	115,512	17,842	4,640	26.0

SOURCE: *The Indian Population of the United States and Alaska, 1930*, pp. 208-15.

NOTE: Data by state are available only for fourteen states with large nonwhite populations.

TABLE A.15
Occupations of Gainfully Employed Indians Over Ten, 1910-30

	1910		1920		1930	
	NUMBER	PERCENT	NUMBER	PERCENT	NUMBER	PERCENT
Male	59,206	100.0	53,478	100.0	80,306	100.0
Professional persons	927	1.6	665	1.2	1,531	1.9
Proprietors and managers	21,765	36.8	21,684	40.5	27,615	34.4
Farmers (owners and tenants)	20,841	35.2	21,097	39.4	26,521	33.0
Wholesalers and retailers	482	0.8	322	0.6	569	1.7
Other proprietors, etc.	442	0.7	265	0.5	525	0.7
Clerks	859	1.5	700	1.3	1,630	2.0
Skilled workers	2,021	3.4	2,097	3.9	4,204	5.2
Semiskilled workers	1,511	2.6	1,887	3.5	4,278	5.3
Unskilled workers	32,123	54.3	26,445	49.5	41,048	51.1
Agricultural laborers	23,293	39.3	16,000	29.9	25,124	31.3
Factory and construction	3,571	6.0	3,826	7.2	6,973	8.7
Other laborers	4,772	8.1	6,244	11.7	8,277	10.3
Servants	487	0.8	375	0.7	674	0.8
Females	14,710	100.0	9,848	100.0	17,842	100.0
Professional persons	357	2.4	339	3.4	824	4.6
Proprietors and managers	1,248	8.5	1,140	11.6	1,665	9.3
Farmers (owners and tenants)	1,156	7.9	1,084	11.0	1,517	8.5
Wholesalers and retailers	38	0.3	20	0.2	56	0.3
Other proprietors, etc.						
Clerks	168	1.1	297	3.0	864	4.8
Skilled workers	35	0.2	67	0.7	24	0.1
Semiskilled workers	6,541	44.5	3,963	40.2	7,477	41.9
Unskilled workers	6,361	43.2	4,042	41.0	6,988	39.2
Agricultural laborers	3,197	11.7	1,849	18.8	3,121	17.5
Factory and construction	85	0.6	97	1.0	111	0.6
Other laborers	101	0.7	60	0.6	46	0.3
Servants	2,978	20.2	2,036	20.7	3,710	20.8

SOURCE: *The Indian Population of the United States and Alaska, 1930*, p. 202.

TABLE A.16
Proportion of Persons Over Ten Gainfully Occupied

	1910	1920	1930
Male:			
All persons	81.3%	78.2%	76.2%
Native white	77.9	75.1	73.4
Foreign-born white	90.0	89.3	88.4
Negro	87.4	81.1	80.2
Indian	61.3	58.4	65.0
Females:			
All persons	23.4	21.1	22.0
Native white	19.2	19.3	20.5
Foreign-born white	21.7	18.4	18.8
Negro	54.7	38.9	38.9
Indian	17.6	11.5	15.4
Total:			
All persons	53.3	50.3	49.5
Native white	49.0	47.4	47.0
Foreign-born white	60.3	57.4	56.1
Negro	71.0	59.9	59.2
Indian	39.2	35.8	41.1

SOURCES: *The Indian Population of the United States and Alaska, 1930*, p. 199; *Fifteenth Census of the United States, 1930, Vol. II: Occupations*, p. 74.

TABLE A.17
Percentage of Indians Gainful Workers: Selected States, 1910-30

State	Male						Female					
	1910			1930			1910			1930		
	TOTAL NUMBER	GAINFULLY OCCUPIED		TOTAL NUMBER	GAINFULLY OCCUPIED		TOTAL NUMBER	GAINFULLY OCCUPIED		TOTAL NUMBER	GAINFULLY OCCUPIED	
		Number	Percent		Number	Percent		Number	Percent		Number	Percent
U.S.	96,582	59,205	61.3	123,469	80,306	65.0	92,176	14,170	16.0	115,512	17,842	15.4
Okla.	24,580	14,177	57.7	32,890	19,997	60.8	24,306	1,750	7.2	32,502	2,866	8.8
Ariz.	10,625	7,008	66.0	16,083	11,153	69.3	9,863	3,169	32.1	14,877	4,467	30.0
N.M	7,240	5,323	73.5	10,568	7,501	71.0	6,861	2,549	37.2	9,840	3,493	35.5
S.D.	7,166	2,907	40.6	8,242	4,952	60.1	7,179	181	2.5	7,627	345	4.5
Calif.	6,458	4,418	68.4	7,811	5,357	68.6	6,148	1,351	22.0	7,013	967	13.8
Mont.	3,978	2,110	53.0	5,525	3,129	56.6	3,961	138	3.5	5,039	236	4.7
Wis.	3,866	2,543	65.8	4,441	2,755	62.0	3,500	331	9.5	3,983	325	8.2
Wash.	4,066	2,346	57.7	4,307	2,761	64.1	4,035	350	8.7	4,022	293	7.3
Minn.	3,290	1,862	56.6	4,025	1,973	49.0	3,218	248	7.7	3,802	250	6.6
N.D.	2,366	1,290	54.5	2,991	1,904	63.7	2,288	88	3.8	2,843	185	6.5
Mich.	3,028	2,268	74.9	2,917	2,087	71.6	2,674	447	16.7	2,348	336	14.3
Nev.	2,120	1,341	63.3	1,960	1,303	66.5	2,070	560	27.1	1,874	335	17.9
Oreg.	1,954	991	50.7	1,856	1,175	63.3	1,950	135	6.9	1,715	134	7.8
Ida.	1,355	752	55.5	1,440	878	61.0	1,349	52	3.9	1,361	59	4.3
Utah	1,232	777	63.1	1,080	723	66.9	1,058	318	30.1	932	136	14.6
Kans.	1,111	465	41.9	1,052	674	64.1	815	47	5.8	818	89	10.9
Wyo.	575	363	63.1	711	463	65.1	523	20	3.8	617	25	4.1

SOURCE: The Indian Population of the United States and Alaska. 1930, p. 200.

TABLE A.18
Median Ages, 1920-30

| | Total | | Males | | Females | |
	1920	1930	1920	1930	1920	1930
All classes	25.2	26.4	25.8	26.7	24.7	26.1
Indian	19.7	19.6	20.4	20.0	19.0	19.1
White	25.6	26.9	26.1	27.1	25.1	26.6
Native	22.4	23.7	22.4	23.6	22.3	23.8
Foreign-born	40.0	43.9	40.1	44.1	29.9	43.7
Negro	22.3	23.4	22.8	23.7	22.0	23.2
Chinese	40.2	32.3	42.7	35.1	19.4	17.3
Japanese	30.2	24.5	34.1	29.7	24.0	15.9

SOURCE: *The Indian Population of the United States and Alaska, 1930*, p. 88.

TABLE A.19
Percentage of Population Over Ten Illiterate

Class	1900	1910	1920	1930
All classes	10.7	7.7	6.0	4.3
Indian	56.2	45.3	34.9	25.7
White	6.2	5.0	4.0	3.0
Native	4.6	3.0	2.0	1.6
Foreign-born	12.9	12.7	13.1	10.8
Negro	44.5	30.4	22.9	16.3
All others	26.6	13.1	14.5	12.3

SOURCE: *The Indian Population of the United States and Alaska, 1930*, p. 143.

TABLE A.20
Percentage of Indians Illiterate for Selected States

State	1910 IO YEARS OLD AND OVER		1930 IO YEARS OLD AND OVER	
	Male	*Female*	*Male*	*Female*
United States	41.5	49.2	24.0	27.6
Arizona	68.4	77.8	49.9	57.2
California	45.4	52.7	18.5	23.7
Idaho	55.6	63.3	26.0	32.8
Kansas	18.7	18.7	9.3	9.4
Michigan	30.1	39.4	13.1	17.2
Minnesota	35.3	45.1	15.4	20.8
Montana	52.1	59.6	21.0	24.4
Nebraska	29.6	41.5	10.2	13.3
Nevada	67.2	76.3	37.7	46.1
New Mexico	78.5	85.0	53.9	61.4
North Dakota	43.6	48.6	20.5	20.9
Oklahoma	22.0	28.4	10.4	12.0
Oregon	29.7	43.5	11.5	19.4
South Dakota	39.0	52.0	13.1	19.5
Utah	80.3	86.2	56.1	58.0
Washington	39.6	52.0	13.7	19.5
Wisconsin	31.2	36.4	12.6	14.5
Wyoming	45.4	57.6	23.2	25.9

SOURCE: The Indian Population of the United States and Alaska, 1930, pp. 144-45.

TABLE A.21
Percentage of the Indian Population Over Ten Unable to Speak English for the United States and Selected States

State	Total 1930	Male 1910	Male 1930	Female 1910	Female 1930
Total U.S.	17.0	27.7	14.8	35.1	19.4
Idaho	19.3	34.9	14.2	45.0	24.6
Kansas	2.1	8.7	1.4	9.2	2.9
Michigan	2.4	14.7	1.0	25.2	4.1
Minnesota	9.0	22.2	5.8	31.5	12.3
Montana	14.9	39.9	12.2	48.2	17.8
Nebraska	7.4	15.3	5.0	30.1	9.9
North Dakota	9.6	39.8	7.0	48.5	12.4
South Dakota	13.5	33.8	10.8	46.3	16.4
Washington	5.1	16.4	3.1	26.8	7.3
Wisconsin	5.2	11.5	2.8	21.6	8.0
Oklahoma	5.2	14.1	3.9	7.3	6.5

SOURCE: The Indian Population of the United States and Alaska, 1930, p. 156.

TABLE A.22

Percentage of Land in the State Improved in 1890: Order of Allotment

Categories	Observations	
	ALL RESERVATIONS	AFTER 1887
Greater than 20.1%	19	11
15.1% to 20.0%	18	18
Less than 5.0%	26	23

ALL RESERVATIONS

N = 63

H (distributed X^2 2 d.f.) = 23.6

Significant at 0.1% level

AFTER 1887

N = 51

H = 20.3

Significant at 0.1% level

SOURCES: Eleventh Census of the United States, 1890, Vol. V: Agriculture: Statistics of Agriculture, p. 74; Annual Reports of the Commissioner of Indian Affairs, 1916-34.

NOTE: Reservations were ranked by the data of allotment, and the percentage of land improved is for the state in which a reservation is located. Statistical test used is the Kruskal-Wallis.

TABLE A.23

Percentage of Land in Crops and Plowable Pasture (by State) in 1930: Order of Allotment

Categories	Observations	
	ALL RESERVATIONS	AFTER 1887
Greater than 50%	17	13
20.0% to 49.9%	30	25
10.0% to 19.9%	16	13
5.0% to 9.9%	11	11
Less than 4.9%	6	6

ALL RESERVATIONS

N = 80

H (distributed X^2 4 d.f.) = 15.5

Significant at 0.1% level

AFTER 1887

N = 68

H = 16.5

Significant at 1% level

SOURCES: Annual Reports of the Commissioner of Indian Affairs, 1916-34; Fifteenth Census of the United States, 1930, Vol. IV: Agriculture, pp. 40-45.

NOTE: See note to Table A.22.

TABLE A.24
Rural Population Density in 1910: Order of Allotment

Categories	Observations	
	ALL RESERVATIONS	AFTER 1887
Greater than 20.1 persons/sq. mile	15	9
10.1 = 20.0 persons/sq. mile	21	18
5.1 = 10.0 persons/sq. mile	21	18
Less than 5.0 persons/sq. mile	23	23
	80	68

ALL RESERVATIONS

$N = 80$
H (distributed X^2 3 d.f.) = 25.53
Significant at 0.1% level

AFTER 1887

$N = 68$
$H = 17.7$
Significant at 0.1% level

SOURCES: *Annual Reports of the Commissioner of Indian Affairs, 1916-34; Thirteenth Census of the United States, 1910, Vol. I: Population.*

NOTE: *See Table A.22.*

TABLE A.25
Value per Acre of Land in Farms in 1910: Order of Allotment

Categories	Observations	
	ALL RESERVATIONS	AFTER 1887
Greater than $40/acre	21	12
$30.01 = $40.00/acre	25	22
$20.01 = $30.00/acre	24	24
Less than $20/acre	10	10

ALL RESERVATIONS

$N = 80$
H (distributed X^2 3 d.f.) = 22.3
Significant at 0.1% level

AFTER 1887

$N = 68$
$H = 18.16$
Significant at 0.1% level

SOURCE: *Annual Reports of the Commissioner of Indian Affairs, 1916-34. Thirteenth Census of the United States, 1910, Vol. V: Agriculture, pp. 82-83;*

NOTE: *See Table A.22.*

TABLE A.26
Original Acreage of Indian Tribal Lands and Deductions Therefrom, by States, up to September 1934

	Gross tribal area			Deductions (other than by allotments)				Allotments		
	ORIGINAL ACREAGE OF INDIAN RESERVATIONS	LAND SUBSEQUENTLY ADDED TO RESERVATIONS	MAXIMUM TOTAL TRIBAL ACREAGE	ACREAGE OF CEDED LANDS[1]	ACREAGE OF SURPLUS LANDS OPENED TO SETTLEMENTS[2]	MISCELLANEOUS[3]	TOTAL	NUMBER MADE	ACREAGE ALLOTTED	ACREAGE ALIENATED BY ALLOTMENTS[4]
Arizona	14,018,029	4,696,404	18,714,433	—	12,160	44,249	56,409	7,110	242,986	40
California	229,852	170,367	470,219	—	—	2,940	2,940	2,887	58,597	15,341
Colorado	584,744	—	584,744	—	—	—	—	375	72,851	33,473
Florida	3,640	122,240	125,880	—	—	—	—	—	—	—
Idaho	2,205,658	640	2,206,298	436,910	242,101	552,656	1,231,667	4,125	628,540	172,843
Iowa	80	3,314	3,394	—	—	33	33	—	—	—
Kansas	116,438	—	—	—	—	—	—	1,305	116,337	81,617
Minnesota	2,180,403	—	2,180,403	—	119,013	757,867	876,880	12,507	892,508	760,110
Mississippi	202	5,706	5,908	—	—	—	—	—	5,706	—
Montana	46,012,169	—	46,012,169	34,380,726	3,870,897	113,243	38,364,866	21,744	6,527,048	1,461,420
Nebraska	500,951	12,348	513,299	—	—	163,650	163,650	4,529	345,403	280,369
Nevada	691,281	7,115	698,396	—	—	—	—	1,654	88,579	1,804
New Mexico	3,805,813	2,237,917	6,043,730	—	—	145,280	145,280	4,697	1,072,220	—
New York[5]	87,677	—	87,677	—	—	—	—	—	—	—
North Carolina	91,035	—	91,035	—	—	—	—	—	—	—
North Dakota	2,037,477	—	2,037,477	—	264,795	417,050	681,845	7,034	1,325,302	348,159
Oklahoma	29,668,760	—	29,668,760	4,000	9,735,162	408,600	10,147,762	119,449	19,488,396	16,601,112
Oregon	3,465,470	17	3,465,487	706,576	—	785,259	1,491,835	5,736	669,858	169,543
South Dakota	12,341,601	—	12,341,601	1,270,897	2,865,770	56,154	4,192,821	32,952	7,445,882	2,834,178
Utah	5,173,180	275,962	5,449,142	—	3,859,463	—	3,859,463	1,375	115,247	29,619
Washington	4,586,526	94,282	4,680,808	1,500,000	224,870	461	1,725,331	11,898	1,199,644	242,562
Wisconsin	570,704	—	570,704	—	—	—	—	4,789	307,287	174,785
Wyoming	2,288,500	1,480,000	3,768,500	—	1,500,427	—	1,500,427	2,403	245,781	18,497
Total	130,730,190	9,106,312	139,836,502	38,299,109	22,694,658	3,475,217	64,468,984	246,569	40,848,172	23,225,472

SOURCE: United States National Resources Board, Land Planning Committee, *Indian Land Tenure, Economic Status, and Population Trends*, 1935, p. 36.

[1]Ceded lands are lands to which title was formally relinquished by treaty.

[2]Surplus lands are those left over after allotment that were opened to white settlement.

[3]Miscellaneous consists mainly of State school lands; purchased for public works, small sales, etc.

[4]Alienated, as here used, means removed from the 25-year-trust status, and includes both white-owned allotment land and Indian-owned allotment land now held under fee patent.

[5]Data incomplete.

APPENDIX B

INTERPOLATION PROCEDURE FOR ACRES PER FARM

For each state, i, the following data are given in the census or can be derived:

I_i = number of Indian farms

NI_i = number of other nonwhite farms in 1910

$r1900_i$ = ratio of Indian to all nonwhite acres per farm in 1900

$r1920_i$ = ratio of Indian to all nonwhite acres per farm in 1920

A_i = acres farmed by all nonwhite farmers in 1910

The following are unknown:

A_{I_i} = average acres per Indian farm

A_{NI_i} = average acres per other nonwhite farm

Let:

$$K = \frac{r1900_i + r1920_i/2}{2}$$

Procedure: Assume that

$$\frac{\text{Indian acres per farms in 1910}}{\text{All nonwhite acres per farm in 1910}} = \begin{array}{l}\text{Average of Indian to all}\\ \text{nonwhite acres per farm}\\ \text{1900 and 1920}\end{array}$$

Then:

$$\frac{(1)\ A_I}{\dfrac{A_I I + A_{NI} NI}{I + NI}} = K$$

[numerator is average Indian acres per farm, denominator is average acres per farm all nonwhite farms 1910]

(2) Solving A_I $\left[1 - \dfrac{KI}{I} + NI \bullet \dfrac{I + NI}{KNI} \right] = A_{NI}$

let term in brackets be Z

Then:

    (3) $A_N Z = A_{NI}$

        total acres farmed by all nonwhites

    (4) $A_I I + ZA_I N = A$

        $\therefore$ Average acres per Indian farm

    (5) $\therefore A_I = \dfrac{A}{(I + ZNI)}$

        total acres farmed by Indians

    (6) Total $= A_I I$

The value per farm calculation was done in an analogous fashion.

SELECTED BIBLIOGRAPHY

Books

Berthrong, Donald. *The Cheyenne and Arapaho Ordeal*. Norman: University of Oklahoma Press, 1976.

Brophy, William A., and Aberle, Sophie D. *The Indian: America's Unfinished Business*. Norman: University of Oklahoma Press, 1966.

Brown, Dee. *Bury My Heart at Wounded Knee*. New York: Holt, Rinehart and Winston, 1971.

Cohen, Felix. *Handbook of Federal Indian Law*. Washington, D.C.: U.S. Department of the Interior, 1941.

Debo, Angie. *And Still the Waters Run*. Princeton, N.J.: Princeton University Press, 1940.

Ewers, John C. *The Blackfeet: Raiders on the Northwestern Plains*. Norman: University of Oklahoma Press, 1958.

Fahey, John. *The Flathead Indians*. Norman: University of Oklahoma Press, 1974.

Fey, Harold E., and McNickle, D'Arcy. *Indians and Other Americans*. New York: Harper and Row, 1959. Revised edition, 1970.

Fite, Gilbert C. *The Farmers' Frontier, 1865-1900*. New York: Holt, Rinehart and Winston, 1960.

Foreman, Grant. *The Last Trek of the Indians*. Chicago: University of Chicago Press, 1946.

Fritz, Henry E. *The Movement for Indian Assimilation, 1860-1890*. Philadelphia: University of Pennsylvania Press, 1963.

Hagan, William T. *Indian Police and Judges*. New Haven: Yale University Press, 1966.

_____. *United States-Comanche Relations: The Reservation Years*. New Haven and New London: Yale University Press, 1976.

Hargreaves, Mary Wilma H. *Dry Farming in the Northern Great Plains*. Cambridge: Harvard University Press, 1957.

Johnston, Mary. *Federal Relations with the Great Sioux Indians of South Dakota, 1887-1933.* Washington, D.C.: Catholic University of America Press, 1948.

Josephy, Alvin M., Jr. *The Indian Heritage of America.* New York: Alfred A. Knopf, 1968.

Karlin, Jules. *Joseph M. Dixon of Montana, Part I: Senator and Bull Moose Manager, 1867-1917.*

Kelly, Lawrence C. *The Navajo Indians and Federal Indian Policy, 1900-1935.* Tucson: University of Arizona Press, 1968.

Kinney, J. P. *A Continent Lost—A Civilization Won.* Baltimore: Johns Hopkins Press, 1937.

Leupp, Francis E. *The Indian and His Problem.* New York: Charles Scribner's Sons, 1910.

Macgreggor, Gordon. *Warriors Without Weapons.* Chicago: University of Chicago Press, 1940.

Mardock, Robert. *The Movement for Indian Reform.* Columbia: University of Missouri Press, 1971.

Meriam, Lewis, and Associates. *The Problem of Indian Administration.* Baltimore: Johns Hopkins Press, 1928.

Meyer, Roy W. *A History of the Santee Sioux.* Lincoln: University of Nebraska Press, 1967.

North, Douglass C., and Davis, Lance E. *Institutional Change and Economic Growth.* Cambridge: Cambridge University Press, 1971.

Otis, Delos Sacket. *The Dawes Act and the Allotment of Indian Lands.* Edited by Francis Paul Prucha. Norman: University of Oklahoma Press, 1973. Originally published as "A History of the Allotment Policy" in U.S. Congress. House. Committee on Indian Affairs. *Hearings on H.R. 7902.* 73rd Cong., 2d sess., 1934, Pact 9, pp. 428–89.

Owen, Bruce, and Braeutigam, Ronald. *The Regulation Game: Strategic Uses of the Administative Process.* Cambridge, Mass.: Ballinger Publishing Company, 1978.

Price, Monroe. *Law and the American Indian: Readings, Notes and Cases.* Indianapolis: The Bobbs-Merrill Co., 1973.

Priest, Loring Benson. *Uncle Sam's Stepchildren: The Reformation of United States Indian Policy, 1865-1887.* New Brunswick, N.J.: Rutgers University Press, 1942.

Prucha, Francis P., ed. *Americanizing the American Indian.* Cambridge: Harvard University Press, 1973.

_____. *American Indian Policy in Crisis: Christian Reformers and the Indian, 1865-1900,* Norman: University of Oklahoma Press, 1976.

Robbins, Roy. *Our Landed Heritage: The Public Domain, 1776-1936.* Princeton, N.J.: Princeton University Press, 1942. Reprint. Lincoln: University of Nebraska Press, 1962.

Schmeckebier, Laurence F. *The Office of Indian Affairs.* Institute for Government Research Monograph, no. 48. Baltimore: Johns Hopkins Press, 1927.

Shannon, Fred A. *The Farmer's Last Frontier, 1860-1897.* New York: Holt, Rinehart and Winston, 1945. Reprint. New York: Harper and Row, 1968.

Simpson, George E., and Yinger, John M., eds. *American Indians and American*

Selected Bibliography   209

Life. The Annals of the American Academy of Political and Social Science
311 (May 1957).

Spicer, Edward H. *A Short History of the Indians of the United States.* New York:
Van Nostrand Reinhold Company, 1969.

Tyler, S. Lyman. *A History of Indian Policy.* Washington, D.C.: U.S. Government
Printing Office, 1973.

Underhill, Ruth. *Red Man's America.* Chicago: University of Chicago Press, 1953.

Washburn, Wilcomb E. *Red Man's Land—White Man's Law.* New York: Charles
Scribner's Sons, 1971.

_____. *The American Indian and the U.S.: A Documentary History.* 4 vols. New
York: Random House, 1973.

_____. *The Assault on Indian Tribalism: The General Allotment Law (Dawes Act)
of 1887.* Philadelphia: J. B. Lippincott Company, 1975.

_____. *The Indian in America.* New York: Harper and Row, 1975.

Wissler, Clark R. *Indian Cavalcade: or Life on the Old-Time Indian Reservations.*
New York: Sheridan House, 1938. Reprinted as *Red Man Reservations.* New
York: Collier Books, 1971.

Articles

Berthong, Donald. "Federal Indian Policy and the Southern Cheyenne and Arapaho—
1887-1907." In *The Western American Indian,* edited by Richard N. Ellis,
pp. 133-34. Lincoln: University of Nebraska Press, 1972. Originally published
in *Ethnohistory* 3 (Spring 1956): 138-48.

_____. "Legacies of the Dawes Act: Bureaucrats and Land Thieves on the Cheyenne-
Arapaho Agencies of Oklahoma." *Arizona and the West* (Winter 1979):
335-54.

Cheung, Steve. "The Structure of a Contract and the Theory of a non-Exclusive
Resource." *Journal of Law and Economics* 13 (April 1970): 49-70.

Coase, Ronald. "The Nature of the Firm." *Economica* 4 (November 1957): 386-495.

_____. "The Problem of Social Cost." *Journal of Law of Economics* 3 (October
1962): 1-40.

Demsetz, Harold. "Towards a Theory of Property Rights." *American Economic
Review* 57 (May 1967): 347-73.

Downes, Randolph C. "A Crusade for Indian Reform, 1922-1934." *The Mississippi
Valley Historical Review* 32 (December 1945): 331-54.

Drozier, Jack, "The Coeur d'Alene Land Rush." *The Pacific Northwest Quarterly*
53 (October 1962): 145-50.

Furubotn, Eirik, and Pejovich, Svetozar. "Property Rights and Economic Theory:
A Survey of Recent Literature." *Journal of Economic Literature* 10 (December
1972): 1137-62.

Gates, Paul W. "The Homestead Act in an Incongruous Land System." *American
Historical Review* 41 (September 1936): 652-81. Reprinted in Vernon Car-
stenson. *The Public Lands: Studies in the History of the Public Domain.*
Madison: University of Wisconsin Press, 1963.

Hagan, William T. "Kiowas, Comanches and Cattlemen, 1867-1906: A Case Study of the Failure of U.S. Reservation Policy." *Pacific Historical Review* 40 (August 1971): 333–55.

Hymer, Steven, and Resnick, Steven. "A Model of an Agrarian Economy with Nonagricultural Activities." *American Economic Review* 59 (September 1969): 493–506.

Lipsey, Richard, and Lancaster, Kevin. "The General Theory of the Second Best." *Review of Economic Studies* 24 (1956-57): 11–32.

Olmsted, Alan L., and Goldberg, Victor E. "Institutional Change and Economic Growth: A Critique of Davis and North." *Explorations in Economic History* 12 (April 1975): 193–210.

Parker, William. "Agriculture." In *American Economic Growth: An Economist's History of the United States*, edited by Lance Davis, Richard Easterlin, William Parker et al., pp. 369–417. New York: Harper and Row, 1972.

———. "Land, Minerals, Water, and Forests." In *American Economic Growth: An Economist's History of the United States*, edited by Lance Davis, Richard Easterlin, William Parker et al., chap. 4, pp. 93–120. New York: Harper and Row, 1972.

Pincus, Johnathan. "Pressure Groups and the Pattern of Tariffs." *Journal of Political Economy* 83 (August 1973): 767–78.

Posner, Richard. "Economic Theories of Regulation." *The Bell Journal of Economics* 5 (Autumn 1974): 335–53.

Sanderson, Warren C. "Does the Theory of Demand Need the Maximum Principle?" In *Nations and Households in Economic Growth: Essays in Honor of Moses Abramovitz*, edited by Paul A. David and Melvin W. Reder. New York: The Academic Press, 1974.

Stigler, George. "The Economic Theory of Regulation." *The Bell Journal of Economics and Management Science* 2 (Spring 1970): 3–21.

Useem, Ruth Hill, and Eicher, Carl K. "The Rosebud Reservation Economy." In *The Modern Sioux*, edited by Ethel Nurge, pp. 3–34. Lincoln: University of Nebraska Press, 1970.

Unpublished Works

Dorner, Peter Paul. "The Economic Position of the American Indians: Their Resources and Potential for Development." Ph.D. dissertation, Harvard University, February 1959.

Eicher, Carl K. "Constraints on Economic Progress on the Rosebud Sioux Indian Reservation." Ph.D. dissertation, Harvard University, December 1960.

Fitch, James B. "Economic Development in a Minority Enclave: The Case of the Yakima Indian Nation, Washington." Ph.D. dissertation, Stanford University, May 1974.

Sanderson, Warren C. "Economic Theories of Fertility: What Do They Explain?" Working Paper No. 36, Mimeographed. New York: National Bureau for Economic Research, March 1974.

Trosper, Ronald L. "The Economic Impact of the Allotment Policy on the Flathead Indian Reservation." Ph.D. dissertation, Harvard University, August 1974.

Government Documents

U.S. Congress. Senate. "Report of Advisors on Irrigation on Indian Reservations," by Porter J. Preston and Charles A. Engle. *Review of Conditions of the Indians of the United States: Hearings Before the Committee on Indian Affairs.* 71st Cong., 2d sess., U.S. Senate Res. 78 and 308, 1930, pp. 2210-2261.

U.S. Department of Agriculture. *Yearbook of Agriculture, 1941: Climate and Man.* Washington, D.C.: U.S. Government Printing Office, 1941.

U.S. Department of the Interior, Board of Indian Commissioners. *Annual Report of the Board of Indian Commissioners to the Secretary of the Interior.* 1915-1930.

U.S. Department of the Interior, Bureau of the Census. *Eleventh Census of the United States, 1890, Vol. V: Agriculture.*

_____. *Eleventh Census of the United States, 1890, Vol. X: Indians Taxed and Not Taxed.*

_____. *Twelfth Census of the United States, 1900, Vol. V: Agriculture.*

_____. "Agriculture on Indian Reservations." In *Twelfth Census of the United States, 1900, Vol. V: Agriculture*, pp. 717-40.

_____. *Thirteenth Census of the United States, 1910, Vol. V: Agriculture.*

_____. *Fourteenth Census of the United States, 1920, Vol. V: Agriculture.*

_____. *Fifteenth Census of the United States, 1930, Vol. IV: Agriculture.*

_____. *Fifteenth Census of the United States, 1930: The Indian Population of the United States and Alaska.*

U.S. Department of the Interior, Office of Indian Affairs. *Annual Report of the Commissioner of Indian Affairs to the Secretary of the Interior.* 1875-1934.

_____. *General Data Concerning Indian Reservations (Revised to June 30, 1929).* Washington, D.C.: U.S. Government Printing Office, October 15, 1929.

_____. *Statistical Supplement to the Annual Report of the Commissioner of Indian Affairs for the Fiscal Year Ended June 30, 1940.*

U.S. National Resources Board, Land Planning Committee, *Indian Land Tenure, Economic Status, and Population Trends.* Washington, D.C.: U.S. Government Printing Office, 1935.

INDEX

About the Author

LEONARD A. CARLSON is Assistant Professor of Economics at Emory University in Atlanta. He has contributed to *Explorations in Economic History*, *The Journal of Economic History*, and *The Southern Banker*.